American Indian Fiction

AMERICAN
INDIAN
FICTION

Charles R. Larson

UNIVERSITY OF NEW MEXICO PRESS

Albuquerque

Library of Congress Cataloging in Publication Data

Larson, Charles R
  American Indian fiction.

  Bibliography: p. 201.
  Includes index.
  1. American fiction—Indian authors—History and
criticism. 2. American fiction—20th century—History
and criticism. 3. Indians in literature. I. Title.
PS153.I52L3   813'.009   78-55698
ISBN 0-8263-0477-X

To Roberta

Acknowledgments

I would like to thank the following people without whose assistance it would have been impossible to write this book: Carlton Stoiber, Mitchell Bush, William Leap, Arlene B. Hirschfelder, Harold S. McAllister, Harvée Schaeffer, Hamlin Hill, Frederick W. Turner, Jeanne Wasile, Lawrence J. Evers, Edward Uhlan, and Helen Oskison Olstad; D'Arcy McNickle, John Joseph Mathews, James Welch, and Chief George Pierre, for generously supplying information about themselves and their writing; John Joseph Mathews and James Welch, for permission to reprint material from their letters; Frank Turaj, Doris Grumbach, Richard Berendzen, and Bernth Lindfors, for giving initial support for the project itself. Lastly, I would like to express my appreciation to the John Simon Guggenheim Memorial Foundation for the fellowship which made it possible for me to complete this book.

Contents

1

The Emergence of American Indian Fiction

The sounds of both Kiowa and Navajo are quite natural and familiar to me, and even now I can make these sounds easily and accurately with my voice, so well established are they in my ear. I lived very close to these "foreign" languages, poised at a crucial time in the learning process to enter into either or both of them wholly. But my mother was concerned that I should learn English as my 'native' language, and so English is first and foremost in my possession—N. Scott Momaday, *The Names*

In the summer of 1972 when I wrote a review essay of Hyemeyohsts Storm's novel, *Seven Arrows*, for *Books Abroad*,[1] I erroneously referred to Storm's narrative of American Indian life as the first novel published by a Native American. As I should have expected, a number of letters to Ivar Ivask, the editor of the publication, pointed out my error and called attention to N. Scott Momaday's *House Made of Dawn*, winner of the Pulitzer Prize for fiction for 1968. I was aware of Momaday's novel when I read *Seven Arrows*—there was, in fact, a copy of the book in my study. Something, however, had made me think of Momaday as a detribalized Native American (I knew that he was a professor of English at some university) and Storm—from the little information I had gathered about him—as an American Indian still living within the tribe. I was wrong on both counts: neither Storm nor Momaday had been the first American Indian to publish a novel, nor was either of them exactly living within the fold. Both of these writers had been vilified by their peers—the question of their

1

"Indianness" (and, therefore, the authenticity of their work) had already been disputed by others. The concept of Indian identity, as I was about to discover, is a difficult one.

The following year, when I began working on a book called *The Novel in the Third World* (which included commentary on *Seven Arrows*), I came across a citation of *Winter Count* by Dallas Chief Eagle, published in 1967 and hence the oldest work of fiction by an American Indian, or so I believed. As in so many instances of literary research, I discoved the reference to *Winter Count* when I was looking for something that had nothing to do with Native peoples. By the time I was able to locate a copy of Dallas Chief Eagle's narrative, I was quite certain that there must be other novels written by American Indians that had long been forgotten.

I began to search at the Library of Congress and to pore over bibliographies pertaining to Native Americans as well as book reviews and catalogs of out-of-print books. Of greatest help in my early work was Arlene B. Hirschfelder's *American Indian and Eskimo Authors: A Comprehensive Bibliography*, published by the Association on American Indian Affairs, Inc., in 1973, and undoubtedly a most valuable reference work for this field. Since novels are identified as such in the Hirschfelder bibliography (which includes all books written by Native Americans), it was a relatively easy matter to track down copies of the works cited and begin reading them. The Hirschfelder bibliography identifies roughly a dozen works as novels—the oldest being Chief Simon Pokagon's *Queen of the Woods*, published in 1899. This was a rather far cry from my earlier assumption that fiction written by Native Americans emerged as recently as the 1970s or even the 1960s. Why, then, have these books remained unknown?

Until Momaday's *House Made of Dawn* and Storm's *Seven Arrows* gained sizable audiences, the earlier novels by Native Americans had met with much the same reception that encountered the works of Afro-American writers. For the most part, that is, they were shunned or politely ignored. Publishers were not especially interested in these books, just as the general reading population was not particularly interested in the American Indian per se. The publisher of Dallas Chief Eagle's *Winter Count* was Denton-Berkland, located in Colorado

Springs, Colorado. Chief Eagle had approached eastern publishing houses and had discovered that they were generally unreceptive to his novel. Ironically, one publisher was interested but said that Chief Eagle would have to change an incident in the story (involving General Custer's suicide), and this he refused to do.

When novels by American Indians did appear, they were often published by obscure publishing houses in unlikely locations: Colorado Springs, Colorado; San Antonio, Texas; Hartford, Michigan. In at least one instance an author decided to pay for the publication of his novel by a vanity press, which meant that the book was ignored by the normal reviewing channels. To be sure, several of the earlier novels did appear on well-known publishers' lists, but here again their general fate was almost immediate obscurity. In a letter to me describing the reception of his novel, *The Surrounded*, published by Dodd, Mead & Co., in 1936 and reissued by the University of New Mexico Press in 1978, D'Arcy McNickle commented with resignation about the fate of his book: *"The Surrounded* made no money, of course, in spite of some excellent reviews. . . ."[2]

It is possible that one or two publishers sensed a general disinterest in fiction by Native Americans and tried to conceal the racial identity of the author—perhaps with the encouragement of the author himself. This appears to have been the case with John Joseph Mathews, whose novel, *Sundown* (1934), was published by Longmans, Green and Co. There is nothing on the book jacket ("A novel of the American Southwest") to identify the author as a Native American. This fact is all the more puzzling since Mathews's earlier work, *Wah'kon-Tah* (1932)—an account of Major Laban J. Miles, the first federal agent for the Osage Tribe of Plains Indians—not only identified the author as an American Indian but became a best seller (and a Book-of-the Month Club selection) *because* of its subject.

The author whose racial identity was most thoroughly camouflaged, however, is not Mathews but John Milton Oskison (1876–1947). The dust jackets of his three novels—*Wild Harvest* (1925), *Black Jack Davy* (1926), and *Brothers Three* (1935)—make no reference to Oskison's Cherokee heritage, though the one for *Brothers Three* goes so far as to state that the author was "born in the old Indian Territory, near the capital of the Cherokee Nation. . . ."[3] Thereafter, Oskison is described as a writer who was educated at Stanford and Harvard before beginning his literary career in New York. Perhaps more interesting is the fact that none of Oskison's novels has much to do with Native American life—something that marks them off from the rest of the novels discussed in this study. The case is once again similar to that of a number of early black American writers. There was a time around the turn of the century when Paul Laurence Dunbar and Charles W. Chesnutt tried to conceal their racial identity, fearing that if it were known, people would not read their works.[4]

Neither Mathews nor Oskison was a full blood, and pictures of them belie their Indian origins. I mention this fact not only because it has influenced the subject matter of their novels but also because it is paramount to the problem of authenticity, to the concept of Indianness. How can we determine that these writers were, in fact, Native Americans? This is not so central a concern with those writers who have tried to conceal or suppress their Indianness as it could be with non-Indians posing as Indians—that is, a writer who claims to be a Native American but is not. In short, how can we determine that the writers discussed in this study are American Indians? How can we be certain, even, that they wrote the works attributed to them? I ask these questions because the two primary qualifications for inclusion of an author in this study are, first, the establishment that he or she is genuinely a Native American; and, second, that he wrote the novel himself without the aid of a collaborator or an amanuensis.

The second of these qualifications is, perhaps, the more difficult to establish. It has been my intention to include in this study only those *novels* written by Native Americans without the aid of a collaborator. I have therefore eliminated the large corpus of American Indian writing that is autobiographical, and an equally large number of works either "as told to" or written with someone else's assistance. Ultimately, I have had to make decisions that only I can account for, though in most instances these have been made because of information revealed within the book itself or on its dust jacket. I have, therefore, excluded several works identified as fiction in the

Hirschfelder bibliography. For example, the curious little novel called *Co-Ge-We-A (The Half-Blood)*, by Hum-Ishu-Ma ("Mourning Dove"), published in 1927—and, regrettably, the only early novel by a female writer—has been omitted from my main discussion because the title page identifies a collaborator ("Given through Sho-Pow-Tan").[5] The title page also states: "With Notes and Biographical Sketch by Lucullus Virgil McWhorter, Author of 'The Crime Against the Yakimas,' 'Border Settlers of Northwestern Virginia,' 'The Discards,' etc.," further suggesting a collaboration or filtering of the original text through another consciousness. Nevertheless, since I believe that *The Half-Blood* is an important work, I include an analysis of it in an appendix.

A more obvious candidate for exclusion—though again a work cited by Hirschfelder as fiction—is *West to the Setting Sun* (1943). Hirschfelder identifies this novel as a work by Ethel Brant Monture "with Harvey Chalmers." Yet Ethel Monture (a Mohawk) is not named on the title page of the volume itself, and the Library of Congress lists *West to the Setting Sun* under Chalmers, who states in an acknowledgment at the beginning of the book:

> Entire credit for the Indian viewpoint, reaction and philosophy in this book is due to Ethel Brant, great-grand-daughter of Jacob Brant, Joseph's second son by Catherine Croghan. Thanks to her manipulation the writer was privileged to meet Indians on a common footing and to see with their eyes and hear through their ears. Before meeting Ethel Brant the writer's ideas about Indians, formed from the descriptions in standard historical romance, were the antithesis of reality.[6]

This is, then, another instance of an obvious collaboration. Despite her significant part in the germination of this work, Ethel Brant Monture had nothing to do with the actual writing of the novel.

A third instance of an exclusion is somewhat different since it involves a work that was published after the Hirschfelder bibliography appeared: *The Reservation* (1976), by Ted C. Williams, who grew up on the Tuscarora Indian Reservation near Niagara Falls, in the 1930s and 1940s. Although at least one reviewer has referred to *The Reservation* as a novel, it is, I believe, more accurately classified as autobiography, since it describes factual incidents from the author's childhood. It appears that Williams's publisher persuaded him to call his book fiction to protect the identities of the people he wrote about who are still alive. This discrepancy between fiction and autobiography is further elaborated in Williams's note to the reader, which begins,

> At first I was sad to have to call this book a work of fiction. But now I don't feel that way anymore. It may, in many ways, be much more accurate this way. This way, many more Indians of the Tuscarora Indian Reservation are in the book. Even the dead are alive again, because names, events, faces, physical descriptions, philosophies, voices, etc., have been resurrected, borrowed, and exchanged among and between those people of the reservation that I have known.[7]

Finally, then, I have excluded *The Reservation* because I do not believe that Williams intended it to be regarded as fiction.

Important as it is to establish that these novels are products of the writer's own genius—and not the result of collaboration—of equal significance is the question of Indian identity. Unfortunately, this is not as easy a matter to determine as it is with black Americans, where the mythical drop of Negro blood has precipitated incredible social inequities. One drop of Indian blood is not so regarded, though it is clear that many of these writers (like many Afro-American writers) are not full bloods. The analogy to Afro-Americans may be a limited one, since a prime distinction for determining "Indianness" appears to be identification with and acceptance by one's fellow tribesmen.

As an initial test for establishing the Indianness of these writers, I have relied on information supplied by the tribes in which the writers are enrolled. The inclusion of a writer's name on the rolls of his specific tribe (compiled by tribal leaders and kept in the tribal headquarters as well as in the Bureau of Indian Affairs) implies a kind of kinship with his fellow tribesmen. Tribal requirements being what they are, the quotas for enrollment vary from tribe to tribe, and an individual who is not a full blood might be included on the rolls of one tribe but not on another; but what actually determines such inconsistencies is not my concern here. Although their importance should not be overemphasized, the rolls are valuable documents for establishing certain factual matters about these writers.

In one instance, the tribal rolls led to my decision to exclude a writer from this study who is included in *American Indian and Eskimo Authors*. Hirschfelder lists Jon Mockingbird's *The Wokosani Road* (1963) and identifies the author as an Apache, yet Mockingbird is not listed on the Apache roll nor is "Mockingbird" a common Apache name. The jacket of the book claims that the novel is largely autobiographical (as a reading of the work also implies); and about a third of the novel is concerned with the main character's activities in World War II. A query at the Veterans Administration further revealed no veteran of World War II by the name of Jon Mockingbird.

All of this is particularly interesting because *The Wokosani Road* was published by the Exposition Press, a vanity publishing house. Correspondence and telephone calls with the publisher, Edward Uhlan, have shown that he is quite interested in the Mockingbird work (Uhlan described himself as an "Indian buff"), but that there are no records to assert anything about the writer's identity. (Uhlan says that all records concerning Mockingbird were among those destroyed in a warehouse fire, that not even an address or a social security number exists for the author.) Uhlan further states that he met Mockingbird and that he looked Indian (?). Although there is a possibility that *The Wokosani Road* was written by an Indian using a pseudonym, I have decided to treat the novel in an appendix, since the author's true identity cannot be authenticated.

What is of especial interest for my study here is the "degree" of Indian blood suggested by the tribal rolls. This is not simply a matter of the earliest writers having increased educational opportunities if they were mixed bloods. Nor am I trying to suggest that the closer the writer is to being a full blood the more truly "Indian" his writing is. For example, John M. Oskison—whose novels are only marginally related to his Indian origins—is one-fourth Cherokee, but included on the Eastern Cherokee roll. John Joseph Mathews is one-eighth Osage, but still included on that roll. Hyemeyohsts Storm— whose novel *Seven Arrows* in many ways seems to be more "Indian" than any of the others—is a mere one-sixteenth Northern Cheyenne, but his name appears on the tribal rolls. These are the oddities of enrollment, and my concern with these figures has only been to suggest that although a significant test of a writer's Indian origins falls back on the rolls themselves, compiled by the tribal councils, the "Indianness" of the writing may have little to do with these figures.

What is of equal importance is historical or documentary information about the writers that attests to their general acceptance by their own people. Thus the first writer, Chief Simon Pokagon, was—as his title suggests—the chief of his people, the Potawatomi; and—to return for a moment to the question of authenticity—there is an abundance of historical information to confirm Chief Pokagon's abilities as an orator and as a writer. Or, to return to John Joseph Mathews, the known fact that he has been a member of the Osage Tribal Council is probably more significant than his genealogy. Known acceptance by one's peers, then, is probably a more meaningful test of Indianness. Along these lines, it should be pointed out that many of the writers discussed in this volume have had their work included in anthologies of American Indian writing, edited by American Indians—a further test of this acceptance.

Moving to more direct matters of literary substance, there is the further question of language. I have already stated that one of the criteria for including a writer in this study is the determination that he actually wrote the novel attributed to him. All of the novels discussed here were published in English, and that also may imply a number of limitations. I am not aware of any novels that have been published by American Indians in their tribal languages, but this is not to suggest that some may not have been written. Furthermore, since the published novels are in English, I suspect that this may wrongly imply that the writer wrote in his second language instead of his first. Again, this is a difficult matter to establish, and only in one instance (the oldest one) is there evidence that the

work was originally written in a tribal tongue. Chief Simon
Pokagon states in an introductory section to *Queen of the
Woods* called "The Algonquin Language,"

> In presenting "Queen of the Woods" to the public, I
> realize that many of its readers will inquire why so many
> Indian words are used. All such will please bear in mind
> that the manuscript was first written in the Algonquin
> language, the only language spoken by me until fourteen
> years of age, and that in translating it into English, many
> parts of it seem to lose their force and euphony, inso-
> much that I deeply regret that "Queen of the Woods"
> can not be read by the white people in my own langauge.
> It is indeed mortifying for me to consider that outside of
> the proper names of lakes, streams, and places, our lan-
> guage is being almost entirely ignored by the incoming
> race, while other languages of foreign birth are entering
> largely into the English dialect; and our children, who
> are being educated in the white man's schools are forsak-
> ing and forgetting their mother tongue.[8]

Pokagon's fears about the loss of one's tribal language are
legitimate, though not fully supported by contemporary evidence. Harold E. Driver, in his book *Indians of North America*, states, "Nearly all Indians today speak English, and about
ninety per cent read and write it to some extent. At the same
time, most of them still speak one of about a hundred Indian
languages still extant in the United States."[9] Many of these
languages have no orthography, and that, of course, has cur-
tailed the possibility of producing literary works in those languages despite their rich oral tradition. There is also a matter
of expediency. If a writer should choose to write a novel in his
tribal tongue, he not only would eliminate the possibility of
non-Indian readers, but he would not be able to establish an
audience with Native peoples who speak another tribal language. As Shirley Hill Witt has written, "The English language has provided the primary means by which intertribal
communication has been made possible."[10] Any successful
movement toward Pan-Indianism will depend upon this common language.

The fact that these novels were written in English may tell

us something about the audience for which they were intended. By extension, we might try to speculate why these
novels were written, though I would be the first to argue that
that kind of question rarely has a satisfactory answer. Why
does any writer write? Partial explanations can sometimes be
made, however, when the writer belongs to a minority group
or has a particular drum to beat. Ethnic literature often has a
didactic or proselytizing bend to it. One thinks of Richard
Wright, who felt that he had made "an awfully naive mistake"
in writing *Uncle Tom's Children*—"a book which even bankers'
daughters could read and weep over and feel good about."[11]
After he read the reviews, Wright says, "I swore to myself that
if I ever wrote another book, no one would weep over it; that
it would be so hard and deep that they would have to face it
without the consolation of tears."[12] The result was *Native Son*
(1939).

With the possible exception of Momaday's *House Made of
Dawn*, there are few instances of this kind of vindictive intent
among the novels written by Native Americans. Rather, these
works were written to give white America a picture of Native
American life, to present the Indians' side of the story—to define Indian consciousness.

With the earliest writers—whom I have called assimilationists—this question of Indian consciousness was, indeed, a
confusing one. The era they wrote about in their novels (generally the years between 1880 and 1920) had been one of
humiliation and defeat, above all one of hopelessness. The
lessons of the recent past had taught them that the Native
American was a dying breed—that survival (if one could call it
that) could only be achieved by accepting the values of the
white man's world. Examined today, the novels by these assimilationists (Pokagon, Mathews, Oskison, and Mourning
Dove) should not be regarded so much as attempts to define
Indian consciousness, then, as cultural artifacts or literary responses to the recent disintegration of the last intact tribal
cultures (those of the Plains Indians).

Still vivid in the memories of these early writers (and in
those of their contemporaries) were the staggering humiliations of the events between 1862 and 1890 which suggested
that assimilation was the only means of survival: the Santee

Sioux war against the white invaders of the Minnesota lands in 1862; the land grabbing of the Indian territories brought about by the end of the Civil War and the subsequent flood of emigration into Indian lands; the Fort Laramie treaties of the mid 1860s, further confining the movement of the Sioux tribes; the Plains wars against the whites, culminating in the Battle of the Little Big Horn in 1876; the decimation of the buffalo herds and subsequent starvation for thousands of Indians; the increasing restrictions of reservation life (and the Dawes Allotment Act of 1887), designed to make Native peoples individual landowners and farmers, without concern for tribal and communal affinities; the final roundup of the renegade Indians (such as Sitting Bull) who refused to be confined to reservation life; and, last, Wounded Knee (1890)—the finale of all these events. With humiliations such as these, it is not difficult to understand why the early writers embraced an assimilationist theme.

When we leave the first group of Native American novelists and pass on to their successors, we begin to notice a sharp change in perspective—in their concern with their "Indianness." Increasingly, as these novels are read in the order in which they were written, we see the writers themselves become aware of their own ethnic consciousness, moving from assimilation, through the equally frustrating period of cultural syncretism (McNickle and Momaday), and finally toward a separate reality. Certainly this sense of Indianness (defined here as a separate life-style rich with its own viable alternatives and realities) permeates the work of all of the most recent writers (Dallas Chief Eagle, Chief George Pierre, Storm, James Welch, Nasnaga, and Leslie Silko), who grew up during a time of greater political and cultural awareness.

The events that influenced these writers began with World War II, when increasing numbers of Native Americans left the reservations and became aware of their dependent status. The youngest writers (Welch, Nasnaga, and Silko) began writing during the 1960s and 1970s, when the civil rights movement and the war in Vietnam spilled over into an emerging period of Indian activism that saw the formation of the National Youth Council (1960) and the more militant American Indian Movement(1969); the takeover of Alcatraz Island in

1969; the "Trail of Broken Treaties" demonstrations on the
eve of the 1972 political elections; the occupation of Wounded
Knee in the early months of 1973. In the novels by these
younger writers one senses the desire to articulate a new national awareness, proclaiming the validity of Red Power.
Though they have not joined together like the writers of the
Harlem Renaissance in the 1920s or the New Black Renaissance in the 1960s and 1970s, the works by these recent Native American novelists cry out as bold assertions of their own
distinct identity.

To a certain extent, the ongoing development of an Indian
consciousness in all of these works is reflected in statements
the writers (and their publishers) have made about the novels
themselves. When Chief Simon Pokagon published *Queen of
the Woods*, literacy in English was somewhat limited among
Native Americans; hence there were few Native readers for his
work. Pokagon states in his dedication,

> As a token of sincere appreciation, I Pokagon hereby
> inscribe "Queen of the Woods" to all societies and indi-
> viduals—benefactors of our race—who have so bravely
> stood for our rights, while poisoned arrows of bitter prej-
> udice flew thick and fast about them, boldly declaring to
> all the world that "the white man and the red man are
> brothers, and that God is the father of all."[13]

His publisher adds in a preface to the work itself (Pokagon
died by the time his novel appeared in print), "His greatest
desire in publishing [*Queen of the Woods*] had been that the
white man and the red man might be brought into closer
sympathy with each other."[14] Furthermore, since *Queen of
the Woods* is a temperance novel, a kind of thesis novel, evi-
dently Pokagon wanted to make a statement about Indian
consumption of alcohol, something I shall discuss later.

In most instances the novels appeared without a preface by
the publisher or an author's dedication that declared his intent, so speculation must remain just that. These writers may
have felt compelled to write about their people, though the
case of John Joseph Mathews may have been more typical.
Answering my letter in which I asked him to describe the
germination of *Sundown*, Mathews wrote,

> . . . after the success of Wah'Kon-Tah I was asked to go to New York and once there the publishers hounded me to write a novel and somehow in the confusion I did promise to write one.
>
> I am a hunter by nature and once home in the Black-jacks the Quail season was open and I found myself wanting to hunt instead of wanting to write. I finally sat down to write the book without any inspiration. Sent it off to the publisher where it was accepted readily.[15]

Oh, that all authors were so candid.

Three of the novels discussed in this book—*Winter Count, Tsali*, and *Seven Arrows*—have a historical thesis that makes it easier to speculate about their authors' intentions. In all three cases, I would suggest, the writers intended to set the past aright, to describe historical events of the white-red confrontation from the Indian point of view. Certainly, this was in part Dallas Chief Eagle's aim when he wrote *Winter Count*: to describe Custer's last stand (and fall) from an Indian perspective. I have already noted that this stance was unacceptable to at least one New York publisher. Jeanette Henry, the editor of the Indian Historical Press, which published Denton R. Bedford's *Tsali*, sounds a similar note:

> *Tsali* is a true story, placed in the warmth and depth of human life itself. Millions of words have been written about the Cherokee Removal of 1838. Facts and figures have been presented. The truth has been shown in research documents, historical essays, erudite legal studies, and learned theses. Falsehood and misrepresentation has also appeared, both in historic accounts and popular writings. In no case has the life of the Indian been described, his thoughts, his feelings, and his philosophy in the face of extreme adversity.
>
> In *Tsali* the author, a Minsee Indian, has shown us the Cherokee "common man" in an act of nobility which compares on an equal plane with that of the world's heroic and epic figures.
>
> James Fenimore Cooper give the world a romantic, one dimensional Indian. Denton Bedford gives us an Indian life in truth, in agony, and in historic perspective.[16]

Hyemeyohsts Storm's explanation for his novel ignores the word "history" yet implies a similar compulsion to correct the record of the past before the oral tradition is forgotten:

> There are many old Stories told within *Seven Arrows*. These Stories were used among the People to Teach the meaning of the Sun Dance Way. They were themselves a Way of Understanding among the People, and also between different Peoples. Because the People did not have a written language, these Stories were memorized and passed down in one way through countless generations.[17]

One can further speculate that at the heart of many of these novels is the author's desire to record an event or historical perspective from the Indian point of view before it is forgotten, to demythify misleading concepts about the past.

How well qualified are these writers to do this? How representative of their cultures are they? Foolish questions, perhaps, like asking how representative any novelist is of the culture he portrays. In theory I believe that asking such questions is a futile exercise. In practice, however, some benefit may be derived from the answer simply because by and large we are dealing with ethnic materials that depict some aspect of the Indian-white confrontation. No doubt we would expect these writers to be true to the cultures they write about, though reading fiction solely to learn about another culture may be misleading. A novel must be something more than an anthropological document if it is to engage our aesthetic sensitivities.

Hyemeyohsts Storm's *Seven Arrows* has an ability to engage us in this way, though it is the one novel out of the sixteen discussed here that has been severely criticized by Native American readers. Storm's novel was published in 1972 as the first title in Harper & Row's Native American Publishing Program. Although it was widely praised by a number of Indian authors (Vine Deloria, Jr., N. Scott Momaday, and Duane Niatum, for example) as well as by scholars who have studied Native American life (such as Dee Brown, Ruth M. Underhill, and Edmund Fuller), *Seven Arrows* caused a furor among the Northern Cheyenne shortly after its publication. It was felt that Storm's novel distorted Cheyenne beliefs. As an article in the Indian publication, *Wassaja*, explained the issue,

Perhaps the most disturbing aspect of . . . *Seven Arrows* is the fact that some of the beliefs which [Storm] presents in his book as having been derived from our spiritual ways are completely unfounded and extremely repugnant to the sensitivities of our people who are knowledgeable and qualified to speak about such things, not merely as the product of imagination, but as the result of actual lived experience.

What has been offensive to them is Mr. Storm's claim that these ceremonial people (many of them now deceased) had been his teachers and the source of his information, when these same people were not even consulted about their true feelings in the matter.[18]

Initial attacks on Storm stated that he was not an enrolled member of the Northern Cheyenne, though that has subsequently been proven incorrect. What appear, in retrospect, to have upset Storm's tribesmen were his free interpretations, what they saw as distortions of Northern Cheyenne traditional life, religion, and values—that is, a kind of tampering with sacred information. Mostly, Storm's difficulties erupted because his critics seemed to think he was attempting to pass off his novel as fact—not as a work of the imagination. Yet, as I have written elsewhere,[19] Storm clarifies his intentions at the beginning of his novel by stating that he has often made up (that is, created) stories from his own imagination—as we would expect any good novelist to do. *Seven Arrows* is also not a novel solely about the Northern Cheyenne but, rather, a composite picture of the Plains Indians—as, again, Storm makes clear in his work.

How representative, then, is Hyemeyohsts Storm of his culture? How typical is John M. Oskison of his fellow Cherokees? How representative is N. Scott Momaday of his people (the Kiowas)? Obviously these are questions best left to cultural anthropologists. If *Brothers Three* (and *Wild Harvest* and *Black Jack Davy*, for that matter) are read for what they reveal about the Cherokees in Oklahoma, the reader will be disappointed. Even N. Scott Momaday—who has been regarded by some critics as the most accomplished Native American writer—has chosen to write not about his own people but about the Navahos. As one critic of Momaday noted when *House Made of Dawn* appeared, "This first novel, as subtly wrought as a piece of Navajo silverware, is the work of a young Kiowa Indian who teaches English and writes poetry at the University of California in Santa Barbara. That creates a difficulty for a reviewer right away. American Indians do not write novels and poetry as a rule, or teach at top-ranking universities either. . . ."[20]

Whenever we discuss a piece of literature, we are talking about something more than cultural background. If this were not the case, then the most representative and, by extension, the most "authentic" Native American novels would be those written by full bloods, still living on reservations. (That would eliminate John J. Mathews, John M. Oskison, D'Arcy McNickle, Hyemeyohsts Storm, Denton R. Bedford, James Welch, Leslie Silko, and Scott Momaday—or at least relegate them to second-class status.) By such measurements Chief Simon Pokagon, Dallas Chief Eagle, and Chief George Pierre would probably be considered the most representative Native American novelists because they are or were at one time the leaders of their people.

Unfortunately (or perhaps fortunately) chieftaincy does not assure literary talent. "Indianness" is present in each and every one of the novels examined in this study—just as cultural elements are unavoidably present in all human artifacts. Our problem is to evaluate the relationship between cultural background and aesthetic temperament. It is possible to study a piece of literature without knowing anything about or paying any attention to the culture that produced it, but I doubt that there is a novelist alive who has been able to escape the more far-reaching constructs of reality that cultural conditioning imposes on each and every one of us.

2

The Children of Pocahontas

Were there two sides to Pocahontas? Did she have a fourth dimension?—Ernest Hemingway, quoted by Philip Young in "The Mother of Us All: Pocahontas Reconsidered," 1962

The Indian is doubtless a gentleman; but he is a gentleman who wears a very dirty shirt, and lives a very miserable life, having nothing to employ him or keep him alive except the pleasures of the chase and of the scalp-hunt—which we dignify with the name of war . . . in his natural barbaric state, he is a barbarian—and it is not possible he could be anything else.—Robert Montgomery Bird, *Nick of the Woods* ("Preface to the Revised Edition," 1853)

Buried deep in our memories is our first piece of "fiction" about Indians: the story of Pocahontas, our earliest tale about red-skinned peoples—a living myth that will not die. Even today she dominates our image of Native peoples; any consideration of the subsequent fiction by her people belongs to the context of its origins: the Pocahontas legend, where the distortions begin—the symbolic beginning of all Indian-white relationships.

Ask any school child: Pocahontas, the beautiful Indian princess, daughter of the cruel chief, Powhatan, intervening in her father's death sentence of the handsome Englishman, Captain John Smith, saving his life before her father's braves would crush the white man's head between two stones; Pocahontas, that sister of mercy, aiding the starving colonists at Jamestown during the dreadful winter of 1607–8—rescuing those pious adventurers who had fled to the New World in search of economic profit and personal glory; Pocahontas, baptized and converted to Christianity, marrying John Rolfe, founding a new dynasty fit for the ideals of the New World, white man and red woman, the brotherhood of man. May their descendants live forever.

It is our oldest myth. Older than Uncle Sam. Older than George Washington chopping down the cherry tree. Older than Paul Bunyan, Rip Van Winkle, and Ichabod Crane—mere fictional characters. It is the story of the beginning of our nation, our tree of life: Pocahontas rescuing John Smith and thereby making the New World safe for Christianity. We tell it to our children, and they pass it on to their children. If they forget, they have only to turn to any one of the countless written versions that have proliferated for more than three hundred years. There is no worry that Pocahontas will be forgotten. She is our Patron Saint. Someone will always write another book about her.

Children know her best. They have been reading about her ever since Noah Webster's *The Little Reader's Assistant* was published in Hartford in 1790.[1] In his provocative article, "The Mother of Us All: Pocahontas Reconsidered," written more than fifteen years ago, Philip Young informs us that "an informal survey of the children's sections of two small Midwestern libraries disclosed twenty-six different books on Pocahontas. . . ."[2] A random dip into one of these (one that tries especially hard to be objective and set the facts aright) reveals how such myths continue to grow, to capture our fancy. Consider, for example, these opening statements about our Indian princess: she "was the very apple of [Powhatan's] eye."[3] That she may have been (though he had many other children). "She was as sweet and pretty as [her father] was ugly and cruel."[4] Or, by implication, Pocahontas did what she did because she was pretty. And Powhatan's wickedness was the result of his unsightliness. What else would you expect from an ugly old man?

Consider the ending of the same book describing Pocahontas's audience with the queen after she has married John Rolfe and gone to England:

> She held her head as high as though she had been born in a snow-white palace. She was proud of being her father's daughter and of having been born in a hut of bark in the midst of the deep, dark woods of Virginia.

Pocahontas herself never returned to her home across the great water. But Powhatan's brave and the other Indians went back, and told such tall tales of the wonders of England, that nobody would believe them. And when Pocahontas's son was a grown man, he sailed to his mother's country. There he became the father of a great, big family, which lives on to this very day.[5]

The work in question is *Pocahontas*, by Ingri and Edgar Parin d'Aulaire, and a notice on the jacket of the book informs us that "*Pocahontas* has received the approval of the National Council of Teachers of English and the Association of Childhood Education International for its high quality." There is nothing in the d'Aulaire book that is an outright violation of the facts surrounding the Pocahontas-Smith-Rolfe triangle. The white men are even described as invaders of Powhatan's land. It is simply that the facts presented here give us only a portion of the story, and, by implication, a distinct racial bias which would appear to be contrary to the goals of the National Council of Teachers of English.

Regrettably, this is true of almost all the books about Pocahontas (whether written for children or adults), as one final example for the moment will illustrate: "Rolfe was a pious young man; the little maid was gentle and good, but after all, she was a heathen. He had himself spoken to her on matters of religion, but she had not said much to him."[6] The quotation, this time, is from a book intended for slightly older children, those in their early teens, yet the ethnic bias is again present. The thirteen- or fourteen-year-old reader does not have to be very perceptive to realize that Rolfe is a good man because he is a Christian, and he is a Christian because he is white. Pocahontas may be gentle, but gentleness is of little value if one is also a heathen. It is a matter of simple logic. Rolfe's religion is superior to Pocahontas's. He can defend his Christianity; she cannot even articulate her paganism. Within the context of the legend, however, this is an obstacle easily surmounted: Pocahontas can be converted and baptized and then she will be a fitting consort for Rolfe.

The Pocahontas myth as it is commonly remembered is replete with factual distortions, racial slurs, and ethnocentric misconceptions. The gentle maid bears little similarity to the

actual person who once encountered Smith and later married
Rolfe. Many of us may even have forgotten that she married
Rolfe, since our sympathies tell us that she should have married Smith. As Leslie Fiedler has written, she married the
wrong man![7] The story isn't really romantic at all; it doesn't
have a happy ending. Pocahontas was only ten (or possibly
twelve) years old when she rescued Smith[8]—*if she did*, and
there has always been some question about that. It was not
exactly, then, love at first sight, as the romanticists would
have us believe. Furthermore, by the time Pocahontas married John Rolfe, she had already been married to an Indian
named Kocoum.[9] And her conversion to Christianity and subsequent baptism were not actually voluntary, since at the time
these events took place, she was a hostage, having been kidnapped by the English as ransom for other white men held by
Powhatan. (Smith had already returned to England.)

About each of the other legendary events in her life—and
the people she encountered—there are similar distortions,
more accurately understood as oversights on the part of Pocahontas's various biographers. One thing is evident, however;
the Pocahontas story as it is commonly related tells us, in
Philip Young's words, that

> Our own ways, race, religion must be better—so much
> better that even an Indian . . . albeit an unusually fine
> one (witness her recognition of our superiority), per-
> ceived our rectitude. But it nicely eases the guilt we have
> felt since the start of its popularity over the way we had
> already begun, by 1608, to treat the Indians. Pocahontas
> is a female Squanto, a "good" Indian, and by taking her
> to our national bosom we experience a partial absolution.
> In the lowering of her head we feel a benediction. We
> are so wonderful she loved us anyway.[10]

It is this absolution—this guilt about the races—that interests
us here.

The Pocahontas myth is difficult to clarify because its origins are obscure. John Smith's *True Relation of such Occurrences and Accidents of note as hath happened in Virginia*,
published in 1608, includes no mention of his rescue by
Pocahontas. Although Smith made reference to the event in a

letter he wrote to the queen (when Pocahontas was in London) in 1616, the first published version of the episode does not appear until *The Capture and Release of Captain John Smith, Including His Rescue from Death by Pocahontas, In His Own Words from the General History of Virginia as Published at London in 1624*. The complete story is slightly more than a hundred words:

> . . . having feasted him [Smith] after their best barbarous manner they could, a long consultation was held, but the conclusion was, two great stones were brought before Powhatan: then as many as could laid hands on him, dragged him to them, and thereon laid his head, and being ready with their clubs to beat out his brains, Pocahontas, the King's dearest daughter, when no entreaty could prevail, got his head in her arms and laid her own upon his to save him from death: whereat the Emperor was contented he should live to make him hatchets, and her bells, beads, and copper; for they thought him as well of all occupations as themselves.[11]

Out of this brief incident Smith published his most popular book, and the myth itself was born.

Smith's rescue by Pocahontas has been in considerable question ever since the 1624 volume appeared. Since he did not describe the incident in the earlier *True Relation*, many critics have concluded that the event never took palce—that Smith simply took advantage of Pocahontas's recent presence in London. (Both Powhatan and Pocahontas were dead when the volume appeared—there was no way Smith could be contradicted.) Why else was it necessary to wait sixteen years to tell the story? Are we to conclude that the 1608 version is fact and the 1624 one is fiction?[12] Are we, therefore, to assume (as numerous people have done) that the rescue of John Smith by Pocahontas constitutes our first piece of American fiction?

Whether fact or fiction, the Pocahontas story fulfills a specific function in our literature. If it is true (and I suspect that it is to a certain extent), it illustrates the ambivalent attitude Europeans held toward Native peoples—wanting to believe that not all Indians were bloodthirsty (as Powhatan was supposed to be). If fiction, it also shows an early American

writer coming to grips with the raw materials and the poten-
tials of a new continent. The Indian was new, different—
something to be written about. Sadly, Smith's first account of
the rescue tells us little about the real Pocahontas (or any of
the other participants, for that matter). Subsequent writers
would embellish the details, but the myth had begun. (To be
sure, there have been attempts down through the years to
separate the real Pocahontas from the mythical one. See, for
example, Henry Adams's "Captain John Smith," *North American Review* 104 [1867]:1–30. Much more recently, in the most
complete account of the Pocahontas story written to date
[Frances Mossiker's *Pocahontas: The Life and the Legend*,
1976], the author suggests that Powhatan never intended to
kill Smith, but, rather, wanted to test the Englishman's courage with a mock execution. If this is so, Pocahontas was part
of the test, and the whole drama was staged by her father.)

We are haunted to this day by the fact that Smith was not
the one whom Pocahontas married. But, after all, even if she
was a heathen, she was an Indian princess, and Smith was a
commoner. When Smith first met her, she was sixteen or
eighteen years his junior and clearly by his mores too young
for any sexual relationship. Nor was Smith exactly known for
his passion. There was a further complication because Smith
returned abruptly to England (wounded and in need of medical care, so most versions say) without telling Pocahontas
about his departure. Unaware of this, Pocahontas probably
concluded that he was dead. Rolfe, in fact, told her this[13]—it
was one of the reasons she married him. By the time of their
marriage, she had also acquired a new name, Rebecca.
(Pocahontas was not her real name either; it was Matoaka.)[14]

Matoaka/Pocahontas/Rebecca married John Rolfe on April
5, 1614, when she was seventeen or eighteen years old. The
year before she had "seen the faith"—a prerequisite necessary
for the marriage, since the church would not have permitted
such an outright violation of the Christian marriage sacrament. Not only did Pocahontas have to be scrubbed and
sanitized, but it was necessary for Rolfe to gain permission
from the Governor of Virginia to marry her. There were
further complications. According to Grace Steele Woodward,
"When King James was told of [the marriage], he was out-

raged and accused Rolfe of committing high treason in marrying the daughter of a savage king. James's Privy Council assured him that Rolfe's heirs would not inherit England's holding's in Virginia. . . ."[15] The king's land would remain secure.

Why did Pocahontas (called Lady Rebecca after her conversion) marry John Rolfe? Besides believing that Smith was dead, she was a bit of a tease—as has been suggested by more than one of her biographers—out from the beginning to catch one of the light-skinned men. Philip L. Barbour, in *Pocahontas and Her World*, gives us this picture from the instant when Pocahontas first encountered the Englishmen. During the winter following the rescue of Smith, Barbour states, "Pocahontas would blissfully do cartwheels around the fort [Jamestown], virtually in the nude,"[16] an image of the young girl that has also been suggested by other writers, including Smith's contemporaries.

In his novel about Pocahontas, David Garnett suggests other reasons for the marriage, namely that both parties had ulterior reasons: "She dreamed of bells, of London churches from whose white steeples, touched by the rosy light of dawn, clouds of white pigeons shot up, spattering the blue sky."[17] Since she had never seen such buildings and steeples, one wonders how she could have dreamed of them, but that is a small matter. More important, Garnett has Rolfe think, " 'If she goes back [to her tribe] she will be married to a painted savage and will become a heathen again. We shall lose the soul we have saved for God!' "[18] And, somewhat later, the pious Rolfe concludes,

> "But if I were to marry her? I should thereby save her immortal soul—(I should save her from the painted Indian.) [Kocoum?] I might be the means of bringing peace to the colony and of converting thousands of savages, doing that work of which so many have spoken and which only here, with Pocahontas, has been begun."[19]

Pocahontas thus became our first Christian convert—a beacon that would bring light to an entire continent of savages. She was living hope for the religious leaders of the colony— proof that savages could be converted.

For a time she lived with Rolfe on his tobacco plantation in Virginia. (In 1614 he was made secretary and recorder of the colony.) Their son, Thomas, was born in 1615, and the following year the three of them sailed to England. Pocahontas was put on display as an exotic, invited to important court functions from which her husband was excluded since he was "a mere gentleman-farmer."[20] In London she also met John Smith again, and it is on record that she was shocked to learn that he was alive. In 1617, as Rolfe and his family were leaving London for Virginia, Pocahontas died, at Gravesend, before the ship left the Thames. (Francis Mossiker suggests that the cause of Pocahontas's death was probably a respiratory or pulmonary infection and not smallpox as others have speculated: "it cannot have been smallpox . . . the symptoms readily recognizable, no smallpox patient would have been permitted to board ship to spread the dread disease among other passengers.")[21] On March 21, 1617, she was buried at Gravesend in the churchyard—in an unmarked grave. She was about twenty-one years old.

The distortions of fact about Pocahontas's life are not limited to her relationship with Smith; they embrace the entire span of her life—up to the time of her death. The problem is that she has become much larger than life. She has come to represent too many differing aspects of our country's nascence, and at this late stage it is almost impossible to separate truth from myth. She has been called "the first lady of America,"[22] a "daughter of Eve,"[23] "a child of the forest,"[24] "an angel of peace,"[25] "a madonna figure,"[26] "the nonparell of Virginia,"[27] "the mother of two nations,"[28] "the mother of us all,"[29] and "the great Earth Mother of the Americas."[30] In a way, of course, she is all of these and more—an Indian princess (one of our few claims to royalty), an ersatz Christian, and, much more important, our first assimilated Indian.

Even more quickly than Pocahontas seemed to embrace English culture was she assimilated into the mainstream of American folklore. Smith's contemporaries never tired of singing her praises.[31] Eighteenth- and nineteenth-century English and American writers never questioned their reading or viewing audiences' voracious appetite for the latest literary work involving the dark heroine.[32] By the mid nineteenth century, theater audiences were so tired of watching still another Pocahontas nuzzle Captain Smith's head in her arms—and in the more extreme versions emit "heighos" and warble romantic ditties—that a string of parodies and anti-Pocahontas plays was produced, beginning with John Brougham's *Po-ca-hon-tas* (1855) and ending—for a time one hopes—with *The Origin of Necking, a Travesty on the Pocahontas–John Smith Episode* (1932), by Boyce Loving.

Pocahontas has appeared even more frequently in fiction than in drama or poetry, and in the most recent embroideries of the myth, the vitality of the story is still in rare form.[33] We have already noted the curious thoughts about London that David Garnett put into her head. What Garnett and others have done, of course, is create a portrait of a westernized Indian. Thus Garnett states of her: "When she had learned to milk, Rolfe taught her to make butter, and before she had mastered the delicacies of handling the churn, he wished for cheese as well."[34] The picture here is of a domesticated Indian, fully integrated into the Anglo-European culture. This is also the core of the confusing relationship implied by all versions of the Pocahontas myth, since they have all been written by non-Indians. Pocahontas becomes the embodiment of all Caucasian desires for the Indian. If every Indian can become a Noble Savage, there will be no Indian problem. If Indians can be domesticated, they will cease being savages and be as good as white people.[35] At its very origin, the Pocahontas myth is rooted in an insidious racism.

To understand these racial implications it is necessary to look more closely at the religious complications that had to be overcome before Pocahontas could be permitted to marry John Rolfe. The Indian represented the darkest aspect of the New World, as he also mirrored the deepest unexplored recesses of the Puritan imagination. As Albert Keiser has written in his early work, *The Indian in American Literature*,

From the very beginning the stern character of the Puritan probably precluded a sympathetic relationship to the race soon to become his opponent and bitter enemy. In his struggle for his very existence the Calvinist who had

looked upon the native as a being to be redeemed from
the power of Satan soon became satisfied that the enemy
of God was to be exterminated at any cost, and that the
only good Indian was a dead Indian. In his peculiar religious intolerance and fanaticism he reputedly fell first
upon his knees and then upon the aborigines, prompted
to do the first in the hope that the second might be more
successful.[36]

In the face of beliefs such as these, the natural-born enemies
of God had little chance for survival.

It is reported by several authorities that Chief Powhatan went
out of his way to be helpful to the Englishmen until he realized
that they were not simply adventurers who would quickly leave
his land and return to their homes across the sea. Thereafter, he
attempted to break off all communication with them, but by then
it was too late. How ironic that his own daughter had already fallen captive to the mysterious qualities of the new dispensation.
Although Powhatan granted her permission to marry John Rolfe
(in a way he had little choice, since she was held in captivity), he
did not attend the wedding. The old chief had become at most a
minor obstacle in the marriage—far less a complication than the
principals themselves.

The ironies here are boundless. In a way, Pocahontas was
more of a Christian than Rolfe, John Smith, and all the Puritan fathers rolled into one. She had played the role of Good
Samaritan without knowledge of the Biblical model. (There
seems to be little disagreement that without her kindness the
Jamestown settlers would not have survived the harsh winter
of 1607–8.) Pocahontas's conversion, then, was to something
she already was—without the doctrine—while the Puritan
fathers themselves were not above engaging in certain un-
speakable acts.[37] Yet Pocahontas had to be converted and
baptized and the marriage approved by the governor and the
church. Once those prerequisites had been realized, there was
no way that she was going to be permitted to return to her
previous dark ways. Although the idea of the marriage may
have been anathema to many of Rolfe's contemporaries, and
even to Rolfe himself, henceforth there was no escape for
Pocahontas. To her own people she was forever lost. The

church needed her as a symbol of its holiness and divine superiority. She had become a living symbol—not, of course, without someone's having to pay a price.

In a way, then, Pocahontas was a kind of traitor to her people. Again and again she let them down. All of the things she has been admired for down through the years (the rescue of Smith, the bringing of food to the starving Englishmen, the conversion to Christianity, the marriage to Rolfe, the excursion to London) must certainly have increased the rancor of her own people—but we have no written accounts of their opinions about these events. All we know is that Pocahontas rejected her own people in favor of the invaders. Perhaps I am being a little too hard on her. The crucial point, it seems to me, is to remember that Pocahontas was a hostage. Would she have converted freely to Christianity if she had not been in captivity? There is no easy answer to this question other than to note that once she was free to do what she wanted, she avoided her own people like the plague. We are told by more than one authority that Pocahontas did not want to return to Virginia,[38] but wished instead to remain in London, though the other Powhatan Indians who were in England at the same time (including one of Powhatan's younger brothers) could not wait to return home.

The problem is that we have never really known how Pocahontas felt about any of these matters (the conversion, her marriage to Rolfe—especially her feelings about her own people). I am simply trying to suggest that if we look at her story solely through the eyes of the white participants (and their subsequent biographers, who have all been white), our conclusions may be rather one-sided. There is that gnawing racist quality about all of these accounts, just as there is about all the participants in the story—except for Chief Powhatan.

Like Pocahontas, John Smith has always been seen as something he was not: a kind of archetypal Englishman—heroic, virtuous, scrupulously moral. Yet he had for years been a crypto-mercenary, a soldier of fortune, engaged in rather shady military matters. Grace Steele Woodward informs us of his most recent difficulty before he arrived in the New World: "En route to Jamestown on the *Susan Constant* he had been arrested and put in irons by Captain Newport,

who had accused him of inciting mutiny among some of the
ship's passengers."[39] Although he was later exonerated, the
fact is that Smith was a rather difficult fellow who frequently
went against the orders of his superiors.

Smith has intrigued his biographers not only because he
failed to marry Pocahontas, but because he never married at
all. Bradford Smith, one of his most sympathetic biographers,
phrases it this way: "That there was a streak of asexual purity
and restraint in Smith is evident both from his works and
from the fact that he never married."[40] (Bradford Smith also
speculates that the reason Smith repressed the rescue by
Pocahontas for so many years was that by publicizing the
event he would be exposing his lauded courage to the gibes of
his contemporaries.) Most of his biographers have agreed that
even though Smith appears to have developed no emotional
attraction for Pocahontas, she did for him. His inability to express his emotions (or even to realize that other people might
possess such feelings), makes it easy for us to understand why
he was able to leave Jamestown without saying farewell to the
young Indian Princess. (Apparently the idea never entered his
mind—a fact that supports the argument that Pocahontas
never rescued him.) Thus, if Smith was not a prude, at the
very least he was a kind of emotional cripple.

The fictions about Smith almost always depict him as a
friend of the Indians—the one Englishman at the Jamestown
settlement who regarded them as something other than unen-
lightened beasts. Yet there is documented evidence that
Smith had killed two or three Indians before the Pocahontas
incident,[41] and I believe we can safely assume that if the
encounter with Powhatan had not occurred, he would have
killed more. Fortunately for the Indians, his last years were
spent as a frustrated hack writer in England trying to capital-
ize on the previous adventures of his life. These writings, of
course, have led to his dubious status as the father of American literature. Although Smith died in 1631 and it was
another eighty-eight years before Daniel Defoe published *Rob-
inson Crusoe* (1719), one cannot help regarding the Pocahontas myth and Defoe's first novel in a similar light. By the time
Defoe wrote his popular work, fiction had already begun to
subsume fact.

John Rolfe is no less a questionable fellow. His reasons for marrying Pocahontas were at best utilitiarian. As John Gould Fletcher wrote in 1928, citing a letter Rolfe wrote to Sir Thomas Dale (the governor) about the forthcoming wedding, "It [the letter] leaves one in complete doubt whether this ageing wooer, already once a widower, felt any attraction towards the Indian girl at all, or whether the whole thing was not a political move inspired by the clever Dale to obtain an alliance with the Indians at little cost."[42] (Fletcher argues that Pocahontas was "effectively sacrificed to the promotion of the prosperity of the Virginia Colony.")[43] "Ageing wooer" may be a little harsh, but there seems to be little question that Rolfe married Pocahontas for personal advantage. As a tobacco farmer, Rolfe may have assumed that marrying the daughter of a chief would in time increase the size of his landholdings. After Pocahontas's death in England, Rolfe left their son, Thomas, with relatives. Then he married for a third time but died without ever seeing Thomas again. (Ironically, Rolfe's death was at the hands of Powhatan Indians, in a massacre led by Pocahontas's uncle.)[44]

By a process of elimination, Powhatan emerges as the only figure in the story who had not been tarnished by history and legend, though he remains under constant attack by almost all writers who deal with the incident. For example, Grace Steele Woodward described the Powhatan culture as one "of dark superstitions and devil worship, a culture of easy cruelty and primitive social accomplishments."[45] Be that as it may, the old chief is the only participant in the story who appears to have remained true to his own convictions. It is easy to forget that his lands were being invaded, that he was lied to by Smith and others, and that he was constantly being duped by the English (who would give him a handful of beads and then demand two or three hundred bushels of corn in exchange). Ironically, he brought about his own decline by aiding the men who later fought against him. Still, when he died in 1618, he directed that a substantial amount of land be given to his grandson, Thomas Rolfe.

Thomas Rolfe, that child of two worlds, quickly decided which side of his heritage was the more important. Some years after his return to Virginia (in 1635), he married Jane

Poythress, an Englishwoman, "and from their union de-
scended seven successive generations of educators, ministers,
statesmen, and lawmakers, among whom were the Blairs, the
Bollings, the Lewises, and the Randolphs."[46] A comfortable
ending to the story—certainly designed to warm the hearts of
true Virginians down to the present day. However, the ending
is not nearly so happy for Native American readers. Today,
nearly two million descendants are able to trace their ancestry
back to Pocahontas (and John Rolfe). Yet only a handful of
so-called Powhatan Indians can be found in Virginia at the
present time, and "these have ceased to function as a culturally definable entity, retaining little more than a tribal name
and a sense of common origin."[47] The children of Pocahontas
are not Indians—they are white.

The story has another irony. In 1641, before he married,
Thomas Rolfe was "appointed Captain of Fort James, [an]
honor requiring his virtual denial of his Indian ancestry,"[48]
and one which effectively cut him off from his Indian heritage. In 1644, he fought against his own mother's people in a
battle against Opechancanough, Powhatan's younger brother.
That battle ended the Indian control of all lands "between the
James and the York, from the fall-line to Chesapeake Bay."[49]
It was the death-knell for Pocahontas's people, ironically participated in by the most celebrated half blood of the time.
Thomas Rolfe's dynasty lives on to the present day scattered
far and wide, bleached whiter and whiter as each successive
generation has diluted the blood inherited from Pocahontas.

Yet the myth lives on, and there is no fear of its demise.
Pocahontas has always been good business: there is no reason
to expect this will change. After all, she is Every Indian, the
archetypal Noble Savage. She was a dea ex machina, rescuing
Smith for reasons she never made public. She appealed to
Englishmen like Rolfe because they were lonely and sex-
starved, surrounded by a masculine community that in turn
was enclosed by a foreboding world of dark shadows. If there
had been more women around, she probably would have been
ignored. (Rolfe wrote to Governor Dale that if he had wanted
to marry someone good looking, he could have found "Christ-
ians more pleasinge to the eye.")[50] Nevertheless, she represents what every enlightened Indian was capable of becoming:

kind, gentle, helpful, rescuing men in times of need, releasing them from the darker shadows of their own innate superstitions and fears. No matter that she has become almost totally an invention of the Euro-American fictive imagination. No matter that she was a traitor to her race. No matter that her earthly existence bears little relationship to the myth she has become.

What we must understand, then, is that Pocahontas ushered in a flood of assimilationist writings, rooted in simplistic logic: if Pocahontas was happy to become white, why shouldn't all Indians be the same? If she could be readily converted to Christianity, why couldn't the others? We have, of course, repressed the fact that in her role as Good Samaritan, she did for us what we would never have done for her. We have always assumed that the Indian would become one of us. We will accept him on no other terms. In the long run, it does not matter that she was never permitted to tell her own version of the story. She would not have been listened to if she had tried to do so.

Pocahontas? She was an Indian we created solely out of our ethnocentric imaginations. She was the shadow in the great forest.

What, then, does all of this have to do with the subsequent novels written by Native Americans?

Like Pocahontas, the Native American has rarely been able to tell his own story. Rather, it has been told for him by others—examined, digested, misinterpreted. With few exceptions, the American Indian has remained a shadow in the great forest—misunderstood, feared, looked at from a distance—always surrounded by a mysterious aura. In our literature (and especially in our novels), our images of Native characters have been created almost exclusively by outsiders, by non-Indians. When we think of popular literary portraits of Native Americans, it is as if a curtain has been drawn before our eyes. When we rack our memories, we can remember only a few images at most: Cooper's redskins, who all merge into one; Hiawatha, the most extreme of them all; Indian Joe (in *Tom Sawyer*), conveniently killed off at the end of the novel; Melville's Tashtego and also Queequeg, a South Sea

Islander, usually classified as an Indian. Cigar Store Indians, all of them, with no more life than the wood from which they were carved. Shadows in the great forest which mirrors the confusion in our minds.

More often than not the shadow in the forest is depicted as a savage. Yet this should be no surprise, since from the beginning, when those earliest Puritans set foot on American soil, the Indian was regarded as a relic from the past. As Roy Harvey Pearce has written in *Savagism and Civilization*,

> . . . the savage would be understood as one who had not and somehow could not progress into the civilized, who would inevitably be destroyed by the civilized, the lesser good necessarily giving way to the greater. . . . For the Indian was the remnant of a savage past away from which civilized men had struggled to grow. To study him was to study the past. To civilize him was to triumph over the past. To kill him was to kill the past.[51]

We have killed him again and again—in a hundred poems, a hundred novels, a hundred movies. Those who were not literally slaughtered by our superior armaments were figuratively murdered by our finest writers, our most talented artists. We commission an artist to paint a picture of the baptism of Pocahontas for the rotunda of the Capitol, while muzzling her compatriots at the same time. We watch a hundred thousand Indians slaughtered on our television sets in late-night movies, never questioning the accuracy of the story, never wondering why one of them hasn't told his own tale.

The Pocahontas myth is the way our fiction about Native Americans begins. And it begins badly. It has little to do with John Smith's rescue. Rather, it is concerned with all the fictions we have evolved relating to the several participants in the story, and all the other fictions about Native Americans which have been perpetrated by non-Indians. Surprisingly, once we turn to those novels written by Native Americans, we encounter no Pocahontas figures. There are few romanticized Indians in these works, yet most of them are concerned, like the Pocahontas tale, with the conflict of cultures, with the coming together of two disparate ways of life. Perhaps there

are no Pocahontas figures in these novels because they generally deal with more recent stages of this confrontation, though
I suspect that if a Native American decided to write a novel
about Pocahontas it would be far different from those versions
of the story we have read in the past, from the myth we are
familiar and comfortable with.

Pocahontas was a white dream—a dream of cultural superiority. The Native American has no more been assimilated
into our culture than we have been assimilated into his. As a
literary subject he is only beginning to be discovered, to be
dealt with in an accurate manner. As recently as 1933, when
Albert Keiser wrote his classic study of Native peoples in literary works written by non-Indians, *The Indian in American
Literature*, he predicted that the Native American would
shortly cease to be a subject of literary concern:

> . . . in his adaptation to [his] new-found freedom [he]
> will more and more cease to be an Indian and become an
> integral part of white civilization. As such he will no
> longer serve as the subject of separate literary portrayal,
> and the picture of the native as reflected in American
> literature will then at last be finished, except in so far as
> master artists of the future may here and there retouch
> the immense canvas.[52]

The novels discussed in this book are a refutation of that
conclusion. The children of Pocahontas are learning to listen.
Powhatan's other children have learned to write.

3

Assimilation: Estrangement from the Land

"Some young men try to talk like white man; they try to act like white man. But they talk like white man who talks like crow, and they act like white man who acts bad, I believe. It is not good for young men to talk like white man who talks like crow. They send our young men off to school and there they learn to talk like white man who knows how to talk, I believe. I believe that is good. But at this school they make our young men do things like white man; but he is Indian. . . . I do not know if it is good for Indian to learn from white man. Indian knows many things, but white says that these things are not good. I believe white man does not know many things that Indian knows."—Big Chief to Major Laban J. Miles, in *Wah'Kon-Tah*, by John Joseph Mathews

The works of the three earliest Native American novelists—Chief Simon Pokagon (1830?–99), John Milton Oskison (1874–1947), and John Joseph Mathews (b.1895)—are representative of the mainstream of American popular writing of the time. (This is also true of the one novel by Hum-Ishu-Ma [Mourning Dove], *Co-Ge-We-A* [*The Half-Blood*], published in 1927, and discussed separately in Appendix 1.) Their works span the period from 1899 to 1935, and include one novel by Pokagon, *Queen of the Woods* (1899), three by Oskison, *Wild Harvest* (1925), *Black Jack Davy* (1926), and *Brothers Three* (1935), and one by Mathews, *Sundown* (1934), though all three writers published other works of nonfiction during their lives. If we did not know that these men were Native Americans, we might conclude from their novels that they were white. Taken together, the novels are conventional in form, traditional in subject, anything but innovative—indistinguishable from hundreds of other fictional works of the time. For the most part, it is easy to see why they have been forgotten. Even when we search for Indian subjects in these works, the results are far less rewarding than for any of the subsequent novels by Native American writers.

As a group, Chief Pokagon, Oskison, and Mathews were all highly educated—certainly by the standards of Indian education of that era, but also by the criteria of all Americans living in those times. Yet, as we will see, the Native American novelist down through the years has tended to be the individual with the exceptional education. Obviously, I am referring to the white establishment's educational measurements— formal education at a public or private institution. Without this training, they would not have become writers. At the time of his death in 1899, Chief Pokagon (of the Potawatomi Indians) was referred to as "the best educated and most distinguished full-blooded Indian, probably, in America."[1] In addition to his own Algonquian language and English, he knew Greek and Latin. His education had been acquired at Notre Dame and at Oberlin College, where he spent three years and one year, respectively. John M. Oskison (a Cherokee), who worked as a professional writer and journalist, received a B.A. from Stanford and went on for advanced work in literature at Harvard. John J. Mathews (Osage) received a B.A. in geology from the University of Oklahoma in 1920, and a second B.A. in the natural sciences from Oxford in 1933.

Writing was important for all three of these men—more than simply a passing fancy. In 1893, Chief Pokagon published a sixteen-page booklet called *The Red Man's Rebuke*, printed on birch bark and sold at the World's Columbian Exposition in Chicago. It was a scathing account of the American Indian's constant betrayal, beginning with the arrival of the white man in his world. (Later reprintings of the work have fatuously retitled it *The Red Man's Greeting*.) Pokagon was also a popular orator and a spokesman for the Native American. (He met with Presidents Lincoln, Grant, and Cleveland.) The publisher of *Queen of the Woods* refers to him as "the redskin bard" and the "Longfellow of his race" (p. 33). Besides publishing three novels, John M. Oskison wrote a number of other works including *A Texas Titan: The Story of*

Sam Houston (1929) and *Tecumseh and His Times: The Story of a Great Indian* (1938), in addition to many short stories and articles on southwestern life. Oskison was an editorial writer and an editor much of his life, working for *The New York Post* and *Collier's Magazine*. John J. Mathews's most widely known book is *Wah'Kon-Tah* (1932), though there are several other significant ones, including *The Osages* (1961), published by the University of Oklahoma Press as part of its American Indian Series.

Taken together, the novels by these three men reveal only a limited concern with the social issues confronting Native Americans of the time. To be sure, Pokagon's *Queen of the Woods* is preoccupied with the evils of alcohol consumption, but this subject in no way is exclusive to American Indian writing. (One thinks of Walt Whitman, whose only work of fiction, *Franklin Evans, or the Inebriate*, published in 1842, was also a temperance novel.) Although it ends as a protest novel, *Queen of the Woods* begins as a romance, presenting a picture of Native American life that was already foreign to many of Chief Pokagon's contemporaries. A sense of artificiality also typifies the works of the other two early novelists. John M. Oskison's three novels have very little to do with American Indian life; rather, Native Americans tend to be used as background for the dramas played out by his Caucasian characters. John J. Mathews's *Sundown* begins to confront more directly those issues facing Native Americans of the time, though the plot of the novel does not always relate to these problems.

In point of fact, the novels of these three writers are basically assimilationist. Their characters accept white values and cultural traits, often rejecting their own traditional way of life. In *Queen of the Woods*, Chief Simon Pokagon is determined to illustrate that he is the same as every American, that he lives similarly to everyone else. Oskison's three novels again and again uphold a conventional belief in the American dream; success, money, riches, he preaches, are available to all through hard work and honest living. In Mathews's *Sundown*, the main character, Chal Windzer, who cannot decide if he should live as an Indian or as a white man, is constantly embarrassed about his Indian "ways."

Chief Simon Pokagon, John M. Oskison, and John J. Mathews were all sophisticated men who moved freely back and forth between the Native American and the white man's cultures. As novelists, however, they were children of Pocahontas, caught in the problems of their dual identities. The horrors of the recent past (the Indian wars of the last half of the nineteenth century) had apparently shown them the total destruction of tribal life and the need for acceptance of the white man's way of life. What more could we expect than their acquiescence in assimilation? Their novels, though lesser works than those of their successors, merit our attention as literary responses to the prevailing registers of cultural demise.

Queen of the Woods

The immediate problem confronting the critic of Chief Simon Pokagon's *Queen of the Woods* is to decide whether to classify the work as fiction or as autobiography. The Preface, written by the publisher, describes the volume as "a real romance of Indian life by Chief Pokagon" (p. i), adding:

> Nearly all the persons mentioned in the narrative bear their real names, and were personally known to many yet living. The reader will bear in mind that in all cases where fictitious names are used, or where the names of persons spoken of are omitted from the narrative, it was purposely done by the author, out of regard for friends and relatives who now occupy the places where certain tragic events occurred. (p. i)

Without this comment from the publisher, I doubt that readers would ever consider the volume as anything other than a work of fiction.

My reasons for classifying the work as a novel are twofold. First, the volume was published several months after Chief Pokagon's death, and I can only conclude that the Preface was a hasty addition by the publisher, who felt some need to pass the work off as fact, rather than as fiction—the old publishing trick of simulating verisimilitude. More important, however, are the facts revealed in the narrative about the

main character (who is called Chief Pokagon). They simply do
not mesh with information known about Pokagon's own life.[2]
Thus I have concluded that *Queen of the Woods* is a romantic
novel which has drawn heavily on certain details from Pokagon's own life, though many of the events described are a free
flight of his imagination—an autobiographical novel, if one
wants to call it that.

The romantic overtones are of especial significance. The
publisher refers to the work as an "interesting Indian romance" and, as already noted, "a real romance of Indian life"
(p. i), the latter a phrase which would appear to contradict
itself. Yet the fact is that without the final sections of the
book, where the temperance theme is dominant, the work
would, indeed, be classified as romance or pastoral, somewhat
in the vein of Chateaubriand's *Atala* (1801) and *René* (1802).
The publisher must have regarded these romantic elements as
central to the story, since there are a number of line drawings
throughout the text which depict the main characters in
highly idealized poses.

The romanticism of *Queen of the Woods* is explicit from the
opening sentence, which introduces both the narrator and a
major theme of the story, the contrast between the Indian's
natural world and the white man's civilization:

> On my return home from Twinsburg, O., where I had
> attended the white man's school for several years, I had
> an innate desire to retire into the wild woods, far from
> the haunts of civilization, and there enjoy myself with
> bow and arrow, hook and line, as I had done before
> going to school. (p. 49)

What follows is the idyllic account of Pokagon's love for an
Indian maiden and the eventual destruction of their relationship because of alcohol—introduced to the Indian by the
white man's civilization.

After his return from the Twinsburg school, Pokagon (the
character) meets the beautiful Indian maiden, Lonidaw, who
lives in the forest with her mother and a white deer. During
the summer, they fall in love, but Pokagon returns to his
classes in the fall. When he is away from Lonidaw, he is unable to think of anything but the virginal young woman. After

their marriage the following spring, the albino deer leaves them out of jealousy and a broken heart, disappearing, never to be seen again. Two years later, a son, Olondaw, is born, followed by a daughter, Hazeleye, three years later. When Olondaw is twelve years old, a Catholic priest suggests that the boy be sent to the white man's school, and shortly thereafter he leaves (against his mother's better judgment and her premonition that he will become an alcoholic). Lonidaw's fear comes true three years later when Olondaw returns home from school, a fifteen-year-old alcoholic. Shortly thereafter he dies from drink. Then the daughter, Hazeleye, drowns because of a freakish accident involving two drunken white men who are boating; Lonidaw dies shortly thereafter out of grief for the loss of her children. (There are only a few parallels here with Chief Pokagon's own life. His first wife, Lonidaw Sinagaw, bore him four children: Cecilia, William, Charles, and Jerome. She died in 1871 and Pokagon raised the children himself until they were old enough to attend Haskell Institute [a school for Indians]. Pokagon remarried much later in his life.) The novel concludes with a lengthy tirade against the evils of drink.

Queen of the Woods is narrated in the first person (by a character called Chief Pokagon), related in strict chronological order, and divided roughly into two parts: the earlier, romantic sections, and the later ones that proselytize about the need for temperance. The tone is didactic throughout, at times giving the impression that one is reading a sermon instead of fiction. Pokagon's use of language is often stilted and awkward, too frequently relying on stock figures of speech: "the curtain of night" (p. 58), "the woodland choir" (p. 58), "the darling of my heart" (p. 119), "my native woodland ways" (p. 120). The dialogue is pompous, imitative, even artificially Shakespearean: "Hark! I faintly hear some muffled footsteps near . . ." (p. 65).

In spite of the rather pedestrian writing, the opening chapters display a certain grace and liveliness, especially those passages treating the natural world. The kind of lush, Rousseau-esque attitude toward nature revealed in these sections is exemplified in the following passage from the opening chapter:

Just as "gi-siss" (the sun) was going down, we reached our landing-place. The shore on either side was fringed with rushes, flags, and golden-rod, and grasses tall between; and scattered here and there wild roses breathed their rich perfume, scenting the evening air. . . . It was indeed a strange, romantic place. (p. 55)

Added to this is Pokagon's frequently implied contrast between the natural world and the white man's artificial one:

While living in that secluded place, I felt a freedom and independence unknown to civilization. There, undisturbed, I could hunt and fish, contemplating the romantic beauties and wonderful grandeur of the forests about me. While in communion with the Great Spirit, I could feel, as my fathers had before me, that I was chief of all I surveyed. (p. 61)

Pokagon uses Lonidaw as an embodiment of the natural order. She is the closest approximation to the stereotyped image of a Noble Savage in all of the novels written by Native Americans; she is a part of the natural world, not removed from it. She could not, in fact, exist in the white man's world. Again and again, Pokagon describes her as something mysterious and beautiful—too perfect, perhaps, for earthly existence. Her purity is symbolized by her companion, the snow-white deer, and the implication of the deer's disappearance is that by marrying her, Pokagon has corrupted her. As we might expect, Pokagon is somewhat jealous of the unusual attraction the deer holds for the young maiden.

Describing Lonidaw's almost mystical unity with the natural world, Pokagon states of her, "She claims all living creatures have a language of their own, and that she can talk with them." In her oneness with the natural order, "She only seeks communion with the Great Spirit through the animal creation . . ." (p. 146). When she dies at the end of the story, at the age of thirty-four, her death unleashes a violent storm. The entire natural world, we infer, aches for her demise.

So thoroughly does the ethereal Lonidaw dominate the narrative that Queen of the Woods might be considered a one-character novel. The energy spent characterizing her makes the minor characters (Olondaw, Hazeleye, Lonidaw's mother, and numerous other Indians who pass in and out of the narrative) unimportant. Even Pokagon himself remains an unconvincing figure, because his primary function (as mouth-piece for the author) is to illustrate the way that liquor has totally destroyed his family. One might surmise from my de-scription of Lonidaw that she is a reincarnation of Captain John Smith's Pocahontas. In fact the two have nothing in common. Lonidaw wants nothing to do with the white man's world, nor does she suffer from any identity problems. Her sole desire is to remain in the wild, as part of nature.

In *Queen of the Woods*, the bridge to the white man's world is education. The opening paragraph of the novel hints that education may become the great confuser for the Indian:

> when our children are educated, and return from school to live among their own people, unless places can be secured for them away from the influences that cluster about them, the result of their education must necessar-ily in some cases prove disappointing to those who have labored so ardently in their behalf. (p. 50)

Not, however, until much later in the story does Pokagon give an illustration of this confusion, and by then the insidious ef-fects of alcohol have begun to infiltrate the narrative. Olon-daw is sent to the Catholic school, at the school's expense, in order "that he might become learned, great, and good, and thereby be of great service to our race" (p. 169). Lonidaw dreams that the school will corrupt her son (expose him to an evil world), but Pokagon convinces her that the boy should leave. It is while he is at school that he becomes addicted to alcohol. As he later tells his parents, the addiction started be-cause he began collecting empty liquor bottles in order to re-deem them for a few pennies' deposit. Later,

> "[by drinking] the rinsing water . . . I began to like it, and after a while I wanted it so awfully bad I could think of nothing else. Then I would go . . . bottle hunting. . . . A big boy used to take my bottle-money and buy whisky for me on the halves, as he called it; as he said I could not buy it, because I was an Indian boy." (p. 174)

Much earlier in the narrative Pokagon has prepared his reader for the horror of Olondaw's addiction. The first reference to liquor appears on the third page of the novel, where Pokagon relates an incident that happened to his friend Bertrand when "he seized [several] bottles [of liquor] and broke them against a rock" (p. 51) because he feared that some Indian women were going to give them to their sons. In the third chapter, we learn that Lonidaw's father died of alcoholism. Thereafter, there are literally dozens of brief asides on the subject of liquor (usually called firewater), drunkenness, and general abuse due to the consumption of whisky and rum. Examples in the text of the novel are supported by footnotes, providing further details about Indian use of alcohol. For example,

> Indian Whisky: The most profitable and the most ruinous trade Mackinaw ever had was in whisky. A well-known recipe among the traders was: "Take two gallons of common whisky, or unrectified spirits, to thirty gallons of water, add red pepper enough to make it fiery, and tobacco enough to make it intoxicating." Its cost was not more than five cents a gallon. Thousands of barrels were sold there every year; the price there generally was fifty cents a quart by the bottle. (p. 107)

In one of the more extreme examples, Pokagon states, "It is well authenticated that many persons addicted to drinking great amounts of stimulants, have taken fire by spontaneous combustion" (p. 196). (I have been unable to establish when Pokagon first became interested in the temperance movement, but it was sometime before the publication of his earlier book, *The Red Man's Rebuke* [1893], which contains a similar attack on liquor.)

After the deaths of Olondaw, Hazeleye, and his wife, Pokagon states, " 'All this trouble now weighing down my soul, has fallen upon me by reason of that curse [liquor] dealt out to our race by the hands of white men' " (p. 183). The remaining forty pages of the novel are one long sermon against the evils of drink. Liquor (now referred to as King Alcohol) is linked to the devil and seen as a monster of uncontrollable proportions that threatens to kill all young Indians.

I saw along *every* trail where the monster wretch had
been, staggering, stalwart young men, and old men with
haggard looks, faces blotched, and eyes bloodshot and
bleared, shrieking and pleading for help, pointing, with
trembling fingers, in mortal agony, whispering, as they
wildly gazed, "See! See! the ghosts of hell, panther-like,
are crouching to pounce upon me."

Some in mad delirium, shook lizards from their
clothes. Others, in desperation, tore coiled serpents from
their necks, and strangling, prostrate fell, and there, like
dying wolves with poisoned "pik-wak" (arrows) pierced,
foam at the mouth. . . .

Among the drunkards in the throng, a few I saw whose
breath took fire within, while from their mouths and nos-
trils issued blue-like sulphurous flames, cremating them
alive, leaving but charred and blackened bones to tell
what they had been. (pp. 195–96)

As if this were not enough, Pokagon lashes out against the use
of tobacco ("cigarette weeds, whisky weeds, and all manner of
vicious weeds are running . . . over, demoralizing alike the
young men and little boys" [p. 208]). The tirade ends with a
call for universal temperance, for legislation to end the sale of
alcohol.

Read out of context, these attacks on liquor appear somewhat ludicrous, and the reader may wonder whatever possessed Chief Pokagon to write a romance *cum* temperance
novel. An initial reading of the novel may suggest that its two
halves (romance and temperance realism) do not belong together. The opening chapters of Queen of the Woods are more
romantic, more idyllic than anything one encounters in subsequent Native American fiction; the concluding chapters are
more farfetched than anything in later American Indian writing. Yet the two halves do fit together, by virtue of Pokagon's
thesis in Queen of the Woods: the romantic world of the past,
the natural order of man living in harmony with his environment, has been destroyed by the white man's greed, most
directly illustrated by the profits derived from the sale of alcoholic beverages to Native Americans.

This thesis is not so far removed from beliefs expressed in

subsequent Native American fiction. In all three of John M. Oskison's novels, drunken Indians appear; in Mathews's *Sundown*, much of the narrative is spent describing the main character's alcoholic stupors. The drunken Indian is, in fact, a stock character in almost all of the later novels by American Indian writers. And 'in at least one of these works (Storm's *Seven Arrows*), a similar economic thesis prevails, though it is extended beyond drink to other debilitating influences from the white man's world. It is not Pokagon's use of the temperance theme in *Queen of the Woods* that is difficult to accept so much as the eventual subordination of the romance once liquor becomes the dominant issue. In less than six pages, drink kills off all of Pokagon's family. Thereafter, the narrator is determined that his position not be misunderstood. The artfulness of the opening chapters is destroyed by the sledgehammer approach toward the end. Artistically, one might say that alcohol has indeed won out in this novel.

The alcoholic theme is also related to Pokagon's assimilationist beliefs. There is a wide discrepancy between what Pokagon (the character) says in *Queen of the Woods* and what Pokagon (the man) professed to believe in his own life. Whereas his novel says that exposure to the white man's world may result in a number of crippling influences for the Indian, the man in fact advocated something else—the white man's education and his life-style in general. It is, after all, not Pokagon, but Lonidaw who fears the white man's world. By the time he meets her, Pokagon has already been exposed to the Western world and apparently has accepted it with few qualifications. Hence, he agrees to send their son to the Catholic school, fully aware of the temptations to which the boy will be exposed. (In an appendix at the end of *Queen of the Woods*, we are informed that Chief Pokagon was "educated [to be] a priest" [p. 238], and that "he was a good Catholic . . ." [p. 239].)

Chief Pokagon's assimilationist beliefs are nowhere more apparent than in the introductory passages that precede the text of the novel. Here we find numerous quotations from the chief's remarks at the World's Columbian Exposition in 1893. Throughout, he expresses a kind of Talented Tenth[3] attitude; let educated Indians be accepted into the mainstream of American life:

"I rejoice that you are making an effort, at last, to have the educated people of my race take part in the great celebration. That will be much better for the good of our people, in the hearts of the dominant race, than war-whoops and battle-dances, such as I to-day witnessed on Midway Plaisance." (p. 12)

Later, determined to prove that Indians are just like everyone else, he states,

"The world's people, from what they have so far seen of us on the Midway, will regard us as savages; but they shall yet know that we are human as well as they, and the children of my father will always love those who help us to show that we are *men*." (p. 13)

Numerous expressions of this attitude are quoted in the Publisher's Notes at the beginning of the novel, all of them suggesting that Pokagon believed that the Indian could be domesticated—remodeled, as it were, to fit the white man's way of life: "We wish to show the world that we are men and brothers, worthy to be called Americans, and fit for citizenship" (p. 16). A few pages later, Pokagon calls for a wholesale renunciation of the Indians' traditional ways:

". . . we *must* give up the pursuits of our fathers. However dear we love the chase, we MUST give it up. We must teach our children to give up the bow and arrow that is born in their hearts; and, in place of the gun, we must take the plow, and live as white men do. . . . Our children *must* learn that they owe no allegiance to any clan or power on earth except the United States. They must learn to love the Stars and Stripes, and at all times to rejoice that they are American citizens.

"Our children must be educated, and learn the different trades of the white men." (p. 21)

The significance of Pokagon's *Queen of the Woods* rests not so much in its dramatic arguments as in its existence as the first novel by a Native American. True, the book established a pattern of assimilationist novels which lasted for roughly the next thirty-five years. After that, however, the Indian novelist was free to reject what his predecessors had embraced; yet, as in so many cases where cultures have undergone rapid social changes, the traces of the past carry over into the present. Pokagon, for all of his extremes, was an optimist; he believed in Christian brotherhood, in the perfectability of man. Later writers were not always so certain about man's ability to improve his lot.

Wild Harvest and Black Jack Davy

Unlike Pokagon's "Indian romance," John M. Oskison's early novels—*Wild Harvest* (1925) and *Black Jack Davy* (1926)—might best be described as romances of frontier life. The setting for both is the Cherokee Indian Territory which became part of Oklahoma when the area became a state in 1907, and the action takes place some years before that date, around the turn of the century. (Oskison was born in Vinita, in the Indian Territory, in 1874.) The locale for both stories is in and around a growing frontier town called Big Grove; and Oskison carries several of the characters in *Wild Harvest* over to *Black Jack Davy*. Both novels describe the hustle and bustle of activity on the frontier (especially the influx of white settlers) shortly before statehood. Unfortunately, they have little to do with Native Americans.

In *Wild Harvest*, the author is concerned about getting fifteen-year-old Nan Forest married to Tom Winger, a handsome cowboy and foreman. This should be an easy matter, since their suitability for each other is established early in the story, but Oskison constructs barriers that postpone the event. First, there is Nan's father, Chester Forest, described as "a fumbler"[4] and not very successful rancher. Oskison dispatches Forest by having him shoot a cattle rustler and then spend most of the story in jail while he awaits trial; eventually he is freed. The obstacles that produce a temporary estrangement between Nan and Tom are Ruby Engle (a seventeen-year-old frontier seductress) and Harvey Stokes (Tom's rival for Nan's hand). While all of these characters are interacting, Nan lives with her aunt and uncle Dines (Forest's older sister and her husband). The plot, for the most part, is unconvincing—needlessly extended so that Oskison can create a narrative long enough for a book. (His previous fiction had been limited to short stories, published in magazines.)

In an attempt to create a sense of life in the Indian Territory, Oskison introduces a number of minor frontier character types and digresses into self-contained substories involving them. There are accounts of cowpunching, cattle rustling, and making money from cattle raising. There are descriptions of roundups, and "neighborhood literaries" designed to bring a little culture to the area, of cutting hay, of cattle stampeding, and like events which Oskison no doubt felt would give a sense of local color for his eastern readers. Other digressions from the main story tell of several murders, a bank robbery, and various events contrived to hold the reader's interest. (The chapter titles also attempt to do this: "Nan Counts Her Chickens," "The Amateur Detective," "The Game of 'I Spy.' ") Mostly, however, these authorial machinations fail, and I think it can safely be said that artistically, at least, *Wild Harvest* is the very nadir of Native American fiction.

Generally speaking, the few Indian characters in *Wild Harvest* are there to provide a kind of backdrop of authenticity, as part of the Indian Territory setting. One of these, named Joe Tiger, moves in and out of the story, usually drunk. Another one, Hank Rosebud, Big Grove's half-blood police officer, periodically helps restore peace and quiet. The few statements about Indians in the book tend to be spoken by the white characters. In the most important of these, occurring at the end of the novel, Nan and Tom foresee the inevitability of allotment,[5] and argue that Indians are ready for assimilation.

> "One of these days, the Indians'll be argued into allottin' all these miles an' miles of prairie, like them Kansas politicians are tryin' to make 'em do now. Then there'll be land for sale, an' the Indians'll have to buckle down to farmin' an' cattle raisin' to keep even with us white folks. Good thing for 'em, too."
>
> "Yes," Nan agreed, "Uncle Billy says Indians like Chief Littlespring, Ross Murray, and 'Sofkey' Horseford are al-

ready showing the way to the others. Uncle Billy likes these Indians; he says they're as smart as anybody—no reason why they shouldn't move ahead with the rest of us."

"An' they sure will," Tom asserted. "At the bank in Big Grove they're already beginnin' to open accounts, make loans an' carry on like regular fellows." (p. 295)

Two significant events in the narrative involve Native Americans. Curiously, it is an Indian who discovers the missing gun that belonged to the man Chester Forest shot; its discovery saves Forest's life, since it frees him from being convicted of shooting a man in cold blood. More important, however, is the wedding ceremony that unites Nan Forest and Tom Winger—presided over by an Indian preacher ("The Indian preacher wore a collarless blue shirt, a short black coat, yellow trousers and weather-stained moccasins; he was completely at ease, smiling, exchanging friendly comment with his Indian neighbors who had come to the wedding" [p. 297].) When his wedding speech is translated into English, we are again aware of the assimilation theme of the novel:

> "He says he is glad to ask God's blessing on this man an' this woman because he loves them both. . . . He says times has changed since he was a young man like him an' his old woman was a girl like her an' they got married out in the woods, but he ain't sorry old ways are goin', because we got to have new ways an' good men an' women from the outside to help build up this Eenyan country. . . . He says the same Great Father loves this girl Nancy an' this man Tom that loves his old woman an' him. . . . He says he gives his blessing on this marriage. Amen." (pp. 297–98)

The novel ends with a particularly revealing comment by Tom Winger: " 'We're elected now to help make this long grass country one of the greatest states in the Union, you an' me an' the folks we know an' them that's comin' after us' " (p. 299). Although it was written after the fact, *Wild Harvest* was propaganda for Oklahoma's statehood.

Black Jack Davy also has a romantic focus—the marriage of Davy Dawes, the main character, to Mary Keene—but the main thrust of the story is to establish peace for the white settler families at Six Bulls River and Horsepen Creek, near Big Grove, in the Indian Territory. Shortly after Jim and Mirabelle Dawes and their foster son, Davy, arrive at Horsepen Creek, Jerry Boyd declares open warfare on the new arrivals. Boyd, who is married to a part-Cherokee woman, and therefore able to own property in her name, decides that if the Daweses and the Keenes (Mirabelle's brother, his wife, and their daughter) can be driven out of the Territory, it will be a simple matter to annex their property. The Daweses and the Keenes both lease land from Ned Warrior, a full-blood Cherokee, and his wife, Rose; so Ned Warrior must also be eliminated before the land-grab will be successful.

The novel concludes with Boyd and his henchmen laying siege to the Keenes and the Daweses, who manage to hold out against the attackers until a posse, led by Tom Winger (and several other characters who appeared in *Wild Harvest*), comes to their rescue. In a sense, Tom Winger becomes the deus ex machina, saving the Daweses and the Keenes from the evil embodied by Jerry Boyd. Ned Warrior enters the final shoot-out also, wounding Boyd and killing his good-for-nothing son, Cale. In the final few pages, Jim Dawes insists that Davy and Mary Keene be married before he dies of gun wounds incurred in the fighting; yet since that is not quite a happy ending, Oskison brings in Davy's real mother (who has appeared earlier in the story) and she stakes Davy and Mary for cattle ranching. (Davy's last name is surely an ironic reference to the Dawes Allotment Act of 1887, which—perhaps more than anything else—led to the breakup of Indian tribal lands.)

The West is wilder in *Black Jack Davy* than it is in *Wild Harvest*. There is a prostitute (who reveals to Davy that Boyd is out to get them), a gambling and drinking house, an excessive amount of shooting, and one violent murder. The general lawlessness of the Indian Territory is contrasted to the superior stock of the settler blood represented by the Daweses and the Keenes. Oskison states of Jim and Davy Dawes: "In their blood was the strain of pioneers who had fought similar battles while waiting for the establishment of organized society: men like Boone, Crockett, Houston and Kit Carson."[6] (Oskison also makes some attempt to romanticize Davy's origins by having Mirabelle connect him to a character in a folk ballad, from whom he derives his name, "Black Jack Davy" [p. 13].)

From this summary of the story, it should be apparent that the Indian characters in *Black Jack Davy* are more important than the ones in *Wild Harvest*. Ned Warrior is the most significant. He is initially pictured as a rather sleazy individual, but by the end of the novel he reforms and not only helps control the lawlessness of the land but settles down and marries Rose in the requisite Christian wedding ceremony. (Shades of Pocahontas?) Ned's reformation is revealed in one of Oskison's final comments about him:

> Ned understood better than ever before why old Running Rabbit and his fellow full-bloods of the hill country met in secret councils and planned to drive out the aliens and close the borders to them. If they only could! Of course, there were many honest whites, good friends of the Indians and good neighbors. . . . But they appeared, sometimes, to be a helpless minority. . . .
>
> Ned himself was no tabby cat. He had walked his own path in defiance of tribal law, had carried Rose Lamedeer off without the formality of marriage, had crippled the deputy Burke in resisting arrest for boot-legging, had all but given up his life in that battle against Cap. Black and his men, has served time in prison. But he was a shining saint compared with these whites. (p. 272)

Rose, Ned's half-blood wife, for a time lures Davy away from Mary Keene, but she is also reformed by the end of the story. As in *Wild Harvest*, Oskison does not make much use of the Indian setting of the story, except for an occasional aside on Indian "progress." One of these comments, spoken by Ross Murray, a "half-blood tribal chief, prosperous cattleman and graduate of the Univeristy of Missouri" (p. 169), returns to the subject of allotment and the Indians' eventual assimilation into the mainstream of American life:

"It is said that the history of a nation is the history of its wars, but in our case it is rather the history of forced cessions of land. That process is now ended, we can cede no more, and the course of our history must change. We must become builders. Put the money you get into the development of good farms." (p. 169)

Regrettably, *Wild Harvest* and *Black Jack Davy* are unconvincing both in plot and character. Events in both novels border on the ludicrous, the unbelievable, the cliché, and I suspect that few readers today would have the patience to struggle through either work. Oskison's characters, whether major or minor, never become anything more than types. His older women are particularly unconvincing. I have a feeling that Oskison recognized this last limitation, since he tended either to kill older women off early in the story (Nan's mother) or relegate them to wheelchairs (Mirabelle), a device he also uses in his next novel, *Brothers Three*. (Usually there is a kind of Old Testament justice for past transgressions. Mirabelle ran off with Jim Dawes against the wishes of her parents. The night of their elopement, she fell from a horse and was henceforth confined to a wheelchair.)

A statement made by Judge Pease early in *Black Jack Davy* conveniently summarizes the subject matter of both these novels: " 'It seems that bad men from the whole United States are flocking into the Indian country' " (p. 17). Unfortunately, Oskison chose to focus both novels upon the incoming whites rather than on the Indians who were already in the Territory. The result was predictable: potboilers typical of mass-market fiction set in the West, with background characters potentially far more interesting than those in the foreground.

Brothers Three

Oskison's *Brothers Three* (1935), which appeared nine years after *Black Jack Davy*, is in every way a more rewarding novel, although it still has little to do with the Native American experience. It is altogether the work of a more mature artist (Oskison was approaching sixty when he wrote it). Though there is still little introspection, the characters are mellower and more believable than in his earlier works; the pace is more relaxed; the story is convincing and reflective. This does not mean that *Brothers Three* is without flaws: it is too long (the longest novel written by a Native American); at times overly sentimental; and in spite of the author's attempts at writing a kind of regional epic, read today the story is dated if not simply boring in places. It is clear that Oskison wanted to write a chronicle of the events of his own family dynasty—a story of the land and its development from Indian Territory to statehood, a little like Edna Ferber's much later novel, *Giant* (1950), though Oskison is writing once again about Oklahoma.

Brothers Three is divided into three sections. In the first of these, called "Timmy," Francis Odell arrives at Redbud Creek in the Indian Territory with his part-Cherokee wife, Janet, and their five-month-old son, Timothy. The year is 1873. The early narrative concentrates on Odell's establishing his ranch and Timmy's later growth into manhood as a leading businessman of the community. Two other sons are born, Roger and Henry ("Mister"), and Janet dies six years after the latter's birth (after being confined to a wheelchair for all six years). Timmy marries May Akers, and the other sons also marry in turn. As the first section ends (immediately after World War I), Francis Odell dies, leaving a large estate which has prospered because of his careful working of the land.

Part Two, "The Herdsmen," shifts to Roger, the second son, the subject turning from farming to money and how to make it. Francis Odell's empire begins to crumble because of the poor management of his sons. Roger makes money in cattle raising, but quickly loses it when the bottom falls out of the market. When he tries to recoup his losses through mining investments, he is swindled out of $130,000 of the family money. In his frustration, Roger begins drinking heavily and eventually becomes paralyzed from an automobile accident that occurs when he is intoxicated. Throughout this section of the novel, May (Timmy's wife) stands for the voice of reason and moderation.

The last part of the novel ("Mister") concentrates on the third Odell son, Henry, whose turn it now becomes to try to salvage the family estate. Living in New York City as a free-lance writer, he is for a time successful in rebuilding the lost fortune by playing the stock market. Eventually, he builds up the estate to nearly a million dollars, but when the market collapses in 1929, almost everything is lost. The novel concludes with May persuading the remaining members of the family to return to the farm, to work the land and pay off the bankrupt mortgage on their property.

Brothers Three is a long novel, influenced by the regional economic novels of Frank Norris and Theodore Dreiser, though Oskison does not share their naturalistic thesis. The theme is simpler than that: the three Odell sons fail because they leave the land, because they want more than their rightful share. Roger's greed leads to his attempts to make a quick profit in cattle raising; he should never have become involved in mining because he knew nothing about it. Mister should have stopped playing the stock market once he recouped the family losses; his error was deciding to stay in and double or triple their money. Only Timmy achieves a margin of success in his business ventures because they are modest transactions. If all three sons had remained farmers, working the land, the farm would have continued to prosper as it did during their father's time.

The attitude expressed toward the land in *Brothers Three* is the one truly Indian aspect of the novel, relating it to Chief Pokagon's sentiments about nature as expressed in *Queen of the Woods*. If the land is respected, not exploited by agribusiness or destroyed by mining, it will supply all of a man's needs—and more. The land is boundless and plentiful if man lives in harmony with it and does not try to conquer it. Oskison's feelings toward farming are consistent with Cherokee beliefs. Before their removal from Georgia in 1838 and relocation in the Indian Territory, the Cherokee Indians were farmers, living off the land, with individual plots designated for specific families. They were not nomads or hunters, as were Indians of many other tribes.

As in Chief Pokagon's *Queen of the Woods*, there is an ironic contrast in *Brothers Three* between the implicit and explicit threads of the narrative. The three Odell sons (Cherokee "blood citizens . . . entitled to land on account of their inheritance from their mother"),[7] have forgotten their Indian heritage and decided instead to pursue the American

Dream. For all practical purposes they have been assimilated into the white economic structure of the country, and for a time they are successful. Oskison, however, makes his position clear. The reader is always aware that it is only a matter of time before the family fortune will be reversed. The mortgaged farm at the end of the story symbolizes this opposition, yet the land remains waiting for their return. As Mister states at the conclusion of the novel,

> "The Farm's a living organism. It's on starvation rations just now, but we've got to do better by it. It's nourished by the lives that are fed into it. If they're clean and sane and competent, like Pa's and Ma's were, the Farm will flourish . . . it's real and solid still—beautiful!" (p. 448)

Other than this attitude toward the land (and the fact that the three Odell sons are one-sixteenth Cherokee), Oskison makes few references in *Brothers Three* to his Indian heritage. As in his two earlier novels, there are a number of allusions to "the invaders of this Indian land, turning it from Indian serenity to white man turbulence" (p. 54). These whites, Oskison tells us,

> were contemptuous of the Indians, and promised to hasten the movement for making the Indian Territory into a "white man's state." They carried on, in grotesque caricature, the tradition that the "savage red man" must, because of his incompetence, give way to the white. Their dirtiest tow-headed moron child of fifteen was taught to feel superior to such boys as Timmy—to any child however slightly "tainted" by Indian blood. (p. 55)

Occasional remarks such as this one suggest that by the time Oskison wrote *Brothers Three* he thought of his Indian heritage as something far back in his past—perhaps almost too painful to write about. It is hard to know how to interpret these asides in light of the three Indian characters he included in the novel: a seventeen-year-old girl, Es-Teece Bellflower, with whom Timmy has a lengthy affair (Timmy thinks " 'It must be the Indian in her that makes her [so loose]' " [p. 117]); Mrs. Elphy Otter, a con artist who helps swindle Roger out of his mining investments; and an unnamed bank robber—a seedy lot, to be sure.

One final aspect of *Brothers Three* deserves mention. Oskison's picture of Henry ("Mister") is highly autobiographical. Like Oskison, Mister went to Stanford and became a writer who lived in New York City, eventually writing two novels set in the Indian Territory: *Prairie Dust* and *Bee Creek Neighbors*. There is an element of self-parody in *Brothers Three* whenever Oskison speaks of Mister's career. Of *Prairie Dust*, he says, " 'It was the brain storm of a victim of the romantic-historic fiction craze that flourished when I was in college' " (p. 344), an apt description of *Wild Harvest* or *Black Jack Davy*. Once he becomes involved in the stock market, Mister suffers from writer's block, yet the novel he is unable to write (called *The Book of Timothy the Second*) is clearly the novel that *Brothers Three* in time became. How ironic that *Brothers Three* not only became Oskison's most successful novel (the only one to go through more than one printing) but also concluded his career as a writer of fiction.

Sundown

In the last chapter of John J. Mathews *Wah'Kon-Tah* (a nonfiction account of life on the Osage Reservation during the tenure of its first federal agent, Major Laban J. Miles), there is a description of an Indian youth who returns from the white world affected by liquor, hot music, and fast cars. He is especially contemptuous of his parents:

> The young man looked with pity upon his parents. He thought of how old-fashioned they were: his father still wearing his buckskin leggings and his beaverskin bandeau, his pale blue silk shirt and his blanket; his mother in her shirt, moccasins and shrouding. They were certainly behind the time, all right. No matter how swell he dressed he was always embarrassed thinking of his parents sitting out at the ranch. They couldn't even speak English. He wished he didn't have to speak Osage with them—it sure made him feel funny when they talked together in public at the Agency.[8]

The youth wears expensive tailored clothes, is indifferent to tribal customs and beliefs, and has become a kind of cultural half-caste, no longer seeing much value in his Indian origins, while aping the worst of the white man's object-oriented world.

Wah'Kon-Tah was published in 1932—two years before Mathews's only novel, *Sundown*. The unnamed Indian youth is easily identified as the precursor of Chal (Challenge) Windzer, the novel's main character. *Sundown* is the story of a mixed-blood Indian, from the night of his birth until his mid thirties, during the Great Depression. It is the first novel by a Native American to follow a character's life from birth to maturity, to give us his story in retrospect with all of its failures and disappointments. Somewhat akin in structure to the traditional *Bildungsroman*, the novel is also the story of the corrupting natures of money and the white man's educational system.

There is not much of a story to *Sundown*; plot has, in fact, given way to character development. In the early chapters we see Chal's confusing feelings about his parents. His mixed-blood father considers himself one of the progressives, working to advance the Indian's standard of living by supporting allotment and the oil development of the Osage Reservation. Initially, he believes that the government in Washington can do no harm, yet by contrast, Chal's full-blood mother distrusts the government and most of the white man's ways on principle. As a child, Chal attends reservation schools and later goes to the state university, though he does not complete his degree because World War I breaks out and he enlists in the air force. The war ends, however, before he is mobilized, and shortly thereafter he returns to the reservation, where he becomes a kind of drifter with nothing to do. (There are a number of parallels here with Mathews's own life. Like Chal Windzer, Mathews also attended the University of Oklahoma, and he joined the air force during World War I.)

Chal's education, Mathews would have us believe, is the primary force that has cut him off from his tribal roots. This is true at every stage of his formal education—from primary school to the university, and even to flight school. Chal's earliest memories of the reservation school are, in fact, of its sinister-looking buildings. Even before he was old enough to attend the school, he had seen Indian boys in the schoolyard; "he had a feeling that they were like animals in a cage, and certainly there seemed to be much sadness in their faces."[9] He thinks of the door of the school "as a mouth into which they [the students] were going; a big, black mouth, bigger and darker than a wildcat's" (p. 23). Mathews's picture of Chal's white teachers is hardly more flattering. One teacher, named Miss Hover, has come to the school because "she fell under the romantic spell of Fenimore Cooper" (p. 26.) When her Indian students do not live up to Cooper's image, she quickly adapts a patronizing attitude toward them.

The reader begins to understand that it is education which is slowly severing Chal's ties to his cultural past. While in high school, on the days he has no classes, he is drawn to the country, where he feels a number of strong, almost uncontrollable forces pulling at him. "One day he stripped off his clothes and danced in a storm and sang a war song" (p. 70). On another occasion, "he took some paints and painted his face . . ." (p. 72). These mysterious sensations come to him only when he is alone on the prairie, yet they continue during his years as a student at the university and later when he attends the air force flight school. Periodically, he has an uncontrollable urge to be alone in the country, where he can be close to the land. As his education occupies more of his time, however, he begins to feel guilty about these sensations, afraid that he is "reverting" to a kind of uncivilized past that typifies his people as a whole. These yearnings, he feels, must be controlled:

> Sometimes as he walked, the urge to pull off his clothes and trot came to him; the desire to play the role of coyote, but he dismissed such desires now with shame, and when they were most disturbing he would murmur aloud to drown the unconventional thought, and he would dismiss the thoughts of his first months at the University in the same manner. He was more civilized now and more knowing, and he was ashamed of his recent past. (p. 152)

By denying his basic affinity with the earth, Chal's education—like Chief Pokagon's in *Queen of the Woods*—cuts him off from the rich heritage of his people. Even worse, the white man's schooling makes him reject his Indian identity: "He didn't want to call attention to the fact that most of his blood was of an uncivilized race like the Osages. He believed that they didn't have any backbone, and he certainly wanted to make something out of himself" (p. 153). In his confusion, he becomes embarrassed that people identify him as an Indian, and he often feels uncomfortable because of the activities of other Indians around him. At the university, when two of his Indian classmates decide to drop out of school, he realizes that he is actually relieved to see them depart—for "fear that they would do something wrong" (p. 112). In time, he feels guilty about his appearance:

> He had often wished that he weren't so bronze. It set him off from other people, and he felt that he was queer anyway, without calling attention to the fact. It was embarrassing to attract attention, and when people looked at him he became shy. He thought he still might have black eyes and straight black hair that shone like patent leather when he put grease on it, if his face were only white. (p. 117)

At the height of his confusion, he mutters to himself, " 'I wish I didn't have a drop of God damn' Indian blood in my veins' " (p. 160).

Eventually, Chal completely rejects his Indianness. The incident takes place at the air force school, when a white woman, with whom he will shortly have an affair, asks him " 'Are you Spanish or something?' " (p. 203). Chal replies, " 'Yes, Spanish' " (p. 203). The narrator comments, "He should like to have indicated that he had a title, as well, but he thought he had better not" (p. 203). Mathews's picture of Chal Windzer is not so different from those of a number of characters in Afro-American novels who are light enough to "pass" as Caucasian. Like them, Chal renounces his racial origins, sides with the white world, and in the process alienates himself from both groups. He becomes a man with no identity at all, a cultural half-caste.

Chal's problems are in no way alleviated when he returns home after the war. His father has committed suicide, after realizing that by siding with the government he acted against his people; allotment and oil development have brought total disruption of traditional life to the Osage Reservation. Ignoring the example of his father's belated insight, Chal continues to be embarrassed by his mother's Indian ways (her manner of dress, the house she continues to live in in spite of the money she receives from the tribal government from its sale of oil). Even at his father's funeral, Chal "had been embarrassed during the ceremony . . . because some of the older Osages had come to the grave, and turning their eyes to the sky, had chanted the song of death" (p. 237). Chal was, in fact, moved by their act, "but there were so many new white people in town now, that he thought they shouldn't have gone through the primitive ritual after the Christian burial" (p. 237). Almost all of his activities are designed so he will not offend the whites around him, yet he has no clear idea what these people are like or what they expect of him.

If education has been the greatest factor in his estrangement from his people, it is money which adds to his total debilitation.[10] From his father's estate Chal inherits $25,000—money that came from tribal sales of oil. There is, in fact, so much money that Chal does not have to do anything to earn a livelihood, yet the money keeps coming in. Mathews uses the black oil derricks as a ubiquitous symbol of the general disruption of traditional life; there is always another one looming on the horizon, no matter in which direction one looks. In one particularly moving incident, lightning strikes a derrick and sets it on fire. One of the Osage elders states that the " 'lightning struck that gas well 'cause the Great Spirit don't want the white people to come here any more' " (p. 82). The earth has been polluted by the white man's rape of the land, and now this greed has spread to the Indians.

Chal's biggest problem is that he does not know "what to do with himself" (p. 262). In the last few chapters of the novel he drifts along, spending his time and money on fast cars, easy women, and binges with liquor that last a week or two at a time. He drives his automobile as fast as it will go; he moves from one woman to the next, finding little satisfaction in either of these diversions. Mathews implies that either liquor—his "senses were dulled . . . he was not acutely aware of anything" (p. 286)—or an automobile accident will finally destroy him.

Abruptly before the end of the novel, Chal makes one final attempt to reclaim his life. With an old friend named Son-on-His-Wings, he goes to the sweathouse to purify his body. For his friend, this is the purification rite that precedes a service of the Peyote Church, but since Chal is not a member, he cannot attend the meeting. In the sweat lodge, one of the tribal elders named Watching Eagle speaks about the havoc that has been brought to the tribe.

> "Long time ago there was one road and People could follow that road. They said, 'There is only one road. We can see this road. There are no other roads.' Now it seems that road is gone, and white man has brought many roads. But that road is still there. That road is still there, but there are many other roads too. There is white man's road, and there is road which comes off from forks. The bad road which no white man follows—the road which many of the People follow, thinking it is the white man's road. People who follow this road say they are as the white man, but this is not white man's road. People who follow this road say that road of Indian is bad now. But they are not Indians any more, these People who follow that road." (p. 271)

The affect on Chal is electrifying: "he was happy and contented, sitting there" (p. 271). He feels free, as if he is flying.

Yet the change is quickly reversed and, ironically, the sweat lodge ritual does not become preparation for spiritual renewal or a return to cultural roots—nothing akin to what Joseph Epes Brown has described as the function of this ritual:

> the "Sweat Lodge" . . . rites are carried out in preparation for all the other major rites, and actually are participated in prior to any important undertaking. They are rites of renewal, or spiritual rebirth, in which all of the four elements—earth, air, fire, and water—each contribute to the physical and psychical purification of man.[11]

For Chal Windzer, the sweathouse cleansing becomes an ironic preparation for his final bodily humiliation. He returns to his bottle, drinking by himself in the countryside. When he is in a state of total inebriation, the old atavistic yearnings return to him; he begins to dance and sing, to feel that he is an Indian again. His body, however, has been destroyed by liquor, and shortly he falls over in a convulsion of great pain. The contrast that Mathews makes here with Chal's earlier yearnings is an important one: Chal has reached the stage where he only feels these forces pulling at him when he is drunk. Earlier, when he was still an adolescent, it was nature alone that created these sensations—not the artificial stimulus of liquor.

The ending of *Sundown* resolves nothing. Chal and his mother are sitting together, having a kind of nonverbal conversation. She breaks the silence and tells him, ' "Many white men are flying across the sea now' " (p. 310). It is her attempt to rekindle his interest in flying, to get him interested in anything, yet Chal resents her remarks. " 'Ah . . . there isn't anything to flyin' " (p. 311), he replies, then adds, " 'I'm goin' to Harvard law school, and take law—I'm gonna be a great orator' " (p. 311). Though his statement silences her, she knows as well as Chal does that he has never thought about law school before, that he has no intention of becoming a lawyer. As the novel ends, she sits watching him ("She saw a little boy in breech clout and moccasins . . ." p. 311) as he falls asleep. For all his indecisiveness, Chal might just as well be a little boy again.

Chal Windzer is a weak character, a questionable hero. He drifts along through life with little purpose or direction, never acting decisively but permitting himself, rather, to be acted upon. He attends the university because some of his high school friends are planning to; he joins the air force at the suggestion of one of his professors; he repeatedly says he is going to start working, but he never does. By the end of the story, he is utterly passive, plagued by guilt because of his feelings about his racial identity. Though he bears a certain affinity to a number of characters in subsequent novels by Native Americans, he is more directionless than they are. He has tried to assimilate into the white man's world, yet he has failed. By the end of *Sundown*, Chal Windzer has become a man without a culture, reduced to a life of frustration and existential loneliness.

Sundown is the most accomplished of the novels written by Native Americans exploring the assimilationist theme, the most significant early account of the clash of cultures, in large part because Mathews has moved beyond the element of plot (so important to Pokagon and Oskison) into the realm of character development. The reader comes away from the novel knowing quite clearly that Mathews never approves of Chal Windzer's attempts to become part of the white man's world, a stance that distinguishes the author from his predecessors. Unlike Oskison's three novels, Mathews's work is almost totally concerned with Native American characters, with the problem of the obliteration of "Indianness" because of the white man's confusing world. Whereas Pokagon uses a proselytizing tone in *Queen of the Woods*, Mathews has chosen to tell his story for the most part without didactic commentary. The result may not always be totally successful; the pace of the narrative at times is slowed down by overwriting and the symbolism is somewhat inconsistent. Nevertheless, John J. Mathews has written a novel which still tells us something vitally important about the Native American and the problems of his identity more than forty years after it was written.

The three earliest Native American novelists followed pathways that were often as confusing as those experienced by their fictional characters. Pokagon, who was raised as an Indian, came to accept a number of white cultural institutions (including the Catholic faith) which ultimately appear to have boxed him into a no-man's-land—a wasteland between cultural traditions. The platitudes he expressed about assimilation late in his life (quoted by the publisher in the introductory sections of *Queen of the Woods*) contradict his earlier, more militant statements on Indian-white relations in *The Red Man's Rebuke*. It is almost as if there were two Pokagons: the earlier, vindictive one, fighting for Indian rights distinct from the white man's tainted benevolence; and the later, more pacified one, arguing for assimilation. It is difficult to put the two together, just as it is difficult not to ask ourselves if there were two Pocahontases, a public and a private one.

Though Pokagon's father, Chief Leopold Pokagon, had

signed the treaty which officially surrendered the tribal lands that became Chicago, it was years before the Potawatomi Indians received payment for this land. Simon Pokagon worked much of his life to see that the terms of the treaty were fulfilled. Honored at the World's Columbian Exposition in 1893, Pokagon, according to Cecila B. Buechner, "died penniless and homeless."[12] Although (like Pocahontas) he adhered to the dictates of Christianity more rigidly than many of his white contemporaries, in time his religion failed him. When he took "a divorced woman for his second wife, he excommunicated himself."[13] The last years of his life were ones of great pain and sorrow; the world he embraced had renounced him.

John M. Oskison's early life was filled with similar confusions. As his three novels illustrate, his Indian heritage played little importance in his upbringing. Yet under the surface Oskison, too, must have been a man delicately balancing opposing identities. A number of short stories he published at the turn of the century, after he graduated from the university, are emphatic statements on the importance of Indianness.[14] They stand in sharp contrast to his later fiction, where he clearly ignores this heritage, again making it difficult to believe that the same person wrote all of these works.

Considering the autobiographical elements in John J. Mathews's *Sundown*, it is impossible not to conclude that this writer also lived through a period of intense personal agony and torture. Chal Windzer is in many ways the archetypal cultural misfit. His identity problems leave indelible scars on his psyche. Although Margaret Szasz did not have Chal (or his creator) in mind when she wrote her book, *Education and the American Indian*, she has perfectly captured the nature of this dilemma:

> The problems faced by this minority of educated Indian youth did not lend themselves to an easy solution. When the pupils returned to the reservation, they often became objects of ridicule. This situation was complicated by the fact that the training they had received had little or no application to reservation life. Thus these pupils became the first victims of the "either/or" policy of assimilation. Their education forced them to choose

either the culture of the white man or the culture of the Indian; there was no compromise.[15]

In *Sundown*, Mathews created an image of his earlier self: the schizophrenic childhood created by one parent's desire to embrace the white man's world and the other's desire to reject it. When he returned to the Osage Reservation after an absence of ten years, Mathews suffered from an identity crisis similar to Chal Windzer's. Unlike the character in his novel, however, Mathews embraced his Indian heritage and articulated this consciousness in all of his nonfictional works.

As novelists dealing with the problems of assimilation, as children of Pocahontas with masked identities, Pokagon, Oskison, and Mathews create fictional characters who rarely appear to reject the white man's world, the status quo. True, Pokagon (the writer) lashes out against the evils of drink, but there are few other influences from the white man's world that he protests so vehemently in *Queen of the Woods*. The same is true of Oskison, though there is a bitterness below the surface of the narrative in the novels by all three of these writers. That acidity is reflected in the ambiguous identities of their characters, caught in the dilemmas the writers themselves experienced in their own lives. Yet if their books depict this commonality of experience, one cannot help concluding that in their own lives, they met the challenge somewhat differently: Pokagon, apparently, remained caught between the two worlds; Oskison clearly identified with the white world; Mathews, with his Indian heritage.

One final comment. Education stands at the center of most of these early novels as it does in each of these writers' own lives. Attending the white man's school results in an estrangement from the land, a severing of the umbilical tie to nature: Pokagon and Olondaw lose the sacred affinity that Lonidaw retains with her environment; the three Odell sons exploit the land instead of respecting it; Chal Windzer's oneness with the natural world is numbed by his addiction to alcohol. Not surprisingly, as Margaret Szasz has written, attitudes toward education and land became the cornerstones of government policy for attaining assimilation:

In the fifty years before the publication of the Meriam

Report [on Indian education, published in 1928], the federal government pursued a policy of total assimilation of the American Indian into the mainstream society. Recognizing the vast difficulties in achieving this goal, Congress and the Indian Bureau adopted a plan to remold the Indian's conception of life, or what came to be known as his "system of values." If this could be changed, assimilationists reasoned, the Indian would then become like the white man. The Indian's system of values was expressed in the education of his children and in his attitude toward the land. Consequently, the assimilationists chose to attack these two concepts as the major targets of their campaign.[16]

Paradoxically, Pokagon, Oskison, and Mathews would not have written and published novels if they had not received the schooling they did and been assimilated (in their varying degrees) into the white man's world. And that, of course, is the crux of their dilemma. Their education took something away from them, yet their writing became a way of reconciling or exploring the problems of assimilation that each man met in his own distinct way.

4

Rejection: The Reluctant Return

When I look back upon those days—days of infinite promise and steady adventure and the certain sanctity of
childhood—I see how much was there in the balance. The
past and the future were simply the large contingencies of
a given moment; they bore upon the present and gave it
shape. One does not pass through time, but time enters
upon him, in his place. As a child, I knew this surely, as a
matter of fact; I am not wise to doubt it now. Notions of
the past and future are essentially notions of the present.
In the same way an idea of one's ancestry and posterity is
really an idea of the self.—N. Scott Momaday, *The Names*

When the sixteen novels included in this study are viewed
as a whole, it is easy to identify several major concerns. The
novels cluster into groups which, by no coincidence, are related to the dates of their publication. The three earliest Native American novelists followed a path which, broadly speaking, embraced cultural assimilation. The characters in their
work accept the white man's world without seriously questioning the destructive influences of this dispensation upon their
traditional life. In all instances, it is the white man's educational system which is responsible for an ironic sense of progress or civilization. Implicit in these works is the assumption
that if a new life-style is going to emerge, something of the
old will have to give.

The two novels examined in this chapter—*The Surrounded*
(1936), by D'Arcy McNickle (1904–77), and *House Made Of
Dawn* (1968), by N. Scott Momaday (b.1934)—are separated
by thirty-two years, and we might easily assume that they are
thematically light years apart. McNickle's *The Surrounded* was

published only a year after Oskison's *Brothers Three* and two years after Mathews's *Sundown*. Momaday's *House Made of Dawn*—coming as it did at the end of a decade of political and racial activism—would appear to herald a new kind of writing by Native Americans (as it does, to some extent), which would imply that its affinities with McNickle's novel would be nonexistent. Yet this is not the case. The two novels, in fact, share a great many structural and thematic similarities, both belonging to what might now be called the post-Momaday era.

To be sure, there is a gap between American Indian fiction of the thirties and the sixties—more than one of years. The hiatus of the forties and the fifties (decades when no novels by Native Americans were published) represents a philosophical and symbolic break with earlier practices, a turn from assimilation to rejection. Like Momaday's *House Made of Dawn*, McNickle's *The Surrounded* is primarily a novel of renunciation—wholesale rejection of the white man's world. The two works illustrate a new ideological stance: repudiation of the white man's world coupled with a symbolic turn toward the life-sustaining roots of traditional Indian belief.

The initial experience in both of these novels reminds one of the works of Chief Simon Pokagon and John J. Mathews: each story begins with the main character's homecoming. In *The Surrounded*, Archilde Leon returns to the valley of his father's ranch. The opening sentence of the novel informs us that "Archilde Leon had been away from his father's ranch for nearly a year, yet when he left the stage road and began the half-mile walk to the house he did not hurry."[1] At the end of the first chapter of Momaday's *House Made of Dawn*, Abel, the central character, stumbles off a bus which has brought him back to the reservation after his experiences in World War II: "The door swung open and Abel stepped heavily to the ground and reeled. He was drunk, and he fell against his grandfather and did not know him."[2] Both of these novels are concerned with central characters who have left their places of birth, gone off for a time and lived in the white man's world, and then returned. That journey Archilde and Abel share with the characters in Pokagon and Mathews's assimilationist novels, but there the resemblance ends.

To a large extent McNickle and Momaday present us with characters who are not certain why they have returned home. All they know is that the white world has not given them solutions to their problems. There is a kind of hesitation on Archilde Leon's part, suggested by his slow pace down the road to his mother's house. His return is a dilemmatic one, as is that of Momaday's inebriated protagonist, who is unable to recognize his grandfather, Francisco. Both protagonists have returned to a world that can never be the same as it was before they left; both novels are about the reluctant return of the native—a theme, of course, ubiquitous in twentieth-century fiction.

The theme of the archetypal return, the end of the journey complete with symbolic new beginnings, relates McNickle's novel to Momaday's. These two novels are thematically united in other ways as well. Each is concerned with Catholicism and the inroads it has made into traditional life, and each makes use of a historical perspective missing from the earlier works by Native Americans. Moreover, the historical framework is so interlocked with the structure each writer has used for his narrative that it is almost impossible to separate the two.

The Surrounded

Like the main character in his novel, D'Arcy McNickle (Flathead) was born in western Montana and attended a government boarding school in Oregon. There, however, the similarities end. The setting of *The Surrounded* is explained in a note opposite the title page of the volume: "They called that place *Sniél-emen* (Mountains of the Surrounded) because they had been set upon and destroyed." McNickle's explanation reads like a warning. This is not only a physical location but also a comment, a judgment of a historical event. From the very beginning of the story, the reader has the impression that the Salish people described in the novel are living in a kind of enclave, surrounded by the white man's universe, from which there is no escape.

McNickle supplies his reader with a number of important facts at the beginning of his story. Archilde Leon (who is half Indian and half Spanish) has returned to his father's ranch after working in Portland as a fiddle player. The time is around 1910. His father, Max, who settled in the area forty years earlier, still thinks of himself as an outsider, and is particularly bitter about his relationship with his eleven children by his Indian wife. There is little or no communication between husband and wife; Max feels his children have reverted to their mother's ways. McNickle symbolizes Archilde's parents' relationship by their dwelling places. When Archilde returns home, he avoids his father's "big house" and immediately heads for his mother's log cabin. His parents have lived separately for years, each determined not to bend an inch toward the other.

The schism within the family, represented by the two houses, is central to McNickle's narrative, for *The Surrounded* is also the story of an extended Euro-Indian family. The author's emphasis on filial affairs has resulted in a story in which character interaction is central. When we have finished reading *The Surrounded*, McNickle's characters remain with us—a marked difference from our memories of earlier Native American novels (except for Mathews's *Sundown*), in which the main narrative interest is plot.

Archilde Leon has returned to his father's ranch for reasons that are not immediately clear to him, though they undoubtedly include the desire to see his mother. He has no intention of staying. As he tells his mother, " 'I had a job. I played my fiddle in a show house. I can always get a job now any time I go away' " (p. 2). Yet he stays longer than he intended, and in time—after a painful reconciliation with his father, who has always considered him a good-for-nothing, like his other sons—Archilde agrees to go to the local mission, where Father Christadore will give him further training in musical theory.

From the very beginning of the story, Archilde is less estranged from his heritage, more sure of who he is, than the protagonists in earlier Native American novels. He appears to have worked out a kind of unarticulated compromise with the white world; he will take from it what it has to offer (music, for example), giving as little in return as possible. He appears

to have an ability to live peacefully in either world. His education has not been solely a negative force; it was at the Indian
school in Oregon that he first became interested in playing
the violin.

Archilde's affinity with his people is nowhere more apparent
than in his relationship with his aged mother.

> As the autumn advanced Archilde felt himself grow
> close to his mother. There had been times in recent
> years when he had felt ashamed of her, when he could
> not bear to be near her. The worst of that phase had
> passed several years before, in his last year of high
> school, and more recently he had not taken it so seri-
> ously; he tolerated her and laughed at some of the cruder
> of her ideas about the world. (p. 113)

One does not find the kind of embarrassment here that
typified Chal Windzer's relationship with his mother. With the
passing of time, Archilde discovers in his mother's world an
almost boundless sense of love and protection: "There in his
mother's tepee he had found unaccountable security" (p. 222).
It is this sense of closeness to his mother that leads to Archilde's agreement to take the old woman on a ritual hunt—
the most important scene of the novel—and the last hunt, he
knows, before her death. The incidents that take place during
the hunt shape almost all of the subsequent events in the
story.

Initially, there is the meeting with Dave Quigley, the
sheriff, who is searching for Archilde's older brother, Louis,
suspected of having stolen a number of horses from a ranch
in the area. Later, Archilde discovers that he cannot kill a
deer—that he has, in fact, lost some of his traditional affinity
with the natural world. At the crucial moment, he cannot pull
the trigger of his gun, yet rather than admit this failure to his
mother, he shoots into the mountainside. It is the sound from
Archilde's gun that brings Louis to their party, "a small deer
across his shoulders" (p. 123). The three of them—Archilde,
Louis, and their mother—are subsequently discovered by a
game warden.

When Archilde learns that the game warden intends to arrest his brother for shooting a female deer, he argues, " 'We're

Indians, and we're free of game laws. . . . Indians are free from all game laws by special treaty' " (p. 125). In the ensuing argument, Louis is shot in the back of the head by the warden, whom Archilde's mother kills with her hatchet. The ritual hunt that the old woman wanted to undertake before her death has revived the old animosities between white man and Indian: in retaliation for Louis's murder, the game warden is scalped. The differing attitudes toward wildlife represent a further attempt by the white man's world to substitute legal control for the Indian's spiritual relationship with his environment. Not only have the white man's laws placed unreasonable restrictions on Indian hunting practices, but they have been imposed from without,[3] once more reinforcing the symbolic meaning of McNickle's title.

The immediate complication that arises from the dual murder is the disposal of the bodies. Fearing the possible consequences of the incident, Archilde tells his mother that both bodies should be buried immediately. His mother, who is Catholic, has other ideas, again illustrating the value systems in conflict throughout the entire hunting scene:

> The old lady's thoughts flew this way and that. She could not let this thing be done. Never in her lifetime had people been buried in the old way. The Fathers had made a special ground and the dead who were not brought there were unhappy. Their souls were tortured. She could not let this happen to Louis. He was her son and some day she could hope to see him again, but only if she brought him to the ground prepared by the Fathers. (p. 129)

Archilde gives in to his mother's request, knowing only too well that there will be consequences.

The repercussions form the denouement of the story and involve a second murder scene that ironically mirrors many of the incidents of the earlier one. At the time of his mother's death, Archilde confesses to Parker, the local government agent, that it was his mother who killed the missing game warden. His confession is due largely to repeated insinuations by Sheriff Quigley that Archilde must have been involved in the events that led to the game warden's disappearance. Al-

though he is supposed to return to Parker for further questioning after his mother's funeral, Archilde lets Elise La Rose
convince him to flee into the mountains, where the two of
them encounter Archilde's young nephews, Mike and Narcisse. When Quigley comes upon their party one night and
tries to arrest Archilde, Elise throws hot coffee in the sheriff's
face and shoots him with her rifle. That is not, however, quite
the end of the encounter. As the novel concludes, Archilde
and Elise discover that Agent Parker and another man have
them trapped—like the Salish people—in a circle from which
there is no escape.

Significantly, Archilde is never the guilty party. He breaks
no laws; he commits no crime; he does nothing he should not
do. Instead, he is a victim of circumstance. It is his mother
who kills the first time and his girlfriend, Elise, the second,
thus making the women the true activists in the novel. By the
end of the story, the theme has been altered from "you can't
go home again" to "you can't leave home." As he tells Elise
after she drags him to the mountains, " 'You can't run away
nowadays, Elise' " (p. 287)—there is no escape into the surrounding world, which offers only a dead end. What is worse,
there is no hiding place in the inner world, the reservation,
where white agents and sheriffs monitor the Indian's every
move—where the Native American is controlled by proxy,
even down to the dictates of what and when he may hunt.
The journey home forces Archilde Leon to realize that the
Native American has few freedoms anywhere, even in his own
territory.

Archilde's mixed-blood origins are at the heart of his initial
problems. From his father he receives his earliest pain, yet
Max Leon is treated as sympathetically as any of the other
characters in the novel in spite of his outsider qualities.
McNickle states of him, "He had been married for forty years
to this woman, she had borne him eleven children, and he
had come no closer to her than that. She would not tell him
what he knew she knew. She did not trust him"(p. 10). He
regards his children—all of whom identify with their
mother—as "sons of bitches." Yet, even in his bitterness, Max
Leon is not denied the insights of old age: "after forty years
[of living with the Salish people] he did not know these people

and was not trusted by them . . ." (p. 75). His painful reconciliation with Archilde comes shortly after his realization that as outsiders he, Father Grepilloux, and Moser (a trader) are responsible for the Indian's condition:

"Do you know what I've been talking about? People are starving! They're freezing to death in those shacks by the church. They don't know why; they had nothing to do with it. You and me and Father Grepilloux were the ones brought it on. For what good? What satisfaction have we got?" (p. 147)

Only Archilde and his mother benefit from the reconciliation, since Max dies shortly thereafter. In their final conversation, Archilde relates what happened on the fatal hunting trip, and Max asks his son to tell his mother to move back into the big house. The symbolic request frees Archilde of the burden of his mixed-blood past and sets the stage for his total identification with his tribal roots. He stops going to the Catholic mission for music lessons, because he realizes the hypocrisy: "The religion of the priests was definitely gone from him" (p. 179).

When his mother dies, he accepts the loss because of the closeness he now feels to his people: "Never had he felt so near to these people as now, when he could do something for them" (p. 269). For the first time, Archilde understands his mother's place in the tribe, her heroic stature. The daughter of a chief, "she had been baptized as Catharine Le Loup" (p. 21) by "the black-gowned priests." Through the years, her piety has earned her the respect of the Christian fathers, who "called her 'Faithful Catharine' and by that name she was known to her people" (p. 21), though her stature with her own people is no less significant. "Archilde's mother occupied a place of distinction in the tribe. . . . she was a woman whose opinions were valued" (p. 61)—no doubt because it is known that outside of her ties with the church, she has never given in to the white man's world. (It is probable that "Faithful Catharine" is a veiled reference to Kateri [Katherine] Tekakwitha [1656?–80], the first Native American presented to Rome for sainthood.)

McNickle's characterization of Archilde's mother is poignant, often deeply moving. After a lengthy passage describing her reactions to her husband's world through the years, McNickle states of her, "Only a small part of what she learned stayed with her. She was an old woman now, and it seemed that the older she got the further she went on the trail leading backward" (p. 173). Her last bow toward her Christian upbringing—the burial of her son, Louis—is also the coup de grâce to her Catholic faith. Thereafter, she rejects the teachings of the black-robed fathers and becomes "a pagan again" (p. 173). In a dream (of the afterlife) which she describes to her old friend, Modeste, she foresees the necessity of returning to her traditional faith rather than remaining cut off from her people forever:

> "I saw none of my friends or relatives there. There were no Indians there at all. . . . It was a good thing there were no Indians there because they would have found nothing to do. Pretty soon the people were saying I did not look happy, so the white God sent for me. He was a kind man. 'Why is it you're not happy?' he asked me. So I told him and he said I could go away and go to the Indian heaven if I wished. Then I went to the Indian place and I could hear them singing. Their campfires burned and I could smell meat roasting. There were no white men there at all. I asked to come in but they told me no. I was baptized and I could not go there. First I would have to return to earth and give up my baptism." (pp. 208–9)

This dream leads to her decision to renounce the teachings of the white fathers and return to those of her own tradition, just as her son Archilde does. Her warning to other converted Indians concludes,

> "You knew my sons and how I prayed for them and tried to keep them from going to hell. It would have been better if they had been given the whip. Praying was not what was needed for them, and it does me no good." (p. 210)

On her deathbed she makes it explicit that she wants no priest offering her the last sacrament. Archilde realizes that "death for his mother . . . was the triumph of one against many; it was the resurrection of the spirit" (p. 272).

Like Archilde's mother, Elise La Rose is also characterized by strength and heroism. The murder she commits symbolically ties her to the old woman since it is committed without forethought against a force she intuitively identifies as evil. In her bitterness about the surrounding white world, she instinctively lashes out at whatever representatives of that world she encounters. Like Archilde, she attended an Indian school in Oregon, where her initial resentments against the white man developed, yet she left the school determined never to return. As the narrator comments, "she was dangerous. . . . She liked action, excitement, recklessness, and the trouble resulted naturally" (p. 249). Like Archilde's mother, Elise La Rose also rejects the white man's religion. She bears a telling similarity to Slim Girl in Oliver La Farge's *Laughing Boy* (1929).[4] She is worldly, much more sophisticated than Archilde. Her desires for revenge create the final trap that ensnares the two of them, as is true of La Farge's novel where the heroine is the more active protagonist.

From the earliest chapters of *The Surrounded*, McNickle makes extensive use of the religious conflict between traditional Indian religion and Christianity buried deep within the Salish people. Father Grepilloux's journals chronicle the events which led to the arrival of the first Catholic priests in the valley of Sniél-emen. The reader detects a subtle discrepancy in the interpretation of these events. Max Leon, for example, "knew in a vague way that the Salish people had a reputation for having met the white men with open friendliness" (p. 48). Father Grepilloux's journal states, "As we had been invited by these Indians to come here and instruct them, we counted on some sort of welcome, yet nothing like what we received" (p. 46). Whatever the case may have been, the St. Xavier Mission establishes a strong influence over the Salish people.

Of Father Grepilloux, the eighty-year-old priest and confidant of Max Leon, the narrator states,

His affection for all Indians was deep and in practical matters he understood them. He saw how admirably adjusted

they were to the conditions under which they lived and he
learned their ways of wilderness travel and existence. He
was at once superior to them and able to place himself on
their level when occasion required it. He despised and
inveighed against those who despoiled the Indians. If the
reservation system must remain, he wanted the agents removed or strictly supervised, and he wanted to see tribal
laws and customs restored and respected. (p. 137)

Like the later Father Olguin in Momaday's *House Made of
Dawn*, McNickle's old priest is not without his redeeming
qualities. His paternalism towards the Indians is touching
though flawed by its ethnocentric bias. His wisdom, like that
of Archilde's mother, is largely one endowed by age.

The theme of rejection in *The Surrounded* is ultimately related to the religion of the black-robed fathers. Since they are
the most visible representatives of white penetration into the
Salish Valley, it is their deity and their world view that must
be renounced. Archilde is the first to come to terms with his
Christian upbringing, during a momentary epiphany in the
church:

What he saw next destroyed one of the last links connecting him with his boyhood, his beginnings. He had
gone to look at the rear of the altar, and there he was
held spellbound. Unpainted timbers, dust, an accumulation of old candle snuffers, flower vases, rags—he had
actually been afraid of those things! He stood motionless
while he tried to reconcile his memory of the rich ceremony which went on before the altar with the shabbiness
which he now saw. In the effort the simple faith of
childhood died quietly.

He had to see the sacristy then. Nothing awed him any
longer. (p. 105)

His mother is the next to revert to her tribal faith, followed by
her faithful friend, Modeste ("he also had turned back to that
world which was there before the new things came" [p. 210]).
Elise (Modeste's granddaughter) has already turned back in
her refusal to return to the Indian school.

McNickle's final image of Christianity, developed in the

substory of Archilde's nephews, Mike and Narcisse, is one of sickness and death. When these two youngsters (who have previously been characterized by their boisterousness and exuberance) return from the mission school, they are strangely pacified—subdued, we learn, by the harsh teachings of the Catholic fathers. Mike, Archilde discovers, was locked up in a dormitory closet where the school prefect told him he would be visited by the Devil for his rowdiness. The experience leads to the young boy's mental sickness. His spirit is totally broken, and it is necessary for Modeste to exorcise his fears. At the end of the story—when Elise persuades Archilde to run away with her to the mountains—it is Mike and Narcisse who join them, the two boys, like Huck Finn, determined to run away from civilization. ("All they asked was to be let alone . . ." [p. 247].) (While Christianity loses its footing among the Salish people, so also do some of the native traditions. Nowhere is this more apparent that at the Fourth-of-July celebrations, which McNickle describes as "a kind of low-class circus where people came to buy peanuts and look at freaks" [p. 216]. Modeste's dance "was a sad spectacle to watch" [p.217], largely because "the spectators laugh[ed]. They were making fun of an old man, too weak to move in the circle, who stood in one place and bobbed himself up and down" [p. 219].)

The pessimistic ending of the novel, the image of death closing in on Archilde and Elise, is consistent with the backlash against Christianity and the violent events described earlier in the narrative. Max Leon, his wife Catharine, and Father Grepilloux have all died from the disease known as old age. Along with Modeste, who is blind and also near death, they represent the passage of an earlier dispensation. It is not, however, a simple matter of the wane of Christianity among the Salish people. Louis is also gone, shot in the back by the game warden, and there is no exit for Archilde and Elise. McNickle, significantly, gives the final word in his story to the white agent, Parker: " 'It's too damn bad you people never learn that you can't run away. It's pathetic—' " (pp. 296–97). The future will only bring further impingements from the white man's world upon the Indians of the valley of Sniélemen.

The Surrounded is the work of a gifted writer. McNickle is a master of short, moving scenes that again and again have the ability to startle (Archilde's encounter with a deaf old woman at the side of the road; a dying mare he is forced to shoot—to mention only two). McNickle is the earliest Native American prose stylist, the earliest craftsman of the novel form. He skillfully incorporates materials from the folk tradition into the narrative, making especially fine use of oral tales ("the story of flint," the story of "the thing that was to make life easy"), as well as bits and pieces of the oral and the written history of the Salish people describing the coming of the white men. He is also master of the unexpected juxtaposition. (At the end of chapter 13, for example, when Louis's body is brought down from the hills, the reader anticipates that the scene will be followed by his funeral; then unexpectedly, McNickle begins the next chapter with a description of the funeral for Father Grepilloux.) *The Surrounded* is also the first novel by a Native American to make a sharp break with traditional chronological narrative—primarily in the use of controlled flashbacks. Though contemporary with Oskison and Mathews, in his handling of form as well as of theme and content McNickle belongs with the writers of the 1960s and 1970s (of the Native American Renaissance) rather than with those of his chronological period.[5]

House Made of Dawn

Momaday's novel is much more radically experimental than McNickle's, belying at almost every juncture the author's formal training in literature. (He has a Ph.D. in English from Stanford University, where he is currently professor of English.) *House Made of Dawn* (1968) is the most complex and the most obscure novel written by an American Indian. Virtually every page of the text illustrates Momaday's fascination with structure: the novel makes use of multiple points of view, stream of consciousness techniques, abrupt changes of time and chronology achieved primarily through the use of flashbacks and flashforwards; it also incorporates ethnic materials (traditional oral tales, fragments of poetry), and historical documents, both oral and written. If there is one major problem with the novel it is its obscurity, which has resulted in a number of ambiguities about factual matters within the narrative. My classroom experience has shown that readers are often confused about important incidents within the story. In an attempt to clarify some of these matters, I shall begin my interpretation with a description of the events in the novel *as they are disclosed*.

House Made of Dawn begins with a three-paragraph prologue which, we later learn, is more accurately an epilogue, since it describes the last incident in the main character's life: Abel's race toward death, a kind of ritual suicide, symbolically occurring at daybreak. The first word of the prologue, "Dypaloh," a Jemez Pueblo conventional form for beginning a story, tells us that Momaday wants us to regard his novel as a traditional story, perhaps part of an oral tradition, designed to teach a moral.

The first major section of the novel is called "The Longhair," and the setting and time are "Walatowa Cañon de San Diego, 1945." This section of the novel is divided into seven "chapters," each one identified by a date: July 20, 21, 24, 25, 28, August 1 and 2. The first of these begins with a brief description of the locale, followed by Abel's drunken arrival home after the war, when he is unable to acknowledge his grandfather.

The second subdivision, July 21, is constructed out of a series of short flashbacks: Abel when he was five years old, playing with his older brother, Vidal; his mother's death (from alcohol), followed somewhat later by Vidal's; Abel's sexual initiation at seventeen; his participation in the Eagle Watchers Society, and subsequent killing of an eagle; a memory of the war. At the end of this series of flashbacks, the narrative shifts to Father Olguin, the local priest, and the arrival of Angela St. John, a white woman from Los Angeles who has come to Walatowa for the mineral baths. At the end of the section, the narrator tells us, "Nothing had yet passed between [Abel and his grandfather], no word, no sign of recognition" (p. 31).

The section for July 24 brings Abel and Angela together; he begins to cut wood for her kitchen stove. July 25 opens with Father Olguin's story of Santiago, a sacred Pueblo bird, followed with a celebration of the feast of Santiago, a symbolic sacrament in which Abel participates, battling against an albino who flails him with a rooster until the bird is dead. Then the story shifts again—this time backward to Father Olguin's perusal of his predecessor's (Fray Nicolás) journals for 1874–75. From these notebooks, incorporated into the text of the story, the reader sees Francisco as a child, as an altarboy; and discovers a reference to the birth of an albino, possibly the one Abel later fought at the Santiago festival. There is also a letter recorded here, written in 1888 by Fray Nicolás to his brother-in-law, which reveals that the old priest was on the verge of a mental breakdown.

July 28: Abel is likened to an eagle in a cage; there is still virtually no communication between Francisco and him. The narrative shifts to Angela, who seduces Abel, though it is difficult to tell who is the seducer. The section ends with Francisco hearing whispers from the cornfields—evil spirits which the narrator hints may be created by the albino hiding there.

August 1: The yearly harvest festivals continue in the village with the Pecos bull run, described as a ritual which has lost its meaning. Abel and the albino sit in a bar drinking. After they leave together, Abel kills the albino with his knife. The next day, August 2, Francisco searches for his grandson.

Part 2 ("The Priest of the Sun") is set in Los Angeles in 1952. There are two dates, January 26 and 27. The first of these sections begins with a reference to "small silversided fish," described as "among the most helpless creatures on the face of the earth" (p. 83). Then the focus shifts to the Rev. J. B. B. Tosamah, the Priest of the Sun, and his basement church. Tosamah (a Kiowa, like Momaday) delivers a sermon to his congregation. When Abel is first described in this section of the novel, he is lying on the beach—like a fish out of water—horribly beaten up. Thus this section of the story announces an abrupt jump in time, since the narrative then flashes back and fills in some of the details omitted at the end of Part 1: Abel's trial for killing the albino, his years in prison, and his subsequent move to Los Angeles. There are a number of other flashbacks, including descriptions of his relationship with Millie, his white girlfriend, and (much earlier) the good times he had with Vidal and Fat Josie. The second date, January 27, returns to Tosamah, giving a sermon which chronicles the history of his people.

In Part 3 ("The Night Chanter"), set in Los Angeles in February of 1952, the point of view shifts from the third person omniscient to the first: Abel's friend Ben (Benally) relates the events of Abel's life after his arrival in Los Angeles. These incidents culminate in an encounter with Martinez, a policeman who beats Abel up, though they include other details about Abel's job, his alcoholism, and his relationships with Millie and with Angela St. John, who visits him in the hospital after he is beaten up. There are also a number of passages from Abel's consciousness, idyllically describing events of his youth. Ben sings the Navaho Night Chanter's song, "House Made of Dawn," part of a traditional purification ceremony, to heal Abel's broken body.

Part Four ("The Dawn Runner"), February 27 and 28, 1952, brings Abel back to Francisco's place at Walatowa. He has returned home to die, yet it is Francisco's death that takes place first. The old man's death is preceded in the narrative by several flashbacks to his youth, describing the ritual killing of a bear (as part of a rite of passage) and his initiation into the kiva society. In one of the last flashbacks, Francisco tells Abel and his brother of the dawn runners. The old man dies the night of February 27, and after Abel has prepared the body in the traditional way (with kaolin and pollen), he takes it to Father Olguin for Christian burial. Then Abel, his body broken from drink and the encounter with Martinez, runs to his death. "*Qtsedaba*," the last word in the narrative, tells us that the story has formally ended.

It is impossible to analyze *House Made of Dawn* without considering two relative points at the outset. First, the meaning or meanings of Momaday's novel are irrevocably bound up in the novel's structure: form and content interlock. Second, the novel should not be interpreted without reference to two other works published by the author: *The Way to Rainy Mountain* (1969) and *The Names* (1976). The first of these has a tripartite interwoven structure involving Kiowa legend, established facts about that legend ("historical" facts), and Momaday's personal experiences with these events or facts. *The Way to Rainy Mountain*, like Tosamah's sermon in *House Made of Dawn*, records the historic movement of the Kiowa people from the Northern to the Southern Plains. *The Names*, a kind of precocious autobiography, covers much the same material.

Momaday was born in 1934; his father was Kiowa, his mother part Cherokee. Both of his parents were formally educated. During the Second World War, the family lived at Hobbs, New Mexico, at the Army Air Base, where his parents were employed and where Momaday was probably first aware of Indians in the armed services. After the war, by which time he had reached the seventh grade, the family moved to Jemez Pueblo, where his parents both taught school. It is apparent from *The Names* that Jemez Pueblo became the setting for *House Made of Dawn*, though many of the Kiowa elements of the novel come from the author's earlier life, when he visited his father's family at Rainy Mountain. In large part, *House Made of Dawn* is a blending of Navaho, Jemez, and Kiowa traditions.

Although Momaday's own childhood was apparently a happy one, and his career as an adult has been highly successful, his overall picture of the American Indian in *House Made of Dawn* is pessimistic—bleaker than that of any of his contemporaries. Although it is one of the most eloquent pieces of writing by an American Indian, it is also one of the most depressing; even many of its poetic sections bespeak an underlying sense of futility, of nihilism. In Momaday's bleak view, the American Indian might just as well beat his head against a wall. The future offers nothing; the past can be recaptured only in fleeting moments. There appears to be little possibility even for simple endurance; the Indian is a vanishing breed.

Almost all of the Native American characters in *House Made of Dawn* are headed toward spiritual suicide, though Abel is the primary example. The reservation has nothing to offer him; the white man's world has mentally and physically maimed him. Although he was regarded by his peers as a brave soldier, Abel returns to the reservation broken by his alcoholism. The job that he takes chopping wood for three dollars a day illustrates the lack of training or technical skills provided by the Army. He is, in fact, the opposite of his name, *unable* to adjust to the world to which he has returned.

Furthermore, Momaday persistently associates his protagonist with trapped, nonhuman creatures. On the reservation he is likened to the caged eagles kept by the Eagle Watchers Society (hence his killing of the eagle rather than keeping it in confinement). Off the reservation, he is described as a fish out of water ("He had the sense that his whole body was shaking violently, tossing and whipping, flopping like a fish" [p. 106]). Neither the reservation nor the outside world offers satisfactory refuge.

Abel's confusion about the white man's world is symbolized by his view of the prison where he spends six years for killing the albino:

> The walls of his cell were white, or perhaps they were gray or green; he could not remember. After a while he could not imagine anything beyond the walls except the yard outside, the lavatory and the dining hall—or even the walls, really. They were abstractions beyond the reach of his understanding, not in themselves confinement but symbols of confinement. The essential character of the walls consisted not in their substance but in their appearance, the bare one-dimensional surface that was white, perhaps, or gray, or green. (p. 97)

The fact that he cannot remember the color of his cell is indicative of his general anaesthetized state; the world has become an abstraction he does not understand. Everything is confused. When he goes to Los Angeles, the years in the prison continue to control his every move: the parole officers and the welfare workers never leave him alone. He cannot hold down a job; he drinks too much. The final blow comes from the hands of an emblem of authority, the sadistic policeman, Martinez. Abel becomes a zombie, dead in mind and body. Momaday states flatly, "He wanted to die" (p. 92). His ultimate deterioration is more than a general crippling from the fight; his addiction has also ruined his mind: "He had never been sick until he was sick with alcohol. . . . His body, like his mind, had turned on him; it was his enemy" (p. 93).

When Ben takes Abel to the bus station so he can return to the reservation, he notes of him, "He looked pretty bad. His hands were still bandaged, and he couldn't use them very well. It took us a long time to get there. He couldn't walk very fast" (pp. 127–28). The return home is the beginning of his final journey. Ben muses on Abel's problems, calling him a longhair[6]—a reservation boy who could not adjust to the outside world—adding, "You know, you have to change. That's the only way you can live in a place like this. You have to forget about the way it was, how you grew up and all" (p. 135). Abel returns home in order to die. The most important quality he needs for survival on the reservation, a healthy body, he no longer possesses.

Abel is not the only Indian in Momaday's novel whose life is out of joint. Benally and Tosamah, examples of "urban" Indians in contemporary society, are also on the verge of spiritual suicide. They have both been cut off from their roots, and their displacement in the city is a terrible existence. It is difficult to tell which is the more pathetic figure, since both have constructed elaborate facades in order to protect themselves.

Ben believes that an Indian has to change if he is going to survive in the city, that it is necessary to forget the "way it was, how you grew up . . ." (p. 135). About his own existence, and the squalid room where he lives, he remarks, "It's a good place; you could fix it up real nice. There are a lot of good places around here. I could find some place with a private bathroom if I wanted to, easy. A man with a good job can do just about anything he wants" (p. 162). Ben lies to himself. He cannot get a good place to stay "just about anywhere" because he is Indian. He has few rights. (Martinez can rob him of his money, and Ben can do nothing about it.) He lives in a slum; his job has made him little more than an anonymous entity. His philosophy hides the realities of life from him:

> You never have to be alone. You go downtown and there are a lot of people all around, and they're having a good time. You see how it is with them, how they get along and have money and nice things, radios and cars and clothes and big houses. And you want those things; you'd be crazy not to want them. And you can have them, too; they're so *easy* to have. (p. 164)

As a relocated Indian, Ben lives in a spiritual vacuum, isolated in a city that has no understanding of or interest in its ethnic minorities.

Tosamah, Momaday's hipster Priest of the Sun, has worked out an even more elaborate system of adaptation in order to endure the horrors of urban existence. He is one of the most fascinating characters in American Indian fiction. His life is a sham, yet Momaday has given him the important role of Kiowa tribal historian. The subject of his second sermon is a tragic story of an earlier Indian "relocation." Tosamah's full name reveals his true identity: "The Right Reverend John Big Bluff Tosamah" (p. 85). He is a bag of wind, "a clown" (p. 165), as Ben calls him, a peyote priest ministering to a congregation of urban derelicts. (In her article, "The Remembered Earth: Momaday's *House Made of Dawn*," Carol Oleson has written of him, "He enjoys verbally tormenting his flock.")[7] Like Rinehart in Ralph Ellison's *Invisible Man*, who is also a storefront priest, Tosamah has worked out an elaborate system of double-talk to disguise his true identity. His character is best revealed by his own words at the end of his first sermon: " 'Good night . . . and get yours' " (p. 91). He is as guilty of misusing the language ("the word") as are the white men he attacks.

It is Tosamah's second sermon, "The Way to Rainy Mountain," that most clearly illustrates Momaday's incorporation of cultural materials (in the form of oral history) into the novel. The sermon chronicles the Kiowa origin myth (their "coming out" from a hollow log); the origin of the Big Dipper; the acquisition of their sacred sun-dance doll, Tai-me; their journey from the Northern Plains to the South. Many of these tales illustrate spiritual decline (the last sun dance, the extermination of the buffalo, the deicide of their god). All of them were later incorporated into *The Way to Rainy Mountain* and *The Names*, sometimes almost verbatim, and Momaday gives Tosamah's ancestors names from his own family lineage.[8] They illustrate Momaday's preoccupation with his own past—a determination to make certain that the treatment of the Kiowas by the white invaders of the plains (representative of the treatment of Native Americans in general) be fully understood.

Momaday's use of Kiowa oral history in *House Made of Dawn* is balanced by his inclusion of written "documents" kept by the Catholic priests on the reservation. (There is, in fact, always a conscientious attempt to balance opposites in the novel: oral history/written history, traditional religion/ Christianity, urban/reservation, Indian/white, and so on.) As in McNickle's *The Surrounded*, the sense of the past is established by Indian oral tales and traditions and the white man's written documents—two often conflicting versions of the "word." These written documents begin with Father Olguin's version of the Santiago myth, describing the way the Spanish (Christian) myth was adapted by the Jemez people. They continue with Fray Nicolás's (Father Olguin's predecessor at the mission) journals and letters. While Tosamah's oral history of the Kiowa people illustrates a movement toward cultural disharmony, Fray Nicolás's written documents illustrate a parallel movement toward spiritual disillusionment and breakdown. His initial trust of the child, Francisco, turns to distrust and paranoia; his Christian "charity" evolves to feelings of cultural superiority.

As they do with Tosamah's story of his people, these written records also reveal a sense of continuity and survival. Things have not actually altered that much. The narrator states,

> The people of the town have little need. They do not hanker after progress and have never changed their essential way of life. Their invaders were a long time in conquering them; and now, after four centuries of Christianity, they still pray in Tanoan to the old deities of the earth and sky and make their living from the things that are and have always been within their reach; while in the discrimination of pride they acquire from their conquerors only the luxury of example. They have assumed the names and gestures of their enemies, but have held on to their own, secret souls; and in this there is a resistance and an overcoming, a long outwaiting. (p. 56)

This state of continuity is also illustrated by the priests themselves; Father Olguin, like his predecessor, is also beset with doubts about his purpose among the Indians. Both priests react similarly when asked to officiate at funerals when they know that the body of the deceased has already been prepared according to Indian tradition.

Historical documents and traditional tales in *House Made of Dawn* are part of the novel's repeated concern with "language" and its all too frequent distortions. We have already noted that Tosamah attacks the white man for diluting and proliferating the word, while violating the language in similar fashion. At his trial, Abel experiences a similar confusion because of the white man's language: "Word by word by word these men were disposing of him in language, *their* language. . ." (p. 95). As the bits and pieces of legal forms and psychiatric tests incorporated into the narrative illustrate (such as Millie's use of IQ tests), the white world is slowly being smothered under a mountain of printed forms and documents. It is Ben, however, who has the last word on language: white people

> can't help you because you don't know how to talk to them. They have a lot of *words*, and you know they mean something, but you don't know what, and your own words are no good because they're not the same; they're different, and they're the only words you've got. Everything is different, and you don't know how to get used to it. (p. 144)

This is the racial core of the story: the subtle and insidious ways that one ethnic group slowly strangles another: by words (legal methods), by deed (historical patterns), by culture (spiritual beliefs). Taken together, along with the overriding images of death and destruction, these issues make Momaday's *House Made of Dawn* the most searing indictment of the white world by a Native American novelist.

In spite of his bitterness, Momaday takes great pains not to stereotype the white characters in his story—another example of his conscious attempt to balance opposites. Except for the sadistic policeman, Martinez, the white characters—Angela St. John, Millie, Father Olguin—are presented without malice. Father Olguin waits and endures; he represents a sense of dogged continuity with the past. Angela, who could easily have been portrayed as a stereotyped white woman out to get her sexual thrills, is strangely moved by her affair with Abel, subdued of her earlier frenzy and made the richer for it,[9] as the tale of the bear and the maiden she tells her son illustrates. Millie, Abel's girl in Los Angeles, is the most sympathetically treated of the three. Her life is much like Abel's—a struggle with the land of her heritage, set against the pain and loneliness of urban living. The account of her daughter's death is certainly one of the most moving passages in the novel.

One other character in the story has often been regarded as a suggestive emblem of the novel's racial theme: the albino, usually described as "a white man." Momaday first describes him as follows: "The appearance of one of the men was striking. He was large, lithe, and white-skinned; he wore little round colored glasses . . ." (p. 42). He is referred to as an albino only once, but his participation in the chicken pull would appear to suggest that he is an Indian and not a Euro-American. The albino flays Abel with a white rooster— according to tradition—until the bird is dead.[10] Seven days later, after drinking with the man at a bar, Abel kills him. Sitting next to him in the bar, Abel detects the albino's "in-human cry. . . . It was an old woman's laugh, thin and weak as water. . . . from the tongue and teeth of the great evil mouth" (p. 77).

A number of readers have placed the murder in a racial context. Jeanette Henry, who reviewed the work for *The Indian Historian*, for example, wrote of the incident: "While drunk [Abel] kills a white man and goes to jail for the crime."[11] Momaday has confused the issue by referring to the birth of an albino child in Fray Nicolás's journal entry for January 5, 1875:

> I heard today of a strange thing here on the 3d & so went to see a child born to Manuelita & Diego Fragua. It is what is called an albino whiter than any child I have seen before tho' it had been of the white race. It is dead & raw about its eyes & mouth tho' otherways hale I think & there is a meagre white hair on its head like an old man & its crying is very little to hear. I advise to baptize this same day & do so at 3 o'clock. It is given a name Juan Reyes. (p. 49)

At Abel's trial, Father Olguin explains to the jury that Abel regarded the albino as "an evil spirit" (p. 94), an argument that is consistent with a passage from Abel's consciousness:

He had killed the white man. It was not a complicated thing, after all; it was very simple. It was the most natural thing in the world. Surely they could see that, these men who meant to dispose of him in words. They must know that he would kill the white man again, if he had the chance, that there could be no hesitation whatsoever. For he would know what the white man was, and he would kill him if he could. A man kills such an enemy if he can. (p. 95)

Tosamah explains the murder, mockingly, by saying that Abel considered the albino a snake—an evil spirit. What leads to further confusion is an incident that takes place between the time of the chicken pull and Abel's murder of the man. While he is working in the cornfields, Francisco hears mysterious whispers. The scene concludes with the figure in the cornfields watching Abel's grandfather leave the fields: "Above the open mouth, the nearly sightless eyes followed the old man out of the cornfield, and the barren lids fluttered helplessly behind the colored glass" (p. 64).

What are we to conclude from this scene and from the passage in Fray Nicolás's journal? Did Abel know that the albino was watching his grandfather from the cornfields? Why does Abel consider the albino a source of evil? If this is Juan Reyes Fragua, he would in fact have to be a contemporary of Abel's grandfather, since his birth in 1875 comes only a few years after Francisco's. If it is not the same man, but an Indian albino, the term "white man" becomes especially confusing since it appears that in neither case does Momaday intend for the murder to be regarded as a racist crime. The fact is that the albino/white man is surrounded by an aura of ambiguities, yet one thing is certain: for Abel, he represents evil incarnate. As such, his color (or lack of color) is emblematic of the greater evil abroad in this world—evil which often wears no conventional cloth.[12]

The general ambiguity enveloping the albino's birth and demise is at the heart of what Martha Scott Trimble has referred to as "the novel's sense of mystery. . . . The scene during which Abel kills the Albino provides the most striking instance of Momaday's refusal to give an explicit explanation of motives, Abel's as well as the Albino's."[13] This "mysteriousness" in fact permeates much of *House Made of Dawn*, though it is most visibly apparent in the conclusion to the novel—after Abel has returned home from Los Angeles.

Generally speaking, the conclusion of the novel—revealed in the prologue—has been interpreted as a kind of "positive" ending to the story, symbolizing spiritual renewal and/or cultural rejuvenation. In her article, "On the Trail of Pollen: Momaday's *House Made of Dawn*," Marian Willard Hylton states of Abel's return: "The Abel who comes back to the reservation to tend his dying grandfather is broken in body but healed in spirit."[14] Of the ending of the novel, she writes: "As he runs, as he becomes a part of the orderly continuum of interrelated events that constitute the Indian universe, Abel is the land, and he is of the land once more."[15] In her monograph on Momaday, Martha Scott Trimble sees the ending of the novel similarly: "Abel's running with the dawn at the end of the last chapter . . . emerges as a religious act leading to self-realization."[16] Similar views are held by Carole Oleson (*House Made of Dawn* is a book of courage, faith, and hope for a 'new world coming' which will be a dynamic, not static, continuation of the old world's wisdom and order")[17] and Harold S. McAllister ("the spiritual redemption he ultimately finds [is] through a return to his own place, his own center, at Walatowa"),[18] though McAllister acknowledges the novel's bleakness and admits that "from a sociological viewpoint, [Abel's] return to Walatowa is a defeat."[19]

Although these interpretations do not take into account the novel's ubiquitous images of death, sickness, and pain, they do admit to its general ambiguity. It is difficult to believe that Abel has come home "to tend his dying grandfather." Rather, it seems that he has returned to the reservation because there is nowhere else for him to go. If there is a sense of recognition at the end of the story, it is that death is the only escape. For the first two days after his arrival home, Abel continues his heavy drinking ("he was sick and in pain" [p. 175]). On the evening of the seventh day, Francisco dies. The following morning, after taking Francisco's body to the priest, Abel prepares for his own death by covering himself with pollen and ashes, symbols of life and death. As he runs, Momaday states of him "his body cracked open with pain. . ." (p. 191).

Momentarily, he falls down into the snow. It is important to remember that seven days earlier, he could hardly even walk to the bus depot in Los Angeles.

That this is a run toward death, a kind of ritual suicide, and not an act of renewal is further supported by earlier references to the "dead runners." Immediately before Francisco's death, there is a flashback describing the time he first took Abel (and his brother) out into the arroyo to explain to them about the dawn runners: " 'Listen. . . . It is the race of the dead, and it happens here' " (p. 186). The dawn runners (running after evil) have an endless task, "running easily and forever" (p. 186), since evil can never be caught. Several earlier references to the runners also identify their goal as death. One of these occurs after Abel kills the albino when he watches several old men participating in the Pecos bull run:

> old men in white leggings running after evil in the night. They were whole and indispensable in what they did; everything in creation referred to them. Because of them, perspective, proportion, design in the universe. Meaning because of them. They ran with great dignity and calm, not in the hope of anything, but hopelessly, neither in fear nor hatred nor despair of evil, but simply in recognition and with respect. Evil was. Evil was abroad in the night. . . . (p. 96)

In the peyote ceremony in Tosamah's church, running is also juxtaposed with death. After eating the peyote buttons, the celebrants feel a momentary peak: "Everyone felt himself young and whole and powerful. No one was sick or weak or weary. Everyone wanted to run . . ." (p. 103). Moments later, when the high wears off, "Everyone thought of death. . . . Everyone was caught up in the throes of a deadly depression. There was a general nausea, and the dullest pain of the mind" (p. 103). So it is with Abel: his running is only a momentary high, a final assertion of body over spirit that cannot be sustained, an act that leads to death.

Much of the tangential symbolism in Momaday's novel also supports the idea of a death run at the end of the story. As in McNickle's *The Surrounded*, death (especially premature death: Abel's mother, his brother, Abel himself) is one of the

most common images, reminding us of the American Indian's
short life-span. Yet the images of death and self-destruction
are prevalent in the descriptions not only of the reservation
but of the outside world. Abel's first encounter with the white
world is during a time of war: "He didn't know where he was,
and he was alone. No, there were men about, the bodies of
men" (p. 26). The dead fish on the beach in Los Angeles
suggest this belief, as do a number of other wasteland images
of the white man's world: "cans and bits of paper and broken
glass" (p. 92). Yet nowhere is the idea of death more obvious
than on the reservation: the carnage of the dead eagle, the
rooster used for the Santiago festival, the murder of the albino, the room "in which his mother and brother died" (p.
176), Francisco's death. By the end of the novel even the title
image of a house made of dawn is used negatively, as a re-
verse symbol, indicating death instead of life. (Momaday appears to be intentionally distorting the Navaho purification
song. Ben sings it to Abel when they are drinking with other
Indians on the hilltop, yet he perverts its function by being
intoxicated and feeling embarrassed that his singing will prevent the others from having a good time. [As a contrast, see
Oliver La Farge's *Laughing Boy*, in which the song is sung at
Slim Girl and Laughing Boy's wedding ceremony.])

Perhaps the most important aspect of the conclusion of
Abel's story (the last event in his life) is its circularity: the
prologue of the novel is actually its epilogue. As in Ralph Ellison's *Invisible Man*, the end is in the beginning. Structure
and meaning have been merged into the novel's opening
sequence: Abel's running at dawn.[20] The circular nature of
Abel's story (his return to the place where his life began) and
the circular structure of the narrative (the conclusion at the
beginning) *are* ambiguous because they can suggest both life
and death. Because of its mythic and archetypal implications,
the circle of life is self-renewing (night/day, dusk/dawn, the
repetition of the seasons), yet a circle—as we have already
seen in the ending of McNickle's *The Surrounded*—can also
be a kind of trap because there is no way out.

How, then, are we to interpret the ending of Momaday's
novel—as an example of "self-realization" and, therefore, as a
return to the life-giving forces within the traditional culture?

Or as an example of defeat, annihilation, of spiritual suicide? Strong opposites these. Why does Momaday persist in calling the albino a white man? Why—almost at the end of the story—does Momaday suggest that Francisco was "sired by the old consumptive priest" (p. 184), that is, Fray Nicolás? All of these questions (and others) can only return us to our opening remarks about the novel: *House Made of Dawn* is the most radically experimental, the most obscure piece of fiction written by a Native American, an intellectual puzzle that engages our attention more completely with each successive reading. Momaday's refusal to explain everything carefully, his determination not to spell out the solutions to our cultural differences—even the novel's dark pessimism—mirror the author's own dilemma of being an educated Indian in modern America. In Momaday's own words,

> The novel is about an Indian who returns from World War II and finds that he cannot recover his tribal identity; nor can he escape the cultural context in which he grew up. He is torn, as they say, between two worlds, neither of which he can enter and be a whole man. The story is that of his struggle to survive on the horns of a real and tragic dilemma in contemporary American society.[21]

Is it as simple as that? I think not, for no matter how we try to explain the novel's many ambiguities, there is still the gnawing realization that Momaday's vision of the American Indian is essentially pessimistic, that again and again he shows us Indians who are the last members of a dying race. Though Francisco's death at the end of the novel heralds the passing of an older way of life, the New Indians (Abel, Ben, Tosamah) have found no satisfactory way of coping with the white man's world. Their existence is not even a matter of simple endurance; rather, they are slowly being obliterated. Their world is dead-ended.

Answering questions after a lecture he gave at Colorado State University, Momaday stated, "I don't know what an Indian is. The 'American Indian'—that term is meaningless; to me it means very little."[22] Momaday was speaking figuratively; he knows very well what the American Indian is. What is worse, he has seen the horror of what the Indian is becoming. What he is not so certain of, it seems to me, is what the American Indian *was*. That past—the end in the beginning— forms the central quest of all of his prose works (*House Made of Dawn*, *The Way to Rainy Mountain*, *The Names*). Reading any one of these volumes is a frightening experience since in each one of them Momaday has created a painful image of his self: a man in search of his roots. I would further suggest that Momaday has yet to solve the dilemma of his own iden- tity. The ending of *House Made of Dawn*—that is, Abel's fate—typifies this dilemma. Is it a positive return to one's roots or a kind of symbolic murder of the past? There is a similar sense of irresolution at the end of *The Names*:

> I bore westward across the Powder River and the Bighorn Mountains, and after many days I took leave of the plains. The way was rocky then and steep, and it seemed that my horse was bearing me up to the top of the world. All the rivers ran down from that place, and many times I saw eagles in the air under me. And then there were meadows full of wildflowers, and a mist rolled upon them, the slow, rolling spill of the mountain clouds. And in one of these, in a pool of low light, I touched the fallen tree, the hollow log there in the thin crust of the ice.[23]

Is this a return to one's roots (to the origin of the Kiowa people)? Or is this meant to suggest a sense of withdrawal (a going back into the hollow log)?

In a profoundly moving account of his travels through Af- rica, *Which Tribe Do You Belong To?*, Alberto Moravia has written of cultural change among the Kikuyu: "There is no greater suffering for any man than to feel his cultural founda- tions giving way beneath his feet."[24] Changing continents and people, it is not difficult to apply Moravia's statement to Abel in Momaday's *House Made of Dawn* or to Archilde Leon in McNickle's *The Surrounded*. Moravia's pronouncement can be transferred to almost all of the novels written by American Indians, for every one of them is concerned in some way or other with cultural confrontation and change.

The novels by D'Arcy McNickle and N. Scott Momaday are the bleakest examples of cultural irreconcilability we will encounter among these works. In their darkest passages, each novel presents a picture of cultural annihilation: McNickle's people are literally surrounded by another universe which is slowly strangling them. Momaday's Indians are either the aged and the dying on the reservation or the younger transplants in the urban ghettos, isolated (like fish out of water) in an environment incapable of nourishing them. In both novels, the circular image of entrapment recurs: the Salish people, caught inside a circle which contains them; Abel's reluctant return (like Archilde's), coming full circle—back to the beginning because there is nowhere else to go. In each work, the ambiguities of the story mirror the novel's experimental structure. For both protagonists, the circle is a death image: for Archilde because there is no crack permitting exit to the outside; for Abel, because he has figuratively been running blindly ever since he first left the reservation.

Yet even in their despair, in their depiction of cultural entrapment and renunciation, McNickle and Momaday admit the possibility of something better, of cultural survival—though it may not be an existence currently understood. McNickle hints at this in his depiction of Archilde's mother (known as faithful Catharine to the priests). Her reversion to her traditional faith suggests that the old traditions will ultimately survive, that Christianity, introduced by the missionaries, will be renounced. Momaday suggests the possibility of a similar endurance in his remark about the survival of the old deities: "in this there is a resistance and an overcoming, a long outwaiting" (p. 56). For both, there is the implication that time is the most important factor; the Native American may eventually win in this numbers game with the white world because his patience is the greater.

There is another important consideration, especially in light of the next group of novels written by Native Americans. *The Surrounded* and *House Made of Dawn* are essentially stories about individuals, isolated Indians trapped in the present world, unable to return to the ways of the past. Although their present existence is individualistic, the past from which they have been severed is collective. The next three novels, in their emphasis upon the wider whole, suggest a solution to this barren existence: the return of the individual, like Archilde's mother, to the life-giving forces of the collective group.

5

History of the People

I am the man, I suffer'd, I was there.—Walt Whitman, *Leaves of Grass*

Indians! There are no Indians left but me!—Sitting Bull, 1889

I want to say further that you are not a great chief of this country . . . that you have no following, no power, no control, and no right to any control. You are on an Indian reservation merely at the suffrance of the goverment. You are fed by the government, clothed by the government, your children are educated by the government, and all you have and are today is because of the government. If it were not for the government you would be freezing and starving today in the mountains. I merely say these things to you to notify you that you cannot insult the people of the United States of America or its committees. . . . The government feeds and clothes and educates your children now, and desires to teach you to become farmers, and to civilize you, and *make you as white men.*—Senator John Logan to Sitting Bull, 48th Congress, 1st Session

If the earliest group of Native American novelists (Pokagon, Oskison, and Mathews) were assimilationists, and the second group (McNickle and Momaday) were reactionaries, the third group of writers I shall discuss (Dallas Chief Eagle, Hyemeyohsts Storm, and Denton R. Bedford) might best be termed revisionists. Central to their novels is a historical event or situation, initiated from outside—inflicted, one might say—upon a group of people. In each of these cases, the historical event (or series of events) may be said to affect a body of people fleeing the onslaught of the white man's advancement upon their tribal lands. The result is removal of the people

97

from their sacred lands to the imposed confines of reservation life.

Broadly speaking, Dallas Chief Eagle's *Winter Count* (1967) relates the same story as Dee Brown's later work, *Bury My Heart at Wounded Knee* (1970): the systematic attempt of the American government during the second half of the last century to obliterate the American Indian from the face of this earth, battle by battle, broken treaty by broken treaty—the humiliating events that were still vivid in the memories of the earliest Native American novelists. Hyemeyohsts Storm's *Seven Arrows* (1972) covers much the same material, though the emphasis is more upon the possibility of cultural eradication than on racial genocide. Denton R. Bedford's novel, *Tsali* (1972), goes back to an earlier event, the Cherokee Removal of 1838, though the author's objective is again historical correction.

All three of these novels return us to an earlier premise of this study: if a Native American were writing a novel about a known historical event or personality, a novel about Pocahontas, for example, it would certainly be a different story from the one with which we are familiar and perhaps more comfortable. That is as it should be since for too many years the Native American's story has been told by someone else. These three novels, however, alter that pattern, and the result is always illuminating.

Although *Winter Count* is ostensibly concerned with a young Indian brave named Turtleheart and his search for his kidnapped bride, Evensigh, Dallas Chief Eagle tells his story against the background of far more significant events: the Indian relocations of the 1870s and 1880s that culminated in the massacre at Wounded Knee in 1890. A number of important historical personalities appear in the narrative, as is true of *Seven Arrows*, though Storm has intentionally shifted his emphasis to lesser-known figures in order to make his story representative of the fate of the Plains Indians in general. Denton R. Bedford's *Tsali* focuses upon a minor character in the Cherokee Removal—a known figure, though a man usually dismissed in a paragraph or two in most studies of the removal—and elevates him to rightfully deserved heroic stature.

In contrast to the novels discussed earlier, the collective situation, the *shared* experience of the group, is much more significant in each of these works than what happens to the individual. The tragedy at the end of *Winter Count* is not simply the deaths of Turtleheart and Evensigh, but the massacre at Wounded Knee, the symbolic culmination of fifty years of bitter warfare between Indians and whites. After Wounded Knee the frontier was forever closed, and Native peoples were reduced definitively to wards of the state, henceforth circumscribed by reservation life. In *Seven Arrows* even more than in *Winter Count* the collective consciousness of the group is the author's concern; there is no single central character. Rather, the focus is upon the "unknown" Indian whose fate is generally represented by a shot in the back. In the case of Storm's novel, the overtones are spiritual as well as historical. The white man's encroachment is depicted as a kind of sickness or disease, threatening to destroy the Native American's culture from within:

> "We are Each a Living Spinning Medicine Wheel, and Each of us Possesses this Power to Destroy or to Create. When Ten of the Hundred do not Care, it Makes our Shield that much less Capable of Stopping Sickness. This Sickness Strikes out at Random, and can Hurt Anyone."[1]

The group experience is equally significant in Denton R. Bedford's novel: Tsali's execution unites the Cherokee Indians in their opposition to the white man's plans for their relocation.

In their concern with the collective whole, with the shared experience of the group, all three of these novels depict aggressive confrontations between Native Americans and Euro-Americans. The relocation of each of these groups of people, however, was far more than a physical uprooting and transplanting from one location to another. The shock of relocation upon the body was secondary to the paroxysm upon the spirit: survival of a people did not always guarantee survival of its culture, of a way of life. In a note appended to the end of his novel, Denton R. Bedford concludes, "Indeed, if one were to consider some of the great achievements of the Cherokee people, it is that they have survived."[2] In their concern with the collective spirit of a people, each of these novels, though outwardly about physical survival, is far more significantly about cultural adaptation and change.

Winter Count

Although Dallas Chief Eagle focuses the beginning and ending of his story on individual characters, much of the narrative is given over to descriptions of the historical confrontations between Native Americans and white Americans, roughly between 1875 and 1890. The novel, which is told in the third person with some flashbacks, opens with Turtleheart and Evensigh's marriage—a time of general festivity. The camp crier announces "the birth of a new family."[3] There is dancing and feasting, a general state of jubilation as the couple depart for their wedding journey. While still enjoying the "ensuing period of blissful seclusion . . . shared by . . . newlyweds until a new crescent moon appear[s] in the western sky" (p. 4), Turtleheart and Evensigh are captured by three white men and a Santee Sioux scout and forced to accompany them to the western goldfields.

The abduction immediately anchors Chief Eagle's story in its historical time frame. The setting of the novel is the land of the Sioux Indians of the West "who were known as the Tetonwan or simply the Teton Sioux" (p. i). The initial conflict occurs because white men en route to the goldfields farther west are trespassing in the Black Hills, the Paha Sapa, on the Sioux reservation (established by treaty in 1868). These white men, we subsequently learn, have deserted from the army—ironically, the same army that would maintain peace between Indians and whites and prevent the latter from entering Sioux lands. As the narrator shows us, however, the treaty of 1868 was meaningless: the Indians had no means of preventing white invaders from entering their land. What is worse, the Santee Sioux scout in the story who guides the three men across the Black Hills reveals the amount of dissension among the Indian tribes themselves; no longer are they united against the white invaders.

At the end of the initial confrontation between Indians and whites, Turtleheart kills one of the white men who would abuse his wife. The two others tie him to a tree, lash him until they believe he is dead, and depart with Evensigh. (The Santee Sioux, Thin Bird, belatedly attempts to aid Turtleheart and Evensigh, but he is killed in the skirmish.) Much of the remaining portion of *Winter Count* is indirectly concerned with the lovers' search for each other. After their eventual reunion (in 1881), the two of them live on the reservation at White Clay Creek until the massacre at Wounded Knee (in 1890), which takes both of their lives.

The historical events of the Indian-white confrontation during the last quarter of the nineteenth century are much more important than the story of Turtleheart's search for Evensigh. Chief Eagle has skillfully mixed the two themes in such a manner that the historical background blends in naturally with Turtleheart's search for his wife. The reader unfamiliar with the events of these years may not even be aware of their magnitude, yet the pages of Chief Eagle's narrative are peopled with the major Indian figures of the period: Gall, Red Cloud, Crazy Horse (one of Dallas Chief Eagle's ancestors), Two Moon, Hump, Chief Joseph, Sitting Bull, Dull Knife, Big Foot. Additional names appear to be variants of those of other Indian leaders of the time: Higheagle (High Hawk?), Crooked Nose (Roman Nose?), Iron Shield (Iron Shell?), Loneman (Lone Wolf?).

The appearance of these historic figures is organic to the main story itself. It is Gall (Sitting Bull's lieutenant, the war chief of the tribe), for example, who discovers Turtleheart after his lashing and nurses him back to good health. Because of an earlier rite (the Hunka ceremony), the two of them have already developed a lasting friendship. Chief Eagle uses Gall as a kind of voice for his people, to articulate the Indians' feelings about the white invaders of the Black Hills:

> "The Paha Sapa is the last remaining symbol of our people's great might. We must not permit the whites to violate this sacred ground by digging for the yellow iron. These hills are sacred because of their symbolic nature, the expression of the Great Spirit." (p. 33)

It is Gall who comments upon the many breaches of the Treaty of 1868 between the Sioux Indians and the whites.

There is no reason to enumerate all the historic events depicted in *Winter Count*. Turtleheart's role as the protagonist is to be the observer of the times during which he lives— somewhat like Jack Crabb, the central character in Thomas Berger's *Little Big Man* (1964). Turtleheart is present in 1876 when the messenger from the Commissioner of Indian Affairs orders Crazy Horse to return to the reservation. He is present at the Battle of the Little Bighorn (1876) and witnesses Sitting Bull's subsequent flight to Canada—even considers going along with him, but returns to the Black Hills in hopes of finding Evensigh. Turtleheart observes Crazy Horse's surrender and subsequent murder, as well as Sitting Bull's arrest and death. He witnesses the defeats of Chief Joseph and Dull Knife; he understands the coercive ways whites manipulate Indians into signing treaties (" 'They used the firewater to get the men to sign' " [p. 193]); he observes the final abortive attempt of his people to restore their vanishing way of life—the Ghost Dance craze of the late 1880s. By the end of the narrative, the role of Turtleheart—the archetypal Sioux, *every* Indian—recalls that of an earlier famous witness of historic confrontation and upheaval: Walt Whitman.

The major historic event in *Winter Count*, the major scene in the novel, is the Battle of the Little Bighorn, commonly referred to as "Custer's Last Stand." Although the author attributes the success of the battle to the skill and confidence of the combined Indian forces, he is careful to present the battle in an objective way. Both sides make tactical errors. (Gall states angrily, " 'I have made a fateful blunder. There are soldiers riding down the other side of the river toward the Cheyenne village and that is where all of the women and children are' " [p. 107].)

No one, of course, can dispute the outcome of the battle itself. What Chief Eagle could not anticipate when he wrote his novel was the hostility of certain publishers to his interpretation of Custer's death: suicide.[4] When Turtleheart and Gall are about to strip Custer (Yellow Hair) of his possessions, Broken Bow tells them, " 'No! No. . . . I say this man shot himself. He destroyed his own life. To take anything of his is bad. It will bring bad things to you, your relatives; all of us. No, you cannot take anything' " (p. 110). Broken Bow further explains,

"In the last of the battle, the white handles on his short guns drew my eyes. He was crouched behind his dead horse and I was over there. . . . I was about out of ammunition, so I lay there waiting for a soldier to die. When Yellow Hair stopped to reload his guns, I took advantage of his distracted attention and crawled closer. When he looked up and saw his forces crumbling all around him, there was terror on his face. He put a gun to his head with both hands and fired. When he did this thing, I knew I did not want his guns. I swear this is true."

Turtleheart looked at Yellow Hair, and noticed that blood had run over his chin and mustache. He was lying on his back, eyes closed. His right hand, covered with blood, still clasped the left hand fingers which still held the gun. (p. 110)

Read today, more than ten years after Chief Eagle published the novel, the incident seems tame enough, hardly worthy of commentary. No one knows exactly what happened to George Armstrong Custer at the Battle of the Little Bighorn except that he (as well as more than two hundred other white soldiers) perished. Chief Eagle's interpetation strikes me as being as reasonable as any other account of Custer's demise—even, perhaps, a healthy corrective to the prevailing interpretation. That the death itself is clouded in confusion is apparent from reading other accounts of the battle. Dee Brown, for example, wryly comments:

Long after the battle, White Bull of the Minneconjous drew four pictographs showing himself grappling with and killing a soldier identified as Custer. Among others who claimed to have killed Custer were Rain-in-the-Face, Flat Hip, and Brave Bear. Red Horse said that an unidentified Santee warrior killed Custer. Most Indians who told of the battle said they never saw Custer and did not know who killed him.[5]

The real issue is one of poetic license, not racial bias. No matter what may have been the conditions of Custer's defeat, white America saw the Battle of the Little Bighorn as a mandate for the final extermination of the American Indian. In a hundred Hollywood movies this attitude has prevailed. Now Chief Eagle confronts us with another version, and all we need remember is that although *Winter Count* is rooted in historical reality, it is still a novel, the product of a creative imagination. Like any other work of fiction, it should not be read as literal fact. George Armstrong Custer may very well have taken his own life—or he may have been killed by an Indian. Since we will never be able to know exactly what happened, there is no reason to repudiate Chief Eagle's interpretation. It is considerably more plausible than other recent novels that have dealt with the subject.[6]

Besides using the fictional Turtleheart as a witness of the tragic confrontations between Native Americans and white Americans, Chief Eagle also uses him to illustrate the strong traditions that bind his people to the past. A lengthy passage, for example, delineates his preparation for and subsequent participation in the Sun Dance—complete with a description of the extremes of physical torture with which the ceremony ended.[7] There is, furthermore, a description of Turtleheart's Vision Quest—similar to descriptions of that central initiation ritual of the Plains Indians in Storm's *Seven Arrows*. From these and other scenes, Turtleheart emerges as a noble young Indian caught up in the major events of his time. His humanity especially underscores many of the most important scenes in the story. After witnessing the Battle of the Little Bighorn, for example, Chief Eagle has Turtleheart reflect: "Do the white women cry for their men who will never, ever return to their arms? In his heart he knew the answer, and the answer made him very sad" (p. 113).

The ultimate humiliations for Turtleheart (and for his people) actually precede the massacre at Wounded Knee by eight or ten years. Forced to remain on the reservation with his people (the only way he knows Evensigh might be able to find him), he reluctantly accepts the position of scout for the white agents—the very people he opposed in earlier battles. Ironically, the government uses reservation scouts to pacify the remaining renegades who have refused to live on the reservation. It is after one of these scouting trips, when Turtleheart helps round up the stragglers of a band of Cheyennes (whom Evensigh has joined), that he is united with his wife.

The reunion, though happy, brings with it a number of subsequent humiliations. Since both Turtleheart and Evensigh have witnessed the futility of trying to live away from the reservation, they decide to accept a parcel of allotted land along White Clay Creek. Henceforth, their life is that of reservation Indians. The buffalo have disappeared; they are expected to till the land while believing that "an Indian belonged on the open prairies, not tied to a plow like a beast of burden" (p. 203); a drought makes it impossible to grow any crops. The natural order of life, the balanced relation to Mother Earth, has been destroyed. Eventually Turtleheart realizes that there is nothing to do but capitulate:

> When the next planting season opened the face of the earth, Turtleheart had given up all hope or thought of farming. By now he had become a regular recipient of dried commodities. His plow lay idle and rusting against the huge cottonwood. (p. 206)

The denouement of the novel once again meshes historical reality with fictive license. In the fall of 1868, the first Blackrobes (Catholic priests) arrived at the reservation. Many Indians, including Evensigh, convert to the new faith, their parched souls unable to endure the harsh reservation existence any longer. Turtleheart, however, holds out (" 'Blackrobe, my old Sioux faith is all I have left of the old way' " [p. 214]), even after the birth of their child, Little Sun. When Turtleheart is sent out on a scouting mission to bring Big Foot and his band of Minneconjou renegades to the reservation, Evensigh learns that Major Whiteside is determined to force a confrontation. She leaves for Wounded Knee (a distance of about twenty miles), where Big Foot and his people have camped overnight. Little Sun is with her in the wagon.

In the morning, just as Evensigh arrives at Wounded Knee, the massacre begins. Evensigh is immediately killed by a cannon blast; Turtleheart is wounded in the general confusion but manages to rescue his son. In the bitter cold and falling snow of the late December day, he carries his son back to the Catholic Mission at White Clay Creek, where he dies from his wounds and exposure shortly after he relinquishes Little Sun (" 'Blackrobe, take my son. Take my son and give him protection, your kind protection' " [p. 229]). The novel concludes with an ironic shift in point of view:

> Looking closely at the blue face of Turtleheart, [the priest] gasped and quickly he signed over the kneeling figure. The lips of the near-frozen hero moved, but there was no sound except a hoarse, indistinguishable word. They formed the word Blackrobe, and the priest knew what he was trying to say.
>
> Gently the Blackrobe put his hand on the frosted head and administered the Christian totem. Turtleheart felt this touch and his tired mind knew that his prayers had been answered. The light faded from his eyes, his labored breathing faltered and stopped, and a small smile of thankfulness appeared as the frozen form fell forward in the snow. His spirit had gone to join his ancestors. (pp. 229–30)

It is a curious ending but one certainly in keeping with the rest of the novel. Chief Eagle never comments directly on the horrors of the massacre at Wounded Knee (never gives a body count or dwells on the grisly details of the holocaust) as he does in describing the Battle of the Little Bighorn. Though Evensigh and Turtleheart might be considered innocent bystanders caught in the crossfire, the pessimism of the end of the novel could not be more apparent. The whites have won both the literal and the symbolic war with the Indians. Out of fear of what may happen to his son, Turtleheart acquiesces to Christianity. Little Sun is sacrificed to the church, left there as an orphan to be raised by the Blackrobes, the rejection of whose religion Turtleheart has previously considered his last holdout against the white onslaught.

Why did Dallas Chief Eagle end his novel in this way? In order to answer that question it is necessary to go beyond the confines of the narrative itself—to the biography of the writer. Chief Eagle was born in 1925. In an interview with Brad Steiger, the author of *Medicine Talk*, Chief Eagle states of his childhood, " 'I was orphaned as a child, and according to our culture, the eldest of the tribe are to raise the orphans.' "[8] Although raised by Indians, he attended mission schools and considers himself "a devout student of nature according to the ancient philosophy of the Amerindian [as well as] a practicing Roman Catholic."[9] He is, in short, a syncretist: "He believes in blending—in one practice and philosophy drawing from another."[10]

This does not mean that he has accepted all the trappings of the white man's culture—only some of the spiritual affinities he sees between his own traditional faith and Christianity. Historically, Chief Eagle accepts the inevitability of cultural change: it was that or cultural extermination. As Strong Echo tells Turtleheart early in *Winter Count*, " 'Turtleheart, you and I and the others must think about the possibility of being conquered. To submit is to change. We will have to find a way to adjust' " (p. 49). Yet in spite of his conversion to Christianity, Chief Eagle remains harshly critical of the white man's treatment of the Native American. Of his childhood experiences on the reservation, he states, " 'The reservations themselves are really set up as stockades. Boarding school was just a little step from the stockade environment into restrictiveness. Boarding schools take you away from people.' "[11] Even more critically, he adds, " 'From the traditional Indian point of view, in a prisoner-of-war camp, you have hope. You know that someday the war will end. On the reservations, there is no hope.' "[12]

Ironically, while that hope may not be possible in the realities of reservation existence, it has been documented by the concerns of Dallas Chief Eagle's own career. For much of his life he has worked for his people. As Brad Steiger notes, "In a special ceremony held in October 1967 the Teton Sioux elected Dallas Bordeaux their chief."[13] The title is largely honorific, yet it illustrates the respect Chief Eagle has earned from his people. *Winter Count* was written because "many years ago, Dallas Chief Eagle made a promise to himself that he would write a book about the Sioux that would be as culturally authentic and historically accurate as he could make it."[14] A number of these facets of *Winter Count* bear directly upon our discussion here.

One of these is the incorporation of the title image—the winter count—into the narrative itself. In her bibliography of Native American writers, Arlene B. Hirschfelder defines a winter count (made from buffalo hide) as

A picture of the main event each winter. Because the Plains Indians traveled far on their long hunts and met people from other tribes, they made wider use of pictographs than did Indians of other regions. Pictographs were also used for messages, warnings, and treaties, as well as histories.[15]

A winter count is thus a kind of visual distillation or cyclical reaffirmation of the health of tribal life—history, one might say, by group consensus. In Dallas Chief Eagle's novel, two winter counts figure importantly in the narrative. After his grandfather (Chiefeagle) is brutally murdered by a group of his own people crazy with firewater, Turtleheart's grandmother gives him the winter count kept by her deceased husband. She also gives Turtleheart a smaller winter count, his own personal one, which was also kept by the old man. The two reappear later in the story, after his grandmother's death, when Turtleheart realizes he will have to record the old woman's demise. In a discussion which ensues at that time, Blue Thunder, one of Turtleheart's companions, spells out the function of the winter count,

> "As you know, winter counts portray history," Blue Thunder explained. "All bands have to have some sort of calendar, a method of recalling events of the past. The winter counts are kept by the winters, not like the white man's calendar of the years, months and days."
> Blue Thunder paused to breathe deeply. "In each band, the keeper of the calendar consulted with the elders to decide the most notable event for that year. When this was done, he drew a picture on the tanned hide. Each picture tells of a year." (p. 138)

The title image, then, returns us to one of the historical aspects of Chief Eagle's novel. A winter count represents the passing of years—especially time experienced as a cycle of repetitions, rather than as linear or chronological development, the more typical Western concept. For the Sioux Indian, the self-renewing aspect of the cycle is typified by each return of winter, when a new picture is added to the hide. Exposure to the white man's world has brought an abrupt stop to this traditional reckoning of time—largely because the Indian's harmony with his natural environment has been destroyed. In the final scene of the novel, at the massacre of Wounded Knee, Turtleheart wraps his own personal winter count around his son's body in order to protect the child both literally and symbolically from the harshness of the elements. Though Little Sun is saved from exposure, the reader knows that no further illustration will be added to the winter count. The cycle of life as Turtleheart has lived it—a closed circle, a self-renewing cycle—has been cracked open by the encroaching white world. Little Sun will be brought up at the mission where, as Dallas Chief Eagle states in *Medicine Talk*, " '. . . the teachings of the whiteman [will] start to show him that he is out of the circle.' "[16]

As in most of the other works of fiction by Native Americans, Chief Eagle's novel illustrates a strong sense of feeling —almost a tenderness—for the land. Another Sioux Indian, Chief Standing Bear, explains this relationship in his autobiography, *Land of the Spotted Eagle* (1933):

> There was a great difference in the attitude taken by the Indian and the Caucasian toward nature, and this difference made of one a conservationist and of the other a non-conservationist of life. The Indian, as well as all other creatures that were given birth and grew, were sustained by the common mother—earth. He was therefore kin to all living things and he gave to all creatures equal rights with himself. Everything of earth was loved and reverenced. The philosophy of the Caucasian was, "Things of the earth, earthy"—to be belittled and despised.[17]

The Sioux Indians considered the Black Hills sacred territory. Gall explains that spiritual legacy to Turtleheart when he speaks of the white man's rape of the land, lamenting the fact that the mineral rights have already been leased to the whites: " 'The Paha Sapa is His sacred ground, and it must not be spoiled by men who worship in mere lodges' " (p. 35), that is, men who worship inside buildings instead of in the natural environment. In *Medicine Talk*, Chief Eagle emphasized this sacrality even further: " 'The Black Hills was the very heart throb of the Earth Mother. I think my book *Winter Count* tells you the feelings of the Indians about the Black Hills."[18]

We have already seen a similar deference toward the land expressed in the novels of Chief Simon Pokagon, John J. Mathews, D'Arcy McNickle, and N. Scott Momaday. In *Winter Count* and (as we will shortly see) in *Seven Arrows* this reverence for the earth, this affinity with the natural world, becomes the basis of the Native American's existence. As Gall tells Turtleheart, " 'The Great One who watches over us, made the earth, so why use things He did not create. We pay homage to Him through His own creations, the sun, the earth, the winds, the thunder, the lightning' " (p. 35). When a thunderstorm overtakes Turtleheart during one of his treks across the prairies, the narrator comments, "Let it rain. He would not seek shelter. This was the prime enjoyment of life, life in the clasp of mother earth" (p. 142). Unlike Western man, whose life has been spent trying to conquer nature, Turtleheart suffers from no ontological gap. The Indian's harmony with the environment is illustrated by Chief Standing Bear in *Land of the Spotted Eagle*:

> We did not think of the great open plains, the beautiful rolling hills, and winding streams with tangled growth as "wild." Only to the white man was nature a "wilderness" and only to him was the land "infested" with "wild animals" and "savage" people. To us it was tame. Earth was bountiful and we were surrounded with the blessings of the Great Mystery. Not until the hairy man from the east came and with brutal frenzy heaped injustice upon us and the families that we loved was it "wild" for us. When the very animals of the forest began fleeing from his approach, then it was that for us the "Wild West" began.[19]

Turtleheart is a part of the great cycle of life, not separate from it. Everything about him, even his winter count is a constant reminder of his closeness to the bosom of the earth.

Yet one of the anomalies with Chief Eagle's story is that the world is not so unified for Evensigh. At the end of the opening chapter, the narrator reveals her racial origins: she is a paleface, white, even though "she has lived as a Sioux since a tiny baby, and has grown up under our culture" (p. 10).

When the three white men abduct Turtleheart and Evensigh, they are confused about the latter's racial identity. They know that she is not an Indian, yet she does not speak English or act like a white woman. Evensigh's several years in St. Louis after her abduction confuse her because of the attentions she receives from a white suitor. In time, she agrees to marry him—after she has made one final check to determine that Turtleheart did not survive the lashing. When she returns to the Indian Territory, however, she learns of Turtleheart's survival, and, thereafter, joining Chief Dull Knife at Fort Reno, she returns to her Indian ways.

Is Chief Eagle's decision to make Evensigh a pale face simply an extension of this belief in cultural syncretism extended to racial blending? In part this may be so, but I suggest that Chief Eagle wants to imply that Indianness is not so much a function of biology as of psychology, a state of the mind.

There is another curious aspect of the story: both Turtleheart and Evensigh are orphans. Their child Little Sun is orphaned at the end of the story, left to be raised by the mission. We are to infer, apparently, that he will be cut off from his people's past. Dallas Chief Eagle, as has already been noted, was also an orphan. Orphanhood is mentioned with such frequency in the novel that it takes on symbolic meaning, suggesting that this is what the white man's world has made of the Native American. All Indians have become orphans, humiliatingly dependent upon the benign paternalism of their unfeeling wardens. When Dull Knife tells Evensigh that they should not give up in their struggle to remain free—that is, to be independent of the white man's so-called protectiveness—he makes reference to the same condition: " 'You have suffered much this journey, but take hope. We are close to home and when we reach there we will be taken in with open arms. We will no longer be treated like orphans by harsh and unloving guardians' " (p. 175).

A harshness, a certain stridency, permeates much of Dallas Chief Eagle's *Winter Count*, a pessimism inherent in the reality of the historical events the novel records. Yet, even though much of the narrative chronicles a general sense of defeat, "a coma of hopelessness" (p. 136), the overall effectiveness of the story as a literary work is still satisfying. Dallas

Chief Eagle knows how to create interesting characters, how to blend historical fact with fictive license. *Winter Count* retains one's interest throughout in spite of its always serious tone. In the face of seemingly insurmountable conditions—relocation, drought, starvation, the extermination of the buffalo, the white man's rape of the land, even the threat of racial genocide—the American Indian will survive. Although the acquiescence to Christianity at the end of the novel may be unsettling to some readers, the author has hinted at a far more satisfying solution to the problem of the Native American's collective fate: tribal unity—today commonly referred to as "Pan-Indianism"—illustrated in the success at the Battle of the Little Bighorn. As Sitting Bull states after that military success, " 'We must unite to survive, to defeat the white man who is our greatest enemy' " (p. 95).

Seven Arrows

Innumerable threads link Hyemeyohsts Storm's *Seven Arrows* (1972) to *Winter Count*. They share roughly the same setting: the environs of the Black Hills in South Dakota and the Powder River area (including the Little Bighorn) in Montana. Many of the same tribal groupings are involved: the Sioux, the Northern Cheyenne (Storm's own people), the Crow, and a number of smaller tribes of the area. The time frame for *Seven Arrows* embraces the same years recorded in *Winter Count*, though Storm's narration begins earlier—perhaps around 1840 or 1850—and extends well into the twentieth century. As noted earlier, certain well-known historical figures (Sitting Bull and Crazy Horse, for example) appear in both works, though by concentrating on figures drawn from his imagination Storm has chosen to make his story more symbolically representative of the fate of all Indian tribal groupings in their first encounter with the white man. The confrontations between Native Americans and Euro-Americans depicted in *Seven Arrows* are generally freed of specific historical trappings in order to make them illustrative of the emblematic nature of those encounters.

Graphically, Storm's novel is unlike anything I have encountered: in shape, more a square than a rectangle; printed in double columns on each page, in brown ink; with dozens of sepia photographs of Indians and the land itself; plus the addition of a number of color plates of medicine wheels. *Seven Arrows* is a visual and verbal experience, owing as much to the climate that produced such works as *The Whole Earth Catalog* (1970) and T. C. McLuhan's *Touch the Earth* (1971) as it does to the novel form itself. I suspect, in fact, that *Seven Arrows'* success has had as much to do with the late 1960s' and early 1970s' return-to-the-land and instant mysticism movements as with the parallel explosion in ethnic studies. Yet *Seven Arrows* loses nothing for these affinities; rather the fusion produced by the interaction of these various movements has resulted in one of the most interesting works of its time. It will be read for generations; probably few people who own copies of *The Whole Earth Catalog* will ever return to them again.

More than in *Winter Count*, time in *Seven Arrows* is perceived as a construct of the natural cycles rather than as a unit measured by clocks and watches. The accumulative effect of time's passing, however, is much the same. Each of these narratives concludes with descriptions of Native Americans living on reservations; the trajectory of the narrative in each case has been toward that final humiliation. Storm's novel, like Chief Eagle's, is a story of the necessity for adaptation and change if the Indian is to survive.

While Chief Eagle makes Turtleheart a kind of historical observer of his people's predicament during the dozen or so years before Wounded Knee, Storm (born in 1933) has chosen the more difficult problem of telling the same basic story without the aid of a central perceiver. There is no protagonist in *Seven Arrows*, no main character we follow from the beginning to the end of the narrative. Rather, Storm creates a dozen or so lesser figures who represent, in their compositeness, the Native American experience of the time. That experience is a horrifying one, bordering at every stage on cultural extermination. *Seven Arrows* is a novel about the survival of a way of life, the survival of the communal spirit, not of the individual himself.

Three introductory sections to *Seven Arrows* prepare the reader to understand much of what follows. In the first of these, "The Pipe," a kind of invocation, Storm describes his novel as "an adventure of the People, the Plains Indian People" (p. 1). The story of these people, he tells us, is the story of the medicine wheel, a way of life, a "Song of the Earth" (p. 1). Storm asks us to join him in "Understanding" (p. 1), and concludes "Let us Teach each other here in this Great Lodge of the People, this Sun Dance, of each of the ways on this Great Medicine Wheel, our Earth" (p. 1).

In "The Circle," the second introductory section, Storm explains his objective: to expand the reader's perceptions, to teach him to perceive in multifaceted ways. *Seven Arrows* should be regarded as a kind of Vision Quest for the reader, just as the medicine shields (the medicine wheels) are intended to serve as teaching examples for the Plains Indians, their function being somewhat akin to the winter count. These sacred shields, however, are only one counterpart to the white man's "talking leaves." Another equally important valence emerges through the oral tales "passed down . . . through countless generations" (p. 10). These stories ("the libraries of our people"[20] as Chief Standing Bear has called them) are teaching ways, "meant to be told, not written" (pp. 10–11). *Seven Arrows*—with its presentation of the pictorial images along with the printed word—is a fusion of these two pathways, designed to enhance the development of our perceptions.

The third introductory passage, "The Flowering Tree," provides a microcosm of the larger narrative that follows. Here Storm describes the tools that are necessary for interpreting his work. First he narrates a traditional tale. Then he interprets it for us, showing how to examine it from several perspectives. In the process of completing this sample "learning experience," Storm introduces many of the later themes of the novel: change, renewal, the circle of life, androgyny, survival, respect for the land, understanding.

There are two parallel narratives in *Seven Arrows*, an outer and an inner story. The outer one is a literal or a factual account of the Plains Indians' gradual exposure to the white man's world; the inner narrative is a much more figurative or symbolic account, told primarily through the collective voice of the past—the oral tradition. The outer narrative begins at a time when few Indians have had any firsthand contact with the white man. They have heard of the white invader—some of his accouterments have been passed along from traders farther east—but few Plains Indians have any true understanding of the white man's world. The outer narrative thus begins at a time when the white man is still a relatively unknown factor.

The inner narrative grows directly out of the oral tradition, from the Native American's storehouse of memories. Storm develops this trajectory by incorporating traditional oral tales into the text of the narrative. As exposure to the white man's world impinges on the Indian's consciousness and begins to bring with it the increasing threat of racial and cultural genocide, the emphasis and space given to these tales increases. As conditions worsen for the Native American, Storm illustrates this tension by having his characters resort increasingly to storytelling. More and more tales, for example, are told to relate and preserve past cultural traditions and achievements.

Seven Arrows thus moves in two directions simultaneously. The outer (historical) narrative line that documents Indian-white confrontation unfolds in a chronological manner, from initial exposure to the white man (when the Plains Indians are still living free on the prairies) to a time of almost total domination by the white world (represented by the reservation system). Concurrently, the inner narrative unfolds backward in time, to an idealized pre-Columbian past, a period when the Native American lived in a holistic and self-contained universe (represented by the circle, the medicine wheel, and the shield). This Plains Indians' concept of circularity has been explained in *Black Elk Speaks*:

> . . . everything an Indian does is in a circle, and that is because the Power of the World always works in circles, and everything tries to be round. In the old days when we were a strong and happy people, all our power came to us from the sacred hoop of the nation, and so long as the hoop was unbroken, the people flourished. The flow-

ering tree was the living center of the hoop, and the circle of the four quarters nourished it. The east gave peace and light, the south gave warmth, the west gave rain, and the north with its cold and mighty wind gave strength and endurance. This knowledge came to us from the outer world with our religion. Everything the Power of the World does is done in a circle. The sky is round, and I have heard that the earth is round like a ball, and so are all the stars. The wind, in its greatest power, whirls. Birds make their nests in circles, for theirs is the same religion as ours. The sun comes forth and goes down again in a circle. The moon does the same, and both are round. Even the seasons form a great circle in their changing, and always come back again to where they were. The life of man is in a circle from childhood to childhood. . . .[21]

There are thus two differing constructs of reality in *Seven Arrows:* a literal one, which may be said to be linear, factual, and time-bound; and a symbolic one, which is cyclical, mythic, and timeless. The outer narrative line is corporeal (ending with the physical reality of reservation life); the inner one is spiritual and intellectual (represented by the imagination). The outer one ends in chaos, the inner one in unification. Fused together, these dualities frame the Native American's difficult quest for coherence within the white man's imposed world.

The central narrative of *Seven Arrows* is composed of twenty-five sections, varying in length from a few paragraphs to fifty or sixty pages. In the opening sections, which begin at a time before the arrival of the white man, Indians are still immersed in the activities of day-to-day living. The first section (somewhat like the opening of *Winter Count*) begins at daybreak, when a camp is waking up. The crier announces the news of the night. Dogs are barking, children are playing, one of the women has given birth to a baby during the night. A feeling of happiness and contentment prevails, yet this mood abruptly changes when several of the warriors jump on their ponies and gallop off.

The reasons for this unexpected change of mood are spelled

out in the second section of the story. Standing Eagle says, " 'Do you not realize that our whole world is falling to pieces? That the People are being exterminated like rabid camp dogs?' " (p. 36). In the conversation that follows, Falls Down and his friends speculate on the possibility of stemming the advance of the white men ("these unnatural white wolves" [p. 36]), heard about but not yet seen. Thereafter, until the end of the narrative, Storm chronicles the steady encroachment of the white men upon the Plains Indians' world until there is no other alternative for these people but acquiescence to confinement on the reservations.

After the opening passages that illustrate an atmosphere of peace and stability, the literal story explodes into one of chaos and warfare, of violent confrontation with the white men. The Sun Dance Way (presented as an era when Indians fought one another only to touch the enemy, to humiliate him) rapidly disintegrates into a period in which killing the enemy becomes the prime objective. The Brotherhood of the Shields collapses; Indians fight not only the white invaders of the land but one another. Always there is an endless advance of white men invading, overtaking the territory, cutting a swathe of destruction. As Lame Bear acknowledges, " 'The whitemen are determined to destroy all People whose Ways do not reflect their own. They have set the People one against the other and will kill whichever is left when the wars have ended' " (p. 67).

Rather than describing specific battles or massacres as Dallas Chief Eagle does in *Winter Count*, Storm often illustrates the effect of the white man's encroachment upon the Plains Indians indirectly. There are, in fact, no famous battles described here, though there are accounts of innumerable skirmishes between Indians and whites. At the end of the fourth section, for example, Storm concludes, "Gray Owl returned to Four Bear's lodge. He was almost asleep when the attack came" (p. 63). This indirect method of referring to a massacre is typical of Storm's ability to startle the reader. Often, we follow a character or group of characters along for a scene or two, become emotionally involved with them, and then see them shot in the back. The result is a disturbing recapitulation of the horrors of the Indian wars. The humanity of the individual is obliterated by the method of destruction: for the white man, the Indian was a disposable object, like the buffalo on the prairie.

The subtler advance force of the Euro-American is illustrated symbolically through the introduction of material objects from the white man's world. Well before the white invaders reach the territory, these possessions have begun to permeate the Indian's spiritual orientation. Storm observes of one of his characters, "Even though Gray Owl had never seen a thunder stick before, he recognized it by the stories he had heard of them" (p. 42).

In *The Soul of the Indian*, Charles Eastman (Santee Sioux) states of the Plains Indians: "His religion forbade the accumulation of wealth and the enjoyment of luxury."[22] In *Seven Arrows*, when Singing Flower asks the Peace Chief why people give away their most prized possessions, the Chief replies, " 'Because the great Spirit gives us so very much. . . . Because the Power is so very rich, it has taught the People to give to one another' " (p. 89). When Bull Looks Around returns from his Vision Quest, he gives away his favorite possessions:

> Four of the things the boy held dearest to him lay on the unrolled robe. He handed the articles one by one to each man until only one remained. It was a bow, one of the finest bows Hawk had seen in his entire life. Bull Looks Around handed it to him and smiled. (p. 130)

The Give Away counteracted materialism so the Plains Indians would not become bound to possessions.

In the face of thunder sticks, stinging water, ba-kits, beads, cloth, and other trade items introduced by the white man, the older spiritualism is rapidly altered to materialism. As Chief Standing Bear has written of the previous order in *Land of the Spotted Eagle*,

> It was not Indian custom for individuals to lay up stores for revenue, to fence land, to capture and hold animals for sale, to fight kith and kin, or to lay by any goods for the sake of mere possession. Any and all goods were to be used by band members at the call of need.[23]

Soon Indians kill each other in order to possess these trade objects, or "gifts," as they are ironically called in Storm's novel. The Peace Chief articulates the basic difference in this attitude toward possessions when he states " 'The gifts to these men overwhelm the mind. . . . Is the love of the universe reflected only in material gifts?' " (p. 67). Hawk replies, " 'Great Father . . . if they have these wonderful gifts, then why do they kill?' " (p. 67). Increasingly, battles are fought for the acquisition of prizes, for objects. Greed and materialism create a new way of life. A basic transformation takes place within the culture itself: the evolution from a spiritually oriented world to an object-oriented one, grounded in the temporal and in the individual's concern for himself.[24]

The objects introduced by the white man are often seen in tandem with his confusing religion—specifically the teachings of the Blackrobes. Rarely have the anomalies of Christianity been delineated so systematically and with such subtle irony. Four Bears tells Grey Owl,

> Whitemen in black robes, and others, move among the People and teach about a new Way, the Way of Geessis. This Geessis appears to be a new Power, one which loves death and rewards mightily those who kill. Because of this, the camps of the whitemen are rewarded most. (p. 62 I)

When a missionary appears at one of the camps, the fusion between Western materialism and Christianity is made explicit. The missionary exhorts, " 'Geessis is heap plenty good power. Kills people who bad are. . . . Geessis give people heap plenty riches. . . . If people Geessis path follow they rewarded rich Gifts' " (p. 192). Charles Eastman has articulated the implicit contradiction in the white man's religion: "They spoke much of spiritual things, while seeking only the material."[25] In the most pessimistic of these observations in Storm's narrative, Pretty Weasel concludes,

> The talkers among them spoke of the Medicine Power that was called Geessis. This Geessis was a Power among them, a chief whom they later killed. He was not surprised that they killed him. After they killed him these men decided he was a Power, and they began to like

him. He came back as a ghost and even now he walks
among them invisible. . . .

This Geessis . . . is the greatest killer of them all. He
kills all of their enemies. And he rewards those who follow his path with many things. Believe me, my brother,
it is a very confusing thing, this Geessis. . . .

These talkers of the Geessis say that it is bad to do
many things. And, believe it or not, killing is one of
them. But, as clearly as I can understand it, this only
means not to kill those who follow the warpath of Geessis. All others are to be feared and killed. (p. 240 I)

Not all of the Indians in *Seven Arrows* are willing to embrace the white man's materialism or his confusing religion,
yet, as Storm shows, those who remain faithful to the old
ways are often mocked by their peers who have transferred
their allegiance to the new dispensation. Storm subtly makes
his own position clear by giving the gift of storytelling to those
who remain faithful to the past (the Peace Chief, Hawk,
Night Bear, Thunder Boy, Hide on the Wind). It is from the
richness of these interpolated tales that the inner narrative
develops. Without them, *Seven Arrows* would be a flat, much
more conventional novel. By incorporating them into his narrative, however, Storm has altered our concept of novelistic
form and written a radically innovative work.

Traditionally, folk tales are designed to teach a lesson or
impart information about a people's past history, traditions, or
values. When a written language is developed, these tales are
often forgotten or transformed. In *Seven Arrows*, one can detect a passionate concern on the author's part to record these
tales before that happens. The result is the dual nature of the
narrative—the "conventional" story moving forward in time,
enhanced by the innovative use of folk materials which provide a vision of the past.

One of the first, longest, and most significant of these tales
is the story of "Jumping Mouse" (the fifth section of the
novel). Many of the novel's major themes—perception,
change, survival—are implicit to the tale which the Peace
Chief relates to Day Woman, Prairie Rose, Hawk, Lame Bear,
and a group of children. As the story goes, once there was a

Little Mouse[26] who heard a strange roaring in his ears. Now a mouse, the Peace Chief tells us, is typified by what is close to him, his nearness to the ground, but this particular mouse was inquisitive. He wanted to learn about the near and the far; he wanted to learn the origin of the roaring in his ears. Thus, first Little Mouse speaks to a racoon who tells him that the noise is caused by the river, but since Little Mouse has never seen a river, he has no idea what it is.

Racoon guides Little Mouse to the river where he meets a frog who tells him that if he will jump up high, he will see a more spectacular sight than the flowing water. When "Jumping Mouse" does as he is instructed, he sees the mountains in the distance. Henceforth, however, Jumping Mouse is unhappy with the world within his immediate view. He wants to see more. He wants to visit the mountains, but he is afraid to go there alone. One day, however, he meets a sick and dying buffalo who tells him, " 'My Medicine has Told me that only the Eye of a Mouse can Heal me. But little Brother, there is no such Thing as a Mouse' " (p. 78 I).

After deliberating for a while, Jumping Mouse gives the buffalo one of his eyes, and as a reward for his Give Away, the buffalo (who is thereby cured of his illness) takes him to the mountains. There he meets a wolf who has lost his memory, and, this time without being asked for anything, Jumping Mouse gives the wolf his remaining source of vision. The wolf is cured, but Jumping Mouse is now blind and frightened that he will be easy prey for an eagle who will swoop down from the sky and devour him. The next morning when he awakens, however, Jumping Mouse detects a blurry shape moving toward him. The shape tells him to jump as high as he can. The Peace Chief's story concludes,

> Jumping Mouse did as he was Instructed. He Crouched as Low as he Could and Jumped! The Wind Caught him and Carried him Higher.
> "Do not be Afraid," the Voice called to him. "Hang on to the Wind and Trust!"
> Jumping Mouse did. He Closed his Eyes and Hung on to the Wind and it Carried him Higher and Higher. Jumping Mouse Opened his Eyes and they were Clear,

and the Higher he Went the Clearer they Became. Jumping Mouse saw his Old Friend upon a Lily Pad on the Beautiful Medicine Lake. It was the Frog.

"You have a New Name," Called the Frog. "You are Eagle!" (p. 85 I)

Storm uses the story of Jumping Mouse to illustrate the central premise of his novel—the need for change, for adaptability, for growth of vision. The Peace Chief tells his listeners that " 'Men are like little Mouse. They are so busy with the things of this world that they are unable to perceive things at any distance' " (p. 70). Like Jumping Mouse, man must learn to conquer his fears, for only then will he be able to identify the roaring in his ears. He must learn to give away a part of himself to help those in need, for in that generosity lies his humanity. By curing others he will cure himself and be transformed in the process.

The values that Jumping Mouse has learned to embrace are reiterated later in the narrative. White Clay, for example, tells Pretty Weasel that " 'Not caring for one another has always caused sickness among a People. . . . Caring is the only way to end sickness completely' " (p. 243 I). When sickness is eliminated the result is wholeness, but that unity must also be balanced with the desire for change. Night Bear tells Green Fire Mouse that a fixed wheel of tradition only maintains itself, " 'It looks back upon itself' " (p. 258). Until the coming of the white man " 'there was only one Way. But now we can learn of the many Ways' " (p. 264). Jumping Mouse not only survived but was transformed in the process of his education.

There are innumerable later references to Jumping Mouse and his ability to "jump up" and expand his perceptions of the universe. They provide a direct contrast to the white man's tunnel vision. Storm suggests, in an ironic way, that the destruction of the Native American has come through the trade of a priceless oral tradition for the valueless material objects of the white world. The little band of Indians who try to keep storytelling alive increasingly relate tales of people torn apart by forces from without over which they have little control ("The story of Fallen Star," for example, told by Hide on the Wind, pp. 286–305), or stories which rely on a hero figure to unify the People ("The story of the Wolf Stick," related by Thunder Bow, pp. 312–27).

Because of the increasing emphasis in the narrative on these tales, in one sense there is no conventional ending to Storm's novel. For the most part, the traditional novelistic unities of character, time, and place are ignored. The denouement involves new characters, a new time, and a new place. There is a sense of irresolution because the reader knows that the cycle will continue: the Native American will experience a series of violent shocks from without, shocks that he will assimilate into his own culture and, even perhaps, eventually conquer. At the same time, however, there is a feeling of resolution at the end of *Seven Arrows*, specifically because of the events described (in both the inner and the outer narrative) in the last two sections of the story.

In the penultimate section, for example, the reader is shocked to discover that time has passed so rapidly that he has suddenly been transported to a much later period. Red Star asks White Rabbit to tell her about the medicine wheels, admitting, " 'When I was little we lived near the forts of the whitemen. The only teachings I received from my mother were those of the stinging water' " (p. 341). Red Star's mother was an alcoholic who " 'made love to many whitemen' " (p. 341). The times have indeed changed: Red Star has grown up without an awareness of the traditional stories. White Rabbit tells her about the peace shields, again transmitting the lessons of the seven arrows.

Later in the same section, when Green Fire Mouse, White Rabbit, Dancing Moon, and the children make camp at the Greasy Grass (significantly, the site of Custer's defeat), they are visited by a man who Dancing Moon thinks " 'must be a thousand years old!' " (p. 356). The ancient little man relates "The story of No Name," a tale about a young man who, after a series of metamorphoses, identifies an old man who has befriended him as his father, as Seven Arrows. As they listen to the story, White Rabbit, Green Fire Mouse, and Dancing Moon also identify the old man as Seven Arrows— the teller of the story he tells. In a final multiplication of the storytelling factor, Seven Arrows incorporates his listeners into the story he is in the process of relating to them, concluding:

That Evening, Green Fire Mouse Went for a Swim
with White Rabbit and Dancing Moon. The Old Man Sat
at the Edge of the River and Watched White Rabbit's
Two Children. The Three Young People Swam Until the
Moon was Bright and Full Overhead. Then, Tired and
Refreshed at the Same Time, they Warmed themselves
by the Fire at the Lodge. They Ate Fresh Berries White
Rabbit had Gathered and Enjoyed the Meat Dancing
Moon had Boiled in Preparation for the Evening. It was
an Evening that would be Remembered Forever.
(p. 367 I)

The characters from the outer narrative thus dissolve into the
inner one; they have been transformed from their corporeal
existence and given immortality in the imaginative domain of
the folk tradition. The two narrative dimensions have been
fused into one; the linear thread has merged with the larger
cyclic and timeless one.

There is one final cataclysm. The one remaining section
catapults the narrative forward into the twentieth century. It
takes place on a reservation many years later, when White
Rabbit and Green Fire Mouse are grandparents. One of their
granchildren, Rocky, asks where they can go fishing. As they
drive along in their pickup truck, Green Fire Mouse smoking
a cigarette, there is a discussion about school (" 'You don't
like school?' Green Fire Mouse answered from under his reservation hat. . .' " [p. 371]). Rocky says that he doesn't like
the white folks' religion, and his grandfather replies, " 'They
haven't understood about the seven arrows yet. . . . What's
happened to Christianity is that it has become an old woman,
a wicked witch' " (p. 371).

Rocky says his grandfather must be kidding—nobody talks
about seven arrows any longer, no one believes in those old
stories. But Green Fire Mouse replies,

"No, I'm not [kidding]. It's a teaching. And there are
seven arrows in the story too. They are called dwarfs.
They give away the gems of wisdom of the north to all
those who understand. And their hair is white, these
seven dwarfs. . . . The name of the story is Snow
White. . . . " (p. 371)

Later, when they are fishing, Rocky asks his grandfather if there are other stories, and the old man replies (and the novel concludes),

"Sure. . . . There is the entire world and everything in it that can teach you much, much more. There are the songs, the bibles, the cities, and the dreams. Everything upon the earth and in the heavens is a mirror for the people. It is a total gift. Jump up! And you will see the Medicine Wheel." (p. 371)

On the literal level, the final section of *Seven Arrows* is a triumph of the white man's material world. Corralled on the reservation, surrounded by newly acquired possessions, schooled by missionaries who force upon their pupils theories of original sin, the New Indians, like Rocky and his sister, now regard the traditional stories as "old time talk"—as a source of amusement. The older language has given way to slang, as Rocky's name indicates. The beauty and profundity of the traditional stories (such as the story of Jumping Mouse) have been cancelled by the temporality of the white man's imagination: the Seven Arrows legend has become Snow White and the Seven Dwarves. Yet this development only represents the literal dimension of the narrative.

More important, the final section of *Seven Arrows* reinforces all the earlier themes of the novel. The Native American has survived in the white man's world precisely because of his ability to assimilate opposites. It is not so much a matter of survival as one of transformation. The oral tradition is so rich, so varied, that it can absorb and even illuminate a story as culturally different as Snow White or an idea as alien to Indian tradition as original sin. (This is also the syncretic world envisioned at the end of Dallas Chief Eagle's *Winter Count*.) Yet Green Fire Mouse's answers to his grandson's questions also imply a warning—not just acquiescence to the white man's world. The white man will also have to learn to assimilate differing attitudes and beliefs if he is going to survive cultural diversity and heterogeneity. The white man also needs to learn how to "Jump Up!" *Seven Arrows* illustrates several ways in which such a transformation may be achieved. The radically innovative form of the novel itself is the perfect embodiment of Storm's message.

Tsali

Denton R. Bedford's *Tsali* (1972) has a much more limited scope than either Dallas Chief Eagle's *Winter Count* or Hyemeyohsts Storm's *Seven Arrows*. Bedford (a Minsee Indian) has concentrated on one limited aspect of the Cherokee migration of 1838: Tsali's private rebellion against that removal. Public opinion about the removal was mixed, to be sure; and a number of leading political and intellectual figures expressed their indignation (Ralph Waldo Emerson published an open letter to President Van Buren, condemning the action), but the president ordered the removal carried out. In May of 1838, the United States Army, under the command of General Winfield Scott, began to evict from their homes and round up 17,000 Cherokee Indians who lived in an area of the Appalachian Mountains that included Georgia, North Carolina, and Tennessee. (The relocation also involved Cherokees living in Alabama but Bedford concentrates on those farther north.) The Indians were placed in temporary stockades, whence, after innumerable delays, they were shipped out to the new reservation 800 miles away in Oklahoma. During the removal, 4,000 Cherokees, primarily the aged and the young, died of exposure, dysentery, and fever.

The event around which Bedford has constructed his novel is limited to Tsali and his family, though it has ramifications which extend to the entire tribe. While they are being rounded up by the soldiers, Tsali kills one of the white men who has been taunting his sickly wife by poking her with his bayonet. Tsali escapes with his family into the mountains, where they meet other Cherokee refugees who have managed to elude the white soldiers. Survival in the mountains is difficult largely because the planting season is over. In the fall, an Indian named Euchela, one of the chiefs, informs Tsali of General Scott's promise that he will stop harrassing the Cherokees who have fled to the hills if Tsali, his two older sons, and his brother (who were involved in the skirmish with the whites) will surrender to him. At the conclusion of the novel, the four men are shot by a firing squad—sacrificed, one might say, in order that the rest of the Cherokees may survive.

The most successful aspect of Bedford's novel is the author's expansion of a minor historical event: Tsali's rebellion, usually ignored or slighted in accounts of the Cherokee removal. In contrast to Chief Eagle and Storm, Bedford, a historian by profession, has written about a much more restricted occurrence. He has embellished a footnote from history into a lengthy narrative in which the personal dimension is as significant as the historical one. In a brief foreword Bedford implies that his intention in part has been to offer a corrective view of the previous treatment of Native peoples in our history:

> History is slanted against the first owners of this land. While Indians are expected to assume all the responsibilities of modern American life, even to dying on a foreign battlefield, they still see their forefathers villified [sic] on the screen. They must study from biased accounts which glorify the white man and demean the Indian. Such great American patriots as Joseph Brant, Tecumseh, Black Hawk, Sitting Bull, Crazy Horse, Chief Joseph, and Tsali are dismissed as "primitive savages" when in truth lessons of great patriotism and devotion to country could be learned from the story of their lives. (p. ix)

Some of the weakness of Bedford's novel is implicit in his statement, for in *Tsali* the historical background often intrudes upon the more interesting dimension of the main character's heroism. There are too many authorial intrusions in the narrative, such as the following, designed to incorporate historical background into the story:

> Can a commanding officer be effectively isolated from the facts? Scott had to know that the original plan for a swift and demoralizing removal was not materializing. He could have ameliorated the harsh conditions had he conducted a personal investigation. In the absence of any attempt to improve the desperate plight of the Cherokees, Scott must be as severely blamed as the lesser offi-

cers involved. The truth of the matter is that the original removal was so badly bungled, the Americans did not know how to handle the mess they had created.

The cruelly victimized Cherokees had lived better than the shiftless and semi-clean white settlers in their native life way. They became understandably embittered when they were herded like cattle into open corrals surrounded by twelve-foot palisades. (pp. 107–8)

Moreover, numerous asides emphasize the perfidy of the oppressors: "Unlike the whites, Indians could be a reasonable people, proud and stubborn though they might be" (p. 8); "These days of the Cherokee round-up left an indelible stain upon America" (p. 56); "The sergeant was the product of a culture which refused to accommodate itself to the Indian in any way" (p. 66). I do not deny the validity of these comments. It is simply that they destroy the dramatic tension of the novel. Because of Bedford's didactic tone, there is none of the subtlety we have seen, for example, in Storm's *Seven Arrows*. Bedford does not show as much as he tells; the white characters in the novel are totally stereotyped. Perhaps Bedford was not certain whether he was writing a novel about an individual's heroism or a revisionist account of the ramifications of the Cherokee removal.

The passages that concentrate on Tsali's private war are by far the most interesting in the novel. Herein also lies the emotional core of the narrative, for while Bedford has written a compelling story of one family's attempt to stifle the forces of evil, at the same time he has written a moving account of the individual's relationship to the collective group of which he is representative. There is thus a kind of double image in Bedford's novel, which relates it to *Winter Count* and *Seven Arrows*.

Tsali himself, Bedford tells us in the foreword, "held no office within the Cherokee tribe, and had no previous mark of distinction" (p. x). Until the time of his private rebellion, he was relatively unknown, "yet he seemed to have acted instinctively, without any peculiar self-consciousness about the importance of his act of defiance" (p. x). Bedford refers to Tsali as a "reluctant hero" (p. x), since he apparently acted instinctively instead of from forethought. At the time of removal,

Tsali was about fifty years old, and although Bedford states that today his name is still not widely known, his killing of the soldier and subsequent execution made him an immediate hero for the Cherokee people.

Tsali's act of self-sacrifice, although intended as an individual gesture, places him at the spiritual center of his people. This question of the individual's relationship to the collective group is first introduced in the narrative by Tsali's wife. " 'What good are Indians without their kinsmen?' " (p. 104), she asks her husband, bemoaning their isolated existence in the hills. Ironically, the murder of the soldier has made them renegades, exiles in their own land, cut off from their people.

The significance of the collective whole is given further expression when Tsali's oldest son, Soquah, complains to Euchela that no one seems to be concerned about the loss of his wife who, because she was pregnant, was separated from him before the removal began. The narrator comments, "The first consideration must always be the tribe and its survival, grievous though individual losses might be" (pp. 121–22). This belief is soon highlighted by the symbolic relationship of Tsali's own family, a social organization that has been explained by Charles Eastman in *The Soul of an Indian:* "The family was not only the social unit, but also the unit of government. The clan is nothing more than a larger family. . . . "[27] If they do not remain together, then what hope is there for the tribe itself? As Bedford observes, "The family was always the basic unit of Indian cohesiveness. When it began to unravel, disintegration seemed imminent" (p. 181). When Soquah returns to his family, after a futile search for his wife, he tells them, " 'I have surely found out that man is no good alone' " (p. 197).

Soquah's reunion with his family prepares the reader for the final scene in the novel: the execution of the four men. Not surprisingly, when Euchela relays General Scott's request to Tsali, the old chief begins by saying, " 'I am forced to come again to ask you to give, that the people may live' " (p. 201). Tsali's subsequent reply reiterates his faith in the collective whole:

"We act this way only because of the people. . . . If we

were alone with only men in the hills, we would give the Unegas [the white men] the bloodbath they deserve, by fighting until we are killed. But there are many women and children in hiding here. They cannot stand the brutality of the white man. It may actually be we are no longer good warriors as you see it, but we surrender and die because the Unegas have promised they will then allow the refugees to remain in those hills. We would do better for the people if we could." (p. 232)

In a symbolic act following the execution, Euchela plants maize (" 'Maize is our life; and while it lives we live' " [p. 36]) over the grave of the four men, proclaiming, " 'I command you, Maize, to lie there until next spring. Then, sprout upon this sad land, so that there may be a rebirth of the Cherokee in the hills' " (p. 252). Tsali thus becomes the life-force from which the Cherokee nation will be reborn. As the narrator concludes, "If maize was the very life of the Cherokee, then the memory of Tsali would never die" (p. 252).

Three important elements bind the novels by Dallas Chief Eagle, Hyemeyohsts Storm, and Denton R. Bedford together and distinguish them from the previous works discussed in this study: the use of the past, the symbolic focus upon the collective whole, and the creation of a heroic figure or figures. The first of these, the use of historical background, is of more direct concern in Dallas Chief Eagle's *Winter Count* and Bedford's *Tsali* than in Storm's *Seven Arrows*. Chief Eagle's and Bedford's intentions are basically revisionist in their corrections of the suppositions which have prevailed down through the years. The primary weakness of each novel is the result of its approach: the historical background at times is heavy-handed, intruding upon the narrative itself, though this is more typical of Bedford's novel than of Chief Eagle's.

In Storm's *Seven Arrows* the historical background is used much more imaginatively than in the other two. The author's intentions are always clear: *Seven Arrows* is an epic history of the People, of the collective consciousness of a people, rather than a meditation upon specific historical events or personalities. Instead of regarding the Indian wars during the second half of the last century as a series of military maneuvers, rooted in the specifics of time and place, fact and figure, Storm presents this confrontation as a series of repetitious acts or cyclical encounters. Individually they may have been unimportant; collectively, they threatened to destroy the Plains Indians' way of life.

That potential obliteration of a way of life and the accompanying challenge of survival is central to all three of these novels, since each in its own way illustrates that survival depends on adaptation and change. At the conclusion of *Winter Count*, following the massacre at Wounded Knee, Turtleheart relinquishes his son to the Catholic mission. It is a symbolic move, to be sure, laden with a sense of pessimism and futility, but Turtleheart's act is also intended as a syncretic move. No other alternatives are available for him; the old kind of "protection" no longer works. The ending of Storm's *Seven Arrows* might be said to expand upon this belief: the new protection is a fusion of the Indian's traditional religion and the Christian tradition introduced in the mission schools. Yet Storm also shows—through the inner narrative of his story—that even though the Native American may be confined to the reservation, the collective spirit of a People, its imagination, is a far more difficult thing to contain.

A similar idea prevails at the end of Bedford's *Tsali*. From the mass execution of Tsali's family, a spirit of renewal arises, revitalizing the imagination of the Cherokee survivors and uniting them forever in their pursuit of freedom. Tsali makes the ultimate self-sacrifice, giving his life for the survival of the wider group. In Storm's more gifted narrative art, this kind of gesture becomes the Give Away, most clearly illuminated in the story of Jumping Mouse. The selfless act is not defeat or acquiescence since it leads to transformation and change. Tsali does not become a martyr as much as a hero, a cultural hero, symbolically united with his people.

There is an important connecting link between Tsali (and his sons) and the protagonists of *Winter Count* (Turtleheart) and *Seven Arrows* (Hawk, Night Bear, Thunder Bow, Left Hand, Green Fire Mouse). In all three of these novels, the authors have developed their stories around strong men who have never lost faith in their traditional culture or shrugged their responsibilities to the collective group. Unlike the central characters in most of the previously discussed novels (Mathews's *Sundown*, Momaday's *House Made of Dawn*, and, to a lesser extent those in the earlier assimilationist works, stories of Indians who often found themselves isolated from their own people), the protagonists of *Winter Count*, *Seven Arrows*, and *Tsali* retain a basic affinity with their people. Nourished by the traditional life-sustaining forces, they fulfill the heroic call by moving to assume the vital center of the spiritual whole.

6

Survivors of the Relocation

And when the last red man shall have perished, and the
memory of my tribe shall have become a myth among the
white men, these shores will swarm with the invisible dead
of my tribe. And when your children's children think
themselves alone, in the field, the store, the shop, upon
the highway or in the silence of the pathless woods, they
will not be alone. At night when the streets of your cities
and villages are silent they will throng with the returning
hosts that once filled and still love this beautiful land. The
white man will never be alone.—Chief Seattle's Speech to
Governor Stevens

Between 1950 and 1970, the official Indian population
more than doubled, and if, by any chance, it should keep
on doubling every two decades while, at the same time, all
other Americans edge toward zero population growth, by
about the year 3000 there would be a hundred million
Indians—conceivably enough to try to take the country
back.—E. J. Kahn, Jr., *The New Yorker* (October 22, 1973)

Thus far in our study of Native American fiction it has
been possible to consider several novels together, to group
them thematically, in order to illustrate the ways in which the
writers have treated a similar topic. In large part these groupings—assimilation, rejection, historicity—mirror the period
during which the writers themselves lived. The characters in
the earliest novels generally accepted the status quo, the
world that surrounded them. The protagonists in somewhat
later novels came to reject that same world—as did the writers
themselves, who saw as their goal the correction of past suppositions and stereotypes. The works themselves evolved from

133

a mood of veiled complaint to one of more overt protest—at its extreme either vindication or historical correction. In all instances, these novels were written in reaction to the white man's world view and the continual debasement of the American Indian by his dominance.

Not surprisingly, the most recent novels by American Indians are much more difficult to classify. They fall into no all-encompassing pattern. The term American Indian Fiction is a limited one, used as a matter of descriptive convenience. Why should we expect that a novel by a Navaho would necessarily reflect the same interests or realities as one written by a Sioux? This is not to suggest that the affinities shared by these works are artificial, but, rather, that Native American fiction is so recent, so young, that the qualities identified here may not seem as significant in the future—once there are fifty or a hundred novels—as they do now. Only one safe generalization can be made at this time: as more and more novels by Native Americans appear, the diversity will become increasingly apparent.

Nevertheless, when we examine the most recent novels by Native Americans (George Pierre's *Autumn's Bounty*, James Welch's *Winter in the Blood*, Leslie Marmon Silko's *Ceremony*, and Nasnaga's *Indians' Summer*) it is possible to identify several marked contrasts between these works and the earlier ones as well as a number of affinities shared by the later works. For example, the element of protest tends to be of lesser importance than in many of the earlier novels, as if these writers have come to accept the social conditions imposed upon them. Stated another way, these novels—especially *Autumn's Bounty*, *Winter in the Blood*, and *Ceremony*—are much more directly concerned with the characters' immediate world than they are with a confrontation with the white man. One finds an increased emphasis upon the family as a unit (already noticed in Bedford's *Tsali*) and the interaction of characters within the familial order. This focus also results in a heightened interest in women, who, as characters, for the first time play more direct roles in the unfolding of the narratives.

In marked contrast to the seriousness of the earlier novels, some of these more recent works tend to be lighter in tone—

on occasion even satirical. This is certainly the primary quality of Nasnaga's *Indians' Summer* (1975), which fantasizes a military confrontation between Native peoples and the United States government during the Bicentennial year. James Welch's *Winter in the Blood*, although ostensibly a serious novel about a young man's identity crisis, is balanced by the author's genius for recording the comic, even the absurd.

One aspect is common to all of these novels: a changed attitude toward life on the reservation. Instead of depicting the necessity for endurance or the despair borne of capitulation, these more recent works tend to illustrate the positive aspects of this "apartheid" system, seeing in it a refuge for spiritual and cultural renewal—both for the family unit and, more important, for the future success of Pan-Indianism. George Pierre's *Autumn's Bounty* is antitermination, offering an argument against the breakup of the reservation system. James Welch's *Winter in the Blood* depicts Indians who have prospered on the reservation. In Leslie Silko's *Ceremony*, the towns that surround the reservation are described as parasites, living off the blood of Indian laborers. Central to Nasnaga's *Indians' Summer* is the author's belief that the Pan-Indian movement will find its greatest number of followers at the grass-roots level on the reservation.

Finally, these recent novels illustrate a further evolution of the syncretic vision developed earlier in the works by Dallas Chief Eagle and Hyemeyohsts Storm. As a character in *Indians' Summer* states,

> "I don't hate the white man; I hate the idea of 'white.' It's not a culture but a machine of destruction. It destroys a man on the inside and leaves an empty shell. I understand how you feel. If I didn't, I don't think we'd be any better off now than before. If we don't profit from the mistakes the white man has made, then we are bigger fools than he is."[1]

Many of the characters in these novels are descendants of those who were relocated—individuals and groups of people who have survived because they adapted themselves to the dual world that surrounded them. No doubt this is true of the writers themselves, who often appear to be infused with a

sense of urgency to proclaim the quality of contemporary Indian life—its ties to the past (particularly through the continuation of ritual) as well as its manifestation in newer life
styles. To borrow a phrase from Leslie A. Fiedler,[2] these more
recent novels are about the return of the vanishing American,
which is to say that they are also about survival.

Autumn's Bounty

Two major confrontations shape George Pierre's *Autumn's
Bounty* (1972): one is filial, the other tribal, though the two
overlap. Both conflicts bear directly upon the main character,
a lonely old man named Alphonse, once a respected hunter
and for the last fifty years the chief of his people. The novel is
set in the Okanogan Valley in the Cascade Mountains, in
Washington. George Pierre refers to the characters in his
story as Okanogan, probably his own people and now a part of
the Colville Confederated Tribes of Washington, of whom he
was once the tribal leader.[3] One suspects that Pierre has been
emotionally involved with a number of issues given fictional
form in his novel, particularly termination and the role of the
chief in contemporary Indian life. (Termination [the breakup
and sale of reservation land and subsequent payment of
monies to each tribal member] first became an issue in the
early 1940s. Like the earlier allotment question, it has often
been regarded by Native peoples as another attempt by the
government to destroy kinship groups, natural communities,
and other groupings that have retained a sense of affinity because of the reservation system.)

At the beginning of the story, Alphonse is isolated from his
family and his people. His granddaughter, Ruby, constantly
browbeats him (" 'Just who are you the chief of? Your old dog
and your old horse?' "),[4] by attacking his chieftaincy and his
renown as a skilled hunter. Many of the other "Indians made
fun of the old man" (p. 13), primarily because he opposes the
movement for termination. Alphonse's only friend is Charlie
Jose, Ruby's twelve-year-old son. The boy's mother has turned
against Alphonse because of their differing attitudes toward

termination. Shortly after the story begins, the old man is mugged by four Indian youths, who try to rob him of his money. The incident is emblematic of Alphonse's pitiful state, his declining influence over his people. The narrator comments,

> No one on the reservation knew if the old man would live or die. Still there was talk that the old man would get somebody into trouble, because the sheriff had been called. So they hated the old man more for it. They blamed him for getting beaten up, as if he had a choice. (p. 28)

After Alphonse is released from the hospital, he decides that despite his age (nearly eighty) he should track down the mountain lion that has been harrassing his people. In actuality, he goes into the mountains to prove to himself that he is still strong (that he can survive in the wild), and to prove to his people that he is still a great hunter. His search for the cougar becomes a test of self-preservation, a matter of pride. Night after night he is attacked by packs of rabid coyotes. He uses up all of his bullets; his horse is killed by the coyotes; he loses his knife. After many days, he is stripped of everything he would use to kill the cougar—except for a snare.

In the encounter with the mountain lion which follows, Alphonse is successful in trapping the animal in his net and subsequently strangling it, though first he is dragged along the ground for a considerable distance. He proves to himself that he is still a great hunter, but his satisfaction is short-lived. At darkness, when he is forced to climb into a tree for safety, the coyotes return, determined to devour the dead mountain lion. The animal is so heavy that Alphonse is unable to pull all of the carcass up into the tree with him. The coyotes bite away at it during the night. In the morning, "When he looked down, all that was left of the cougar was its head" (p. 141).

Although Alphonse regains the respect of his family and his people, the author's more central concern is the old man's test of endurance in the wilderness, an episode somewhat reminiscent of Archilde's mother's ritual hunt in McNickle's *The Surrounded*. It is important that Alphonse encounter the mountain lion (who is also old) with his bare hands, on an elemental level, instead of killing him with a gun or a knife. The slaughter of the animal thus takes on a ritualistic meaning, the retesting of his manhood ("he raised his head and knew that he had to go on with the hunt, because he was a hunter. He was born a hunter, a son of a chief, a chief. He had to hunt the mountain lion and kill it" [p. 113]). One cannot help noting the resemblances between *Autumn's Bounty* and Ernest Hemingway's *The Old Man and the Sea* (1952); like old Santiago in that work, Alphonse is sustained by his pride, and by a twelve-year-old-boy, the only support he has left.[5]

A metaphor of sickness and disease highlights the conflicts in Pierre's story. Alphonse himself suffers from arthritis and a limp resulting from a World War I injury. Both become obstacles in his physical struggle with the mountain lion. More important, the rabid coyotes that attack him nightly are not so different from the pack of young punks that beat him up for his money. (At the hearing for the mugging, when Alphonse refuses to identify the boys as his attackers, one of them yells at him, " 'You stink, old man' " [p. 36]). The pack of diseased coyotes who devour the mountain lion are determined, like Alphonse's own tribesmen, to nullify his heroism. Pierre shows (as Storm does in *Seven Arrows*) that it is greed and materialism—manifested in sickness and disease—that destroy the harmony of a people. Grandchildren turn against grandparents; youngsters no longer respect their elders—not even the tribal chief.

The question of termination is developed in a prolonged scene that takes place among the other members of the tribe while Alphonse is away in the mountains, stalking the cougar. The issue itself is second only to the story of Alphonse's own testing, uniting as it does two lesser themes of the novel: the disintegration of filial and tribal loyalties because of the increased conflict between generations, the demise of traditional attitudes toward land. Alphonse wants the reservation to remain in common trust for all of his people. Ruby is protermination; she wants the land broken up and sold off so that each Indian will receive a lump sum of money.

The question of termination is at base an attitude toward the land, toward traditional life. When Alphonse first argues with his granddaughter, he refers to the issue as one of future economic exploitation by the white man: " 'It is the white people who want you to sell out the reservation so they will get rich—that is the way it has been with the tribes that sold out' " (p. 5). During the old man's absence, at the termination hearing, a character named Horse McLain (a state representative and spokesman for George Pierre) voices his beliefs: " 'Termination is not a panacea. Termination is not the gateway to utopia in the Indian country' " (p. 75). Another tribal member concludes, " 'None of the tribes that have been terminated have gained self-sufficiency as the policy is purported to bring in its wake. Rather the tribes have ceased to exist as cohesive communities with their own culture and history' " (p. 77). Once the sacred lands are parceled out, the culture and traditions of the people will again be threatened with fragmentation and potential obliteration. The survival of a tribe depends on the survival of its land holdings.

The question of termination further highlights the conflict between present and past ways of life. Like Storm's *Seven Arrows*, the narrative in *Autumn's Bounty* unfolds in two directions simultaneously. As Alphonse tries to hold onto the past way of life, his people move blindly toward a future which contains the final threat of tribal disintegration. While Alphonse's memories provide a bridge to the past, his more vocal tribesmen dream of a time in the future when termination will reward each of them with a substantial sum of money. Though Pierre's picture of Alphonse is largely one-dimensional, the author gives his protagonist a number of insights. Alphonse knows that once the termination money is spent, there will be nothing left—not even any land to sustain future generations.

Since it is designed to bring about a happy ending, the resolution of *Autumn's Bounty* is vastly oversimplified. Charlie Joe, who is injured by a fall in the mountains searching for Alphonse, survives his wounds. Alphonse states of him, " 'He lives. He will not sell the land. He will not sell the bones of our fathers and mothers' " (p. 153). One of the tribal elders tells Alphonse of the results of the meeting: " 'The congressional hearings went well. Termination is dead. Now maybe we will not hate or suspect our brothers and our sisters. Maybe we can love one another again' " (p. 153).

Although the central encounter in *Autumn's Bounty* (the struggle between Alphonse and the mountain lion) is skillfully handled, the dramatic effect of the novel is weakened by a number of artificial scenes and dialogues. Famous speeches by past Indian leaders (Chief Joseph, Chief Seattle, Tecumseh, Chief Logan, Washakie) have been incorporated into the text verbatim, placed there supposedly as some of the thoughts that pass through Alphonse's consciousness while he stalks the cougar. The story is also undermined by an unconscionable number of biblical paraphrases and religious symbols. For example, just as he kills the cougar, Alphonse dreams that he is Christ crucified—rejected by his people. Largely these weaknesses of the novel—especially its didactic and often bitter tone—are a matter of distance. One cannot help concluding that when Pierre wrote his narrative he was still too close to his material, still too involved in the issues of termination and tribal leadership.

Winter in the Blood

In contrast to *Autumn's Bounty*, James Welch's *Winter in the Blood* (1974) is an almost flawless novel, certainly one of the most significant pieces of fiction written by an American Indian; yet the experiences recorded in the story extend far beyond those of Native peoples, as a number of reviewers noted in praise when the book was first published. Welch (who is half Blackfoot and half Gros Ventre) was born in Browning, Montana (on the Blackfoot Reservation) in 1940. The setting for his novel is the nearby Fort Belknap Indian Reservation and a number of adjacent towns: Havre, Harlem, Dodson, Malta.

The story is deceptively simple. As in so many contemporary American novels, very little seems to happen. Rather, much of the action is limited to what transpires in the unnamed narrator's mind—a question of subtlety, nuance, and tone. Welch's artistic control may remind one of the early works of John Steinbeck, such as *The Red Pony*, or the short stories of Ernest Hemingway, though he is perhaps closer to a number of earlier American writers who also wrote about

growing up on the land: Hamlin Garland, O.E. Rolvaag, Willa
Cather. The author's vitality is apparent in every page of the
novel, in every paragraph and sentence. (Since Welch published the opening chapters of his novel several years before
the entire work appeared, it is possible to examine this early
version of his work-in-progress and notice the extensive
amount of revision the novel underwent. See "The Only
Good Indian, Section I of a Novel in Progress," *South Dakota
Review* 9 [1971]: 55–74.)

Like several earlier novels we have examined, *Winter in the
Blood* begins with the main character (the narrator) returning
home to the reservation. Immediately, however, there is an
ironic twist. This is not a return from the war (like Abel's in
House Made of Dawn) or from a job in one of the big cities
(Archilde in *The Surrounded*), but, rather, from a few days of
drinking, fighting, and fornicating in one of the nearby towns
("My right eye was swollen up, but I couldn't remember how
or why, just the white man, loose with his wife and buying
drinks. . .").[6] In the remaining few paragraphs of the opening
chapter the narrator broadly announces that "coming home
was not easy anymore. It was never a cinch, but it had become a torture" (p. 3). His conflict is largely a private one,
not so much a response to the people around him ("the distance I felt came not from country or people; it came from
within me" [p. 4]). While he was still writing his novel, Welch
described his work as follows: "[It is about] an Indian man in
his early thirties who is haunted by abstract furies and the
emptiness of his relations with other people. He is a do-
nothing low-life, but in the end, he will discover that he is
human if insignificant."[7]

At the beginning, however, there is a sense of emptiness, of
depression bordering on paralysis, reflected in the narrator's
isolation from himself. He returns home to his mother and his
grandmother only to learn that Agnes, the Cree girl with
whom he has been having an affair, has run off in his absence, taking with her his gun and electric razor. Although
much of the remainder of the story outwardly focuses on the
narrator's search for Agnes, in time he discovers that what he
is searching for is himself. Like lost pieces of a jigsaw puzzle,
the panorama of his present life is riddled with holes because

he has failed to exorcise the demons of his past. The stolen gun and electric razor (his masculinity?) are the easiest objects to replace. Far more difficult are the relationships with his family, including the guilt he harbors about his father's and his brother's deaths.

Once again the literal trajectory of the narrative moves forward in time, recording several weeks in the narrator's life on and off the reservation, while the internalized narrative loops back into the past, to those deaths long ago. The chronological events begin when Teresa, the narrator's fifty-five-year-old mother, marries Lame Bull. Subsequently, the narrator works in the fields with his stepfather for several days during the harvesting season. Three times he goes into neighboring towns, where he drinks, fights, spends the nights with bar girls, and strikes up a rather absurd relationship with a fugitive from the FBI (known simply as "the airplane man") who is trying to escape over the border into Canada. When he finally locates Agnes in a bar, he suffers from a strange feeling of embarrassment—a recognition that he has never been certain what he wanted from their relationship. (" 'Do you think I care about that gun? . . . I couldn't even find a plug-in for that electric razor. I won it' " [p. 122].)

Often these scenes that take place away from home, off the reservation, are heightened by a sense of absurdity, of surreality. An old man (who the airplane man says is a spy) dies in a restaurant, his head crashing forward into his plate of soggy oatmeal; the narrator walks through the streets of Havre, carrying a large purple teddy bear, won by the airplane man at a punchboard game; when the protagonist hitchhikes back to the reservation, a university professor asks if he can take his picture. Throughout the novel, people talk at each other, but rarely with each other, as if they were carrying on separate conversations with themselves, oblivious of each other's existences.

While all these superficial encounters take place, the narrator's consciousness slowly grapples with the blurred events of his past. He is constantly bombarded by outer sensations that stir up associations from his earlier life. A movie marquee advertising an old Randolph Scott western triggers the cinema in his mind, recalling an incident twenty years earlier when he and his brother, Mose, discussed Scott's skill with a six-shooter. ("Randolph Scott had plugged me dead with a memory I had tried to keep away" [p. 12].) The memory of that discussion in turn reminds him of other movies from his own past, before his brother's death, when the two of them were boys growing up on the reservation. Mose was then fourteen; the narrator was twelve.

These memories ultimately crescendo with the narrator's understanding of his part in Mose's death, but first Welch fills in his puzzle with the images of several other deaths, both from the immediate world and from the past. These images begin in the opening paragraph of the novel when the narrator passes the borrow pit at the Earthboy place. "On the hill behind the cabin, a rectangle of barbed wire held the graves of all the Earthboys. . ." (p. 3). It is not until somewhat later in the story that the reader discovers that the borrow pit[8] on the Earthboy property is where the body of his father, First Raise, was discovered frozen to death one winter morning ten years ago when the temperature hit thirty degrees below zero. The narrator remarks rather flatly that he didn't really know "the man who froze in the borrow pit" (p. 26). His father was always in transit, never able to settle down; he froze to death while he was drunk. Yet even though he never understood his father, the narrator has become much like him—living in a kind of frozen state, incapable of responding to much in his life: "Ten years had passed since that winter day his wandering ended, but nothing of any consequence had happened to me" (p. 28).

When the narrator returns home from his third visit to one of the neighboring towns, the house is empty. For the first time he can remember, the living room is devoid of his grandmother's presence, and he concludes that the old woman (who was nearly a hundred) has died and that Teresa and Lame Bull have taken her to the mortuary. When they return, the men dig the grave for the old woman's casket, and in the process of digging, the narrator's consciousness returns again to the more painful death of his older brother, Mose. Earlier it has been revealed that in the accident that claimed Mose's life, the narrator had injured his kneecap. Although he subsequently underwent two operations on his leg, it constantly hurts him—a continual pain keeping alive the remorse he feels about his brother's death.

As one eventually learns through the narrator's journey into his past, the accident that he has repressed for so many years occurred during a winter twenty years earlier when the narrator and his brother were rounding up cattle. It should have been an easy matter, but one of the cows led the others out onto the highway. The boys followed the loose herd and an automobile struck Mose, on his horse, and killed him. While digging his grandmother's grave, the narrator thinks, "We shouldn't have run them . . . it wasn't good for them" (p. 159). If they hadn't been running the cows so fast, the accident might not have occurred.

> "What use," I whispered, cried for no one in the world to hear, not even Bird, for no one but my soul, as though the words would rid it of the final burden of guilt, and I found myself a child again, the years shed as a snake sheds its skin, and I was standing over the awkward tangle of clothes and limbs. "What use, what use, what use . . ." and no one answered, not the body in the road, not the hawk in the sky or the beetle in the earth; no one answered. And the tears in the hot sun, in the wind, the dusk, the chilly wind of dusk, the sleet that began to fall as I knelt beside the body, the first sharp pain of my smashed knee, the sleet on my neck, the blood which dribbled from his nostrils, his mouth, the man who hurried back from his car, his terrible breath as he tried to wrestle me away from my brother's broken body. (p. 168)

The "survival guilt" that has gnawed at his consciousness for twenty years has become frozen into his personality, cutting him off from the people around him as if he were the one killed in the accident.

After this vivid recollection of the real circumstances of his brother's death—that he was partly responsible for it, that he survived while his brother died—the story abruptly shifts from the past to the present, from the inner to the outer narrative. When the grave for his grandmother is finished, the narrator visits Yellow Calf, a blind old Indian who lives in a cabin by himself some miles away. It is the second visit in recent weeks, and this time the narrator tells the old man " 'My grandmother died. . . . We're going to bury her tomorrow' " (p. 172). During the cryptic conversation that follows, Yellow Calf reveals that he was the old woman's lover, that is, Teresa's father. In losing his grandmother, the narrator gains a grandfather. During the earlier visit, the narrator had acknowledged his respect and affinity for the old man by calling him "grandfather."

> And so we shared this secret in the presence of ghosts, in wind that called forth the muttering tepees, the blowing snow, the white air of the horses' nostrils. The cottonwoods behind us, their dead white branches angling to the threatening clouds, sheltered these ghosts as they had sheltered the camp that winter. But there were others, so many others. (p. 179)

The world of ghosts is ubiquitous; the images of death are overriding. When the narrator leaves Yellow Calf and returns home, he discovers that a cow is caught in the slough, "lying on her side, up to her chest in the mud" (p. 187). In his anger, he wants to ignore the beast ("I wanted to go away, to let her drown in her own stupidity" [p. 187]). His memories converge again on the details of Mose's death; the present is infused with a sense of the past. Ironically, it is the same cow that ran onto the highway twenty years earlier and caused the accident. ("I had seen her before, the image of catastrophe, the same hateful eye, the long curving horns, the wild-eyed spinster leading the cows down the hill into the valley" [p. 188].)

In the scene that follows—certainly the most powerful in the novel—all the major images and subplots of the story are carefully drawn together. Somewhat like Alphonse in his determination to kill the mountain lion, the narrator of *Winter in the Blood* decides to rescue the old cow from the slough. When he is unable to lasso her horns with his rope, he wades into the mud and ties the rope around her. At the other end of the rope is Bird, the horse he had ridden the day of the accident. Yet while he is in the mud, something gives out in his knee: "it wouldn't bend. . . . My whole leg was dead" (p.

189). Then it begins to rain, and just as the cow is successfully freed from the mud, he hears a rumble in the horse's guts. The cow is rescued; the horse dies from overexertion. As it was with his grandmother's death, one thing is taken away and another assumes its place. It is the law of nature—a matter of balance, replacement, and change. Yet in rescuing the cow, the narrator also atones for Mose's death—for whatever part he feels he played in it—and is released from the slough of his own despair. He stands in the rain, thinking of his father and his brother: "I wondered if Mose and First Raise were comfortable. They were the only ones I really loved. . ." (p. 193).

The brief epilogue describes the old woman's funeral the following day. The symbolic change that has taken place in the narrator—his sense of maturity gained through his reconciliation with his own past history, his recognition of what he has become—is indicated by his attire. He wears a suit and tie that belonged to his father. When Teresa sobs, and Lame Bull delivers an absurd eulogy (" 'Not the best mother in the world . . . but a good mother, notwithstanding . . . who could take it and dish it out . . . who never gave anybody any crap. . .' " [pp. 198–99]) the cinema in the narrator's mind produces a series of memories of the past juxtaposed with events of the future: his leg will have to be operated on again, his relationship with Agnes (and other people) will be more active. As a final gesture to his grandmother, he throws the old woman's tobacco pouch into the grave, thus acknowledging the role of the dead, the spirits of the past, and their ability to influence the living. (The burial of the tobacco pouch thus becomes a kind of traditional propitiation ritual, in this case releasing him from the ghosts of his frozen past.)

The fact that this most recent death takes place in summer, instead of winter, suggests another change or break from the patterns of the past. The title image, used throughout the narrative primarily as a symbol of death and emotional coldness, takes on renewed significance at the conclusion of the story. Earlier the narrator spoke of a feeling of winter in his bones; his father and Mose both died during the winter; Yellow Calf began his relationship with the narrator's grandmother during the harsh winter months (" 'My people starved that winter; we all starved but they died. It was the cruelest winter. My folks died, one by one' " [p. 173]). Winter kills, yet from that terrible period the union began that led to Teresa's birth, just as the narrator's rebirth begins with his grandmother's death. Winter is the end of the growing cycle, but from one end there is always a new beginning. Nature takes away but provides something fresh as a replacement. (The images of death in Welch's novel—radiating from the title itself—were also implied by the author's earlier title for the work: *The Only Good Indian* [is a dead Indian]. The subtlety of the final title is an improvement, though one wonders whether Welch's earlier projections for the novel would have included a different ending from the one in the final version.)

The style and the tone of Welch's *Winter in the Blood* are more relaxed than the work of most of his Native American contemporaries. In spite of the underlying seriousness of the story, many of the activities engaged in or witnessed by the narrator are suffused with a gentle, carefree quality. At its extreme, this lightness approaches the ridiculous, often juxtaposing a sense of absurdity with the more serious implications of his story. During the funeral scene, for example, Lame Bull discovers that the grave for the old woman's coffin is too short: "Lame Bull lowered himself into the grave and jumped up and down on the high end" (p. 198). I have already noted several of the more absurd incidents in the novel, and the entire subplot with the airplane man has an element of slapstick to it. So ubiquitous are these comic and ridiculous overtones that I cannot help believing that Welch is even lampooning his main character's accident (wounded knee?), or at least pulling the reader's leg.

Much of the novel is also a celebration of life—of those brief but unforgettable moments that evoke a sense of transcendence. The day of his initial return home, the narrator comments, "The evening was warm and pleasant" (p. 14), a remark that applies to the weather but also extends to the warm relationship which exists among his mother, his grandmother, and Lame Bull. There is a sense of filial compatibility—of people in Teresa's family actually enjoying each other's presence, in spite of the tragedies of the past. (The drinking scene in chapter 11, in honor of Teresa and

Lame Bull's marriage, is one of the comic highlights of the
story, rooted in a sense of humanity.) Nowhere is the sense of
brotherhood more apparent than in a number of flashbacks
from the past, describing the narrator's loving relationship
with his brother, Mose:

> I sat up and looked about the dark room. When I was
> young I had shared it with Mose and his stamp collection
> and his jar full of coins. In one corner against the wall
> stood a tall cupboard with glass doors. Its shelves held
> mementos of a childhood, two childhoods, two brothers,
> one now dead, the other servant to a memory of death.
> Mementos. I slipped from beneath the sheet and tiptoed
> to the cupboard. Two brown duck eggs lay in a nest of
> hay. Albums full of stamps lay beside the nest and, on a
> lower shelf, a rusty jackknife that we had found in an
> Indian grave pointed solemnly at a badger skull. Shell
> casings from different-caliber guns circled neatly within a
> larger circle of arrowheads. In the center a green metal
> soldier crouched, his face distorted in a grimace of anger
> and his rifle held high above his head. (p. 45)

Collecting stamps and tin soldiers—even Indian arrowheads!
These activities are not unlike those of thousands of other
boys who have grown up in the country. Welch's novel is a
song in praise of life—a link it shares with the greatest works
of all our disparate cultures.

The general feeling of goodwill that Welch displays toward
his characters and their lives is unique for the picture it gives
of reservation life itself. Not surprisingly, the female characters contribute much to the sense of fulfillment that Welch
sees as the potential for this life. Although Teresa is a difficult
person to live with, her acumen and practicality (especially in
business matters) give her a sense of strength. She is one of
the most fully realized female characters in all of the novels
examined in this study. What is especially significant is
Welch's use of her as an example of prosperity—not only of
survival but of making the reservation experience into something tangible and worthy of her talents. Throughout the
story, minor characters whom the narrator encounters speak
of Teresa as a strong, fulfilled woman. To a lesser extent,
those qualities are also true of her mother, largely because of

her ability to endure all those lonely years after the death of her first husband (when the relationship with Yellow Calf began). One cannot help but conclude that these two women, taken together, define a broader, more active role that female characters will play in subsequent Native American fiction.

Looking at it after *Autumn's Bounty*, one realizes that Welch's picture of the reservation makes explicit the antitermination position argued less artistically by George Pierre. The reservation, Welch tells us, permits one to retain an affinity with the land. The successful characters in this novel, like Teresa and Lame Bull, are farmers whose livelihood comes from the soil. If some of the earlier novels hinted at a sharp dichotomy between life on and off the reservation, in *Winter in the Blood* this demarcation is more fully and persuasively conceived. Of the four parts of the story (excluding the epilogue), three (the first, third, and fourth sections) are primarily confined to the reservation itself. Part 2, however, except for the opening sections on the land, is concerned with the sleazy towns that surround the reservation, living off it like a parasite, sucking away its vital juices. Welch creates a sense of exile for his narrator during these episodes in the neighboring towns, of estrangement from the heartbeat of Indian life. In the last chapter in Part 2 as he leaves Havre to return home, the narrator states,

> I had had enough of Havre, enough of town, of walking home, hung over, beaten up, or both. I had had enough of the people, the bartenders, the bars, the cars, the hotels, but mostly, I had had enough of myself. I wanted to lose myself, to ditch these clothes, to outrun this burning sun, to stand beneath the clouds and have my shadow erased, myself along with it. (p. 141)

True, there is still a sense of his own estrangement here, but the narrator now recognizes that he cannot discover the pieces of his puzzled past in these two-horse towns. When he arrives home he states matter-of-factly, "It was good to be home. The weariness I had felt earlier vanished from my bones" (pp. 151–52). In *Winter in the Blood* the reservation is not only home, a safe refuge from the outside world, but also a place of warmth and fulfillment, where the survivors of today find a life-affirming sense of belonging.

Ceremony

In Leslie Marmon Silko's *Ceremony* (1977) the reservation—Laguna Pueblo, where the author was born (in 1948) and has spent much of her life—emerges as a refuge from the outside world, though the evil from that world has begun to permeate this haven and undermine the characters' lives. The source of the disease is World War II and the exposure it brought to Indians who fought in the armed services—a theme that connects Silko's novel with Momaday's *House Made of Dawn*. Silko, however, goes beyond Momaday's implications to suggest that the origins of evil were brought about by the Indians themselves. As in *Winter in the Blood*, the conflict is never a simple matter of Indian versus Caucasian, of right against wrong. Life is a continual struggle, a never-ending ceremony necessary to purify the world around us.

The story embodies a number of mythic overtones: a venture into the unknown (the war), a descent into the underworld (madness), and a ritual cleansing or purification. The narrative structure is elliptical, developed through flashbacks and spatial juxtapositions, abrupt changes in time and point of view; the chronology of the events must be reconstructed from Silko's dense and often obscure narrative.

The story begins shortly after World War II. An American Indian named Tayo (half Laguna and half white) returns home to the reservation after a period of time in a hospital in Los Angeles. He suffers from battle fatigue and frequent hallucinations which pull him back to the horrors of the war. The land is parched and barren, threatening to dry up completely and destroy his people's livelihoods; and Tayo believes he is responsible for the drought because he prayed the rain would go away when he was in the South Pacific ("the rain had stopped coming because he had cursed it").[9] Furthermore, in his hallucinations he mistakes his own people for the Japanese he fought against in the South Pacific. As the story evolves, however, the reader realizes that Tayo's guilt goes back much further than the events of the war.

Flashbacks take the story back to the more distant past and establish a number of events responsible for Tayo's feelings, such as the origins of his birth (his father was white, his mother a prostitute who left Tayo with her sister, Auntie, when he was four years old). Auntie never lets Tayo forget that his blood is mixed, that his mother (Laura) was a tramp. She lavishes her love and attention on her own son, Rocky, who she believes will erase the blot on the family name brought about by Laura's promiscuity. Rocky will go to the university, become a football star—in short, do all the accepted things and thereby assimilate into the white world. Tayo will remain on the land and raise cattle. But the war nullifies all of Auntie's plans. Tayo and Rocky both enlist and leave to fight for America (" 'Anyone can fight for America,' " the recruiter tells them, " 'even you boys. In a time of need, anyone can fight for her' " [p. 64]). Rocky is killed in the fighting; his death—like Mose's in *Winter in the Blood*—results in the protagonist's survivor guilt, since Tayo had promised Auntie he would protect her son. A further source of guilt develops because Tayo promised Auntie's brother, Josiah, that he would help raise his Mexican cattle. While Tayo is away, Josiah dies; later, in his hallucinations, Tayo watches his uncle die in the South Pacific jungles.

Tayo's wise old grandmother suggests that a medicine man be called in to try to cure him; the subsequent encounter with the medicine man, old Betonie, facilitates Tayo's purification. From the elaborate ceremony, imaginatively woven into the texture of Silko's narrative, Tayo discovers that the evil within him can only be eliminated by recognizing all matter as a part of the whole, as a kind of great chain of being: evil, like good, is part of the great design of creation. If one part of the organism is contaminated, the entire system eventually becomes polluted.

Silko's use of language bristles through in almost every scene of the novel. The experimental structure enhances the complexity of the narrative, yet the author's supreme achievement is her ability to create startling poetic images[10]—whether in the form of entire poems incorporated into the story (reminiscent of Jean Toomer's use of poetry in his novel, *Cane*, published in 1923), or the delicate, poetic images that explode into the prose sections:

> "But you know, grandson, this world is fragile." The word he chose to express "fragile" was filled with the intricacies of a continuing process, and with a strength in-

herent in spider webs woven across paths through sand hills where early in the morning the sun becomes entangled in each filament of web. It took a long time to explain the fragility and intricacy because no word exists alone, and the reason for choosing each word had to be explained with a story about why it must be said this certain way. (pp. 35–36)

Because of a core of recurring images, such as the spider web in the passage above, in one sense *Ceremony* has no conventional beginning and end. It would be possible to begin reading the novel at almost any page and continue from there since the images are circular, related to one another by imaginative association. Like these interwoven images, the subject of *Ceremony* is the "continuing process," the interconnectedness of everything in our universe and our lives. The form of Silko's novel, then, reduplicates its meaning. Tayo discovers that his so-called madness, his sense of repetition, is the accurate way to observe the world and not the abnormal one.

Early in the novel there are hints that his distortion is in fact a valid way of perceiving the world, but Tayo is not able to understand this; he has yet to begin the ceremony of his reeducation. Lying on his bed at home, he is aware of Japanese voices becoming "Laguna voices" (p. 6), of a dead soldier's white skin becoming the color of his own ("even white men were darker after death" [p. 7]), of Josiah lying there next to the dead Japanese soldiers. The fusion of his own people with the Japanese confuses him: "the tall [soldier] looked like a Navajo guy from Fort Defiance . . . even shook his head like Willie Begay did. . . . It was then Tayo got confused, and he called this tall Jap soldier Willie Begay. . ." (pp. 43–44).

The interconnectedness of the rains in the South Pacific and the drought at Laguna Pueblo is similarly beyond Tayo's comprehension. Rather than seeing these events as part of a great cycle of natural occurrences, he regards them as cause and effect. In the miasmic jungle on that South Pacific island, Tayo curses uncontrollably, exhorting the rains to cease forever:

He damned the rain until the words were a chant, and he sang it while he crawled through the mud to find the corporal and get him up before the Japanese saw them. He wanted the words to make a cloudless blue sky, pale with a summer sun pressing across wide and empty horizons. The words gathered inside him and gave him strength. He pulled on the corporal's arm; he lifted him to his knees and all the time he could hear his own voice praying against the rain. (p. 12)

Tayo knows from earlier events in his life that he has strange powers as a rainmaker.

Tayo's guilt about the drought, ultimately a statement about the land, illustrates Silko's concern with the collective whole, and relates her novel to Storm's *Seven Arrows*, which also teaches that the power of the whole is diminished by the dissent of one single individual. From Ku'oosh, Tayo learns that "it took only one person to tear away the delicate strands of the web, spilling the rays of the sun into the sand, and the fragile world would be injured" (p. 38). Tayo thinks, ". . . he had not killed any enemy. . . . [But] he had done things far worse, and the effects were everywhere in the cloudless sky, on the dry brown hills, shrinking skin and hide taut over sharp bone" (p. 36). Though the focus is often limited to Tayo's own thoughts, *Ceremony* is as much concerned with the group-felt experience as are a number of the earlier Native American novels. Tayo *believes* that his actions have had far-reaching ramifications for all of his people, that he is responsible for their current condition; the rain he seeks to water his parched soul will also bring a resurrection for his people, a new era of plenty.

Initially, it is Josiah who teaches Tayo to respect the land: " 'There are some things worth more than money. . . . This is where we come from, see. This sand, this stone, these trees, the vines, all the wildflowers. This earth keeps us going' " (p. 45). Josiah also warns Tayo about abusing one's symbiotic relationship with the earth: " 'The old people used to say that droughts happen when people forget, when people misbehave' " (p. 46). Before the war, it was Josiah's intention to breed his Mexican desert cattle—capable of sustaining themselves in a world of dry sand and scrubby mesquite—with domesticated Herefords and produce a new breed of hearty beasts able to withstand the erratic fluctuations of drought and fecundity, to endure the extremes of the elements on the poor reservation land. The cattle are a part of his people's future. When they disappear after Josiah's death, Tayo feels he has let his uncle down. By ignoring his responsibility to Josiah's cattle, Tayo feels he has not only neglected his responsibility to his people, but severed his relationship with the land.

The cycle of restoration and purification—the ceremony Tayo undergoes with Betonie's guidance—unites all of the major themes in the novel (the cyclical nature of the drought, the source of fulfillment from the land and the cattle, Tayo's estrangement from his people and his environment, his mental "illness" and confusion about nature's capacity for reduplication, the private "war" he has fought against the background of the more public one) and restores Tayo to the center of traditional life.

The ceremony itself begins with Betonie stressing the need for change:

> "At one time, the ceremonies as they have been performed were enough for the way the world was then. But after the white people came, elements in this world began to shift; and it became necessary to create new ceremonies. I have made changes in the rituals. The people mistrust this greatly, but only this growth keeps the ceremonies strong." (p. 126)

Tayo asks what good Indian ceremonies can be against the sickness that comes from war, bombs, and lies—perpetuated by the white man's world. Betonie replies that the original source of evil is from the People themselves:

> "That is the trickery of the witchcraft . . . . They want us to believe all evil resides with white people. Then we will look no further to see what is really happening. They want us to separate ourselves from white people, to be ignorant and helpless as we watch our own destruction. But white people are only tools that the witchery manipulates; and I tell you, we can deal with white people, with their machines and their beliefs. We can because we invented white people; it was Indian witchery that made white people in the first place." (p. 132)

The idea is expanded in one of the novel's more lengthy poems:

> They see no life
> When they look
> they see only objects.
> The world is a dead thing for them
> the trees and rivers are not alive
> the mountains and stones are not alive.
> The deer and bear are objects
> They see no life. (p. 135)

White people have become machines, estranged from the natural world, and these machines have poisoned the environment. The poem projects a vision of destruction, sterility, and drought—a self-perpetuating wasteland

> Set in motion now
> set in motion
> To destroy
> To kill
> Objects to work for us
> objects to act for us
> Performing the witchery
> for suffering
> for torment
> for the still-born
> the deformed
> the sterile
> the dead. (p. 137)

When he enlists in the armed services at the outbreak of the war, Tayo becomes a part of this self-renewing cycle of death and destruction, an extension of a machine.[11]

Betonie's vision—the prophecy of the poem—takes us back to the opening passages of the novel, which depict Tayo's war buddies (Emo, Harley, Leroy, and Pinkie) as the cultural fallout of the war. Spending their days and nights drinking, they try to recapture the period during the war when they thought they were important. ("They spent all their checks trying to get back the good time . . . feeling they belonged to America the way they felt during the war" [pp. 42–43].) Silko injects a sociological comment about their conditon: " 'Reports note that since the Second World War a pattern of drinking and violence, not previously seen before, is emerging among Indian veterans' " (p. 53). The land registers their condition: "Since the men came back from the war [there was] broken bottle glass all over the reservation" (p. 250). Only Tayo, because of his vision of the interconnectedness of all life, has comprehended the forces that are slowly destroying the Indian veterans. He knows they must be stopped before they contaminate everyone and everything on the reservation.

Tayo's ceremony, then, is more than a recognition of Indian witchery in the creation of white people, more than an acknowledgment that this sorcery in time circled back upon itself and began to destroy the Indian world. It involves a personal purification and epiphany, as well as a destruction of those violent forces which have gotten out of check. On the individual level, the ceremony is necessary to purge Tayo's sense of guilt; on a collective level, the veteran rampagers must be destroyed before they bring total havoc to the reservation.

With the aid of his assistant, Betonie cleanses Tayo, informing him, however, that his total release from the nightmares of the past will depend on his locating Josiah's cattle. After Betonie predicts where the cattle may be located, Tayo leaves the reservation, climbs high into the mountains east of the Rio Grande to an area where "there was no sign the white people had ever come" (p. 184), and searches for the cattle. His quest culminates in an idyllic affair with a mysterious Indian woman in the hills (possibly a spirit woman), which frees him from his emotional instability and makes him whole. He is released from his tortured past; the cattle are located where Betonie predicted ("He would take the cattle home again, and they would follow the plans Josiah had made and raise a new breed of cattle that could live in spite of drought and hard water" [p. 187]).

In the summer that follows, Tayo continues to live with the woman in the hills, far away from his family and the other Indian veterans. Though the drought ends as the rains return, the cycle of restoration is not complete. Auntie's husband, Robert, visits Tayo and tells him that the other veterans have started rumors to the effect that he is still unbalanced from the war and that he should be sent back to the hospital. Robert recommends that Tayo return to the reservation, live with his people for a time, and thereby prove his normality.

The reunion with his family is forestalled by Tayo's final encounter with Emo's claque of war buddies, now determined to kill Tayo because they regard his "madness" as an embarrassment. Before they can destroy him, however, Tayo escapes to an abandoned mining camp, and there he experiences the epiphany that completes his own personal ceremony and permits him to comprehend the totality of evil in the world. The mining camp, an abandoned uranium shaft, is situated between White Sands, "where they exploded the first atomic bomb" (p. 245), and Los Alamos, "where the bomb had been created" (p. 246). The war, the Japanese faces duplicated in the Laguna ones, the wholesale destruction of the earth with machines and other scientific "achievements" from the white man's arsenal—all of these elements fall into perspective for him:

> There was no end to it; it knew no boundaries; and he had arrived at the point of convergence where the fate of all living things, and even the earth, had been laid. From the jungles of his dreaming he recognized why the Japanese voices had merged with Laguna voices, with Josiah's voice and Rocky's voice; the lines of cultures and worlds were drawn in flat dark lines on fine light sand, converging in the middle of witchery's final ceremonial sand painting. From that time on, human beings were one clan again, united by the fate the destroyers planned for all of them, for all living things; united by a circle of death that devoured people in cities twelve thousand miles away, victims who had never known these mesas, who had never seen the delicate colors of the rocks which boiled up their slaughter. (p. 246)

As he examines the mine shaft carefully, Tayo glances at a piece of uranium ore: "the gray stone was streaked with powdery yellow uranium, bright and alive as pollen. . ." (p. 246). Life (the pollen, sacred to his people) and death (the uranium, converted into a tool for slaughter by the white people) converge in the core of the earth. It is man's choice to make of them a living or a dead thing.

Tayo hides from his attackers and watches them turn against each other. Harley and Leroy are violently murdered by Emo and Pinkie, because they let Tayo escape. As the narrator comments, "It was not much different than if they had died at Wake Island or Iwo Jima: the bodies were dismembered beyond recognition. . ." (p. 259). Pinkie is later killed by Emo, the victim of an "accidental" gunshot; Emo is forced to leave the reservation and told never to return again. As Betonie had predicted, evil destroys itself.

> Whirling darkness
> started its journey
> with its witchery
>   and
>   its witchery
> has returned upon it. (pp. 260–61)

In the aftermath of this violence, Auntie changes her attitudes toward Tayo, finally accepting him as one of the family, as her surrogate son. Thus the family unit is restored; there is a modicum of hope for the future, embodied in the return of the cattle from the hills, Tayo's Indian woman (described as a source of life), the promise of a new day:

> Sunrise,
>   accept this offering,
>   Sunrise. (p. 262)

The complexity of Silko's novel is intensified by the poems she has incorporated into her story, recalling Storm's use of oral tales in *Seven Arrows*. The fusion of poetry and prose is intertwined with the circularity of the narrative itself, though when the poems are examined separately, they reveal a picture of displacement and drought and the eventual cycle of restoration that brings rain and stability to the once-barren land. The poems fall into three separate stages—an invocation, a central body or story with its own thematic variations, and a resolution—all three divisions running parallel to the main prose narrative.

In the first three poems of the novel (preceding the prose

sections) Silko, in a kind of traditional epic invocation, creates a persona of herself (Ts'its'tsi'nato, Thought-Woman), the singer of the song, the storyteller of what will shortly become the novel itself. Silko has thus projected two voices of herself in the novel: we know she is the author of the wider narrative called *Ceremony*, yet she has secreted a second persona of herself into the poems. Thought-Woman "is sitting in her room/ and whatever she thinks about/ appears" (p. 1). The emphasis is upon the imagination—the poet's gift to the world. Whatever she thinks of is created in the process of this thought. As she names these objects, they appear.

> She is sitting in her room
> thinking of a story now
>
> I'm telling you the story
> she is thinking. (p. 1)

The second poem ("Ceremony") delineates the traditional function of poetry and oral stories: "They aren't just entertainment" (p. 2), she tells us, "They are all we have . . . to fight off/ illness and death" (p. 2). The poet's function is similar to the shaman's: he purifies the world of evil by telling his tales, by reciting his poems. By writing this novel, Silko is exorcising the past—purifying the world of its wickedness. Poetry is so important that without it "You don't have anything" (p. 2). The poem ends with a plea for change ("the rituals and the ceremony/are still growing" [p. 2]). The brief poem that follows ("What She Said") reiterates the poet's belief in the healing power of poetry:

> The only cure
> I know
> is a good ceremony
> that's what she said. (p. 3)

The poet—the artificer of words—has become a verbal medicine man; his poetry is as important to his people as the shaman's curative powers. One heals the body, the other the mind. The balancing effect of the two is important since Tayo's problems, though psychological, were brought about by his physical involvement in the war.

The themes that connect the poems in the central narrative

of the novel are many of the same ones that concern Tayo and his people: neglect of one's traditional roles in life, the cyclical patterns of drought and fertility, the abuse of power (through magic and witchery), the need for atonement or purification before the natural harmony of the earth can be restored. (Several poems also relate incidents concerning GI's during the war.) The poems vary in length and style from several short imagistic lines to much longer narrative ones, relating traditional folk myths and stories. The dominant theme of many of the early ones, however, is tradition and duty. Reed Woman and Corn Woman argue about their work in the world (p. 13); the warriors of the Scalp Society know that if they ignore their traditional duties, havoc will be unleashed (p. 37); interest in Ck'o'yo magic makes the people in Reedleaf town neglect the mother corn altar (pp. 46–48). In all of these instances, the poet stresses that people must work hard to reaffirm their natural relationship with the land. If this work is ignored, drought and starvation prevail.

The later poems illustrate various means of propitiation, for restoring the unity lost through neglect. Hummingbird flies to the Fourth World below as an emissary to plead the case for rain (p. 82); fly and hummingbird tell their people of the need "to purify/ the town" (p. 106); Sun Man rescues his people from Ck'o'yo Kaup'a'ta, the Gambler (pp. 170–76); hummingbird and fly are eventually successful in their sacrifice to old Buzzard:

> Everything was set straight again
>   after all that ck'o'yo' magic.
>
> The storm clouds returned
> the grass and plants started growing again
>   There was food
>   and the people were happy again (p. 256)

Evil (the "whirling darkness" that Betonie described) is destroyed at the moment when Tayo comprehends the mystery of the universe (life or destruction) in the uranium shaft. The poetic and prose sections of the narrative are thematically meshed together:

> Whirling darkness

> has come back on itself.
> It keeps all its witchery
>   to itself (p. 261)

The novel concludes with a warning that although this evil is "dead for now" (p. 261), even the offering of sunrise may not be able to hold these forces in check forever.

Leslie Silko's *Ceremony* should be cause for general cele-bration. Like a clever trickster (with a constantly changing persona) Silko (the author/poet/prophet) has created a wild phantasmagoria in which structure and meaning are almost impossible to separate. Tayo's journey away from his people and subsequent rediscovery of the traditional life-force is also the journey of the collective spirit from exposure to evil in the universe, through purification, to redemption. The ceremony that old Betonie uses to cleanse Tayo of his illness is much the same as the author's belief in the curative power of the word, rendered through image and form.

Silko's affinities with her contemporaries (especially Moma-day, Storm, and Welch) are difficult to dispute, yet in a way she has reached beyond them because of her faith in the re-deeming value of language and ritual. The bleakness of Momaday's narrative is matched by Silko's violent images of a war-ravaged world—extending far beyond the delineated battlefronts of physical warfare—yet her final image of dawn is, indeed, one of hope. Storm's belief that cultural survival depends on cultural change is qualified by Silko, who stresses the need for continual renewal and awakening. Welch's sur-vivors on the reservation in the 1970s find their fulfillment there largely because other Native peoples have already fought some of their most important battles. *Ceremony*, I cannot help thinking, is the kind of story Pocahontas would have told us if her voice had been her own.

Coda: Indians' Summer

In Nasnaga's (Roger Russell's) satirical spoof, *Indians' Summer*, the reservation is also seen in positive terms, as a center for future political activity: "The reservations, once hated and scorned as ghettos without buildings, now offered a land base, a ready-made country" (p. 131). The success of the confrontation between Indians and the United States government is dependent upon the existence of the reservation system: "The territory was outlined and occupied; only the borders needed to be secured and that had been accomplished within the first forty-eight hours" (p. 131).

The story (published in 1975) takes the form of a fantasy set in the immediate future—the summer of 1976. Indians forcibly occupy several areas of the country, asserting their sovereign rights: "On July 4, 1976, right in the middle of the two hundredth birthday of the United States of America, the Navajo, Sioux, Mohawk, Apache, and Pueblo nations had declared their independence" (p. 4). Much of the guerrilla warfare activity is organized and led by Indians who fought in Vietnam. At the United Nations, the newly formed nation of Anishinade-waki (Land of the People) wins the support of the Third World bloc. The governments of the USSR, India, Ghana, Sweden, and France make overflights to the Indian areas. The Canadian prime minister commits suicide, since the Indians in his country also claim their independence and he fails in his confrontation with them. At the end of the story, the Indian leaders call the president's bluff (by convincing him that three Minuteman missiles are pointed at Washington) and win his guarantee to recognize their lands as an independent nation: Red Power has had its day.

The story develops from a number of short, choppy scenes that switch back and forth among the various participants and their respective settings: the Oval Room of the White House, the occupied Indian areas, the Security Council of the United Nations, and so on. As is often true of satire, the characters are cardboard, though there are a number of ironic reversals. (It is the white characters who drink in this novel, not the Indians.) The narrative itself is largely rhetoric—written, it appears, as a reaction to the 1973 Wounded Knee confrontation (which is referred to several times). Largely because the author has taken a one-gag idea and stretched it out for nearly two hundred pages, the humor quickly collapses. Even the quips and puns are often strained: "the feathers had hit the fan" (p. 4), "the president . . . saw red" (p. 33), "The U.S. talks with two faces, and one of them spits bullets" (p. 115).

In spite of its many artistic limitations, Nasnaga (a Shawnee) has written a novel that touches several of the more important themes and issues from earlier fiction by Native Americans. The success of the takeover is largely dependent upon the unification of the various Indian tribal groupings ("Unity among tribes was once unheard of; today it was a reality" [p. 129]). Tribal cohesion is seen as an extension of the individual's place within the tribal group: "Nothing worse could happen to an Indian than to be cut off from his people" (p. 40). These ideas are interwoven with continual diatribes against white America, such as the following observation about nature:

> "In truth, the American wilderness did not exist until the white man came to this land. The native American found no wilderness here. He found oneness with nature's own plan. He grew and developed in the folds of her valleys. He lived and died in the softness of the vast forest which once covered this land. Within the context of nature and those gifts the Creator had placed at his disposal, the native American wove his culture to enhance his mind, his body, his soul. He did not destroy the work of those natural forces of which he was so much a part. But the beauty and dignity of native American culture was no match for European guns and greed." (p. 76)

These attitudes toward land and cultural and tribal unity in *Indians' Summer* provide an interesting example of the potential force known as Pan-Indianism—the major theme of Nasnaga's novel ("The Indians' summer was over. Far off in an eastern forest a hawk cried. It was a time of the People" [p. 195]). (The Pan-Indian theme is also of primary importance in Jon Mockingbird's *The Wokosani Road* [1963], discussed in appendix 2.)

In spite of the widely differing novels by the four writers discussed in this chapter, a compelling sense of urgency unites much of their work. George Pierre, once the appointed leader of his people, projects his main character back into the past when the chief was still a unifying element for his tribe, when the individual achieved his greatest respect in traditional ways. *Autumn's Bounty*, for all its glaring nostalgia, asserts the significance of traditional life as an ideal worthy of emulation. A similar attitude permeates James Welch's *Winter in the Blood*. The author, a highly gifted writer probably more widely known as a poet than as a novelist, has perfectly captured the existential dilemma of the contemporary Indian. Because of his frozenness, Welch's unnamed narrator is a poor imitation of those giants of the earlier generations who nurtured him. In *Ceremony*, Leslie Marmon Silko, also widely known as a poet, cries out for the need for renewal and reinvigoration of the older rituals that kept Indians alive and strong. All life, she tells us, is a ceremony, an elaborate ritual to ward off evil, to assure one's relationship with the land and one's people. Even Nasnaga (an artist and a draftsman by profession), for all his artlessness, proclaims the need for intertribal cohesion if Native Americans are ever to regain control over their collective destiny.

Fused together, these four novels share a common warning or prophecy: don't push us any longer, don't try to take away any more of our land. We have been pushed too far already, and soon we will begin to fight back. Certainly that is the warning sounded in Pierre's *Autumn's Bounty*: termination must be resisted because it will break up the Native American's final refuge, the reservation. That land is all we have left to claim, and we intend to keep it. Both Welch's *Winter in the Blood* and Silko's *Ceremony* expand upon this belief, hinting at a more rewarding life for the Indian on the reservation than has previously been suggested. We like it here, and we're certainly not going to sell out to those two-bit towns that surround us. The reservation is home. Nasnaga's *Indians' Summer* develops this idea so that the reservation becomes the focal point of future political activity. Any successful Pan-Indian movement will not begin with Native peoples who have fled to the white man's cities, but rather with those still on the land. The Native American has no intention of vanishing (that attitude has always been a white concept anyway), nor will he tolerate any definition that relegates him to invisibility, or sees him as a shadow of the dominant culture.

The time of the People has come.

7

The Figure in the Dark Forest

> If you and I were sitting in a circle of people on the prairie, and if I were then to place a painted drum or an eagle feather in the middle of this circle, each of us would perceive these objects differently. Our vision of them would vary according to our individual positions in the circle, each of which would be unique. . . .
>
> The perception of any object . . . is ultimately made a thousand times more complicated whenever it is viewed within the circle *of an entire People as a whole*.—Hyemeyohsts Storm, *Seven Arrows*

In my earliest assumptions about Native American fiction —based solely on readings of N. Scott Momaday's *House Made of Dawn* and Hyemeyohsts Storm's *Seven Arrows*—I envisioned a literature radically original in form and content, distinctly shaped by cultural constructs and differences, something removed from the mainstream of American fiction. How wrong those assumptions have proved to be! The novels by Momaday and Storm are not exactly random samples of the body of Native American fiction. By chance, my initial exposure to American Indian fiction placed me in a kind of cultural cul-de-sac whence it was difficult to catch a glimpse of the more representative terrain.

Looked at as a totality, the novels by American Indian authors are not very different from a great deal of fiction written by other American writers. Often, in fact, Indian novelists have written works that bind them to their Euro-American contemporaries; except for the fact that their works are usually concerned with Indian characters and the situations of their lives, it would be difficult to identify the racial origins of the writers were they not already known. One thinks particularly of the earliest writers, who often tried to emulate the work of their contemporaries: Pokagon's use of the temperance theme in *Queen of the Woods*, Oskison's regional romances, Mourning Dove's Western melodrama. Even some of the later novelists (D'Arcy McNickle and George Pierre) appear consciously to have patterned their narratives after the works of their white contemporaries, as if to assert the homogeneity of Native Americans and their pale-faced brothers.

The similarity between the earliest novels by Native Americans and those of their Euro-American contemporaries is the easiest to identify, since they were written for a predominantly white reading audience. When he wrote *Queen of the Woods*, Pokagon knew that few American Indians would be able to purchase a copy of his book, much less read it. Oskison, Mourning Dove, Mathews, and McNickle all published their novels before Indian education assured the artist a reading audience of his own people. Even some of the most recent novels by Native Americans give the impression of being written for a non-Indian readership. *Seven Arrows*, with its instructions and guiding interpretations, comes immediately to mind—in spite of the fact that the author has relied so centrally on the oral tradition to give the narrative its innovative shape. Even Momaday's *House Made of Dawn*, because of its technical obscurity, would seem to appeal only to the most patient of readers—those as much interested in the form of the novel and its structural possibilities as in Native American culture. I suspect that numerous readers of Momaday's novel, both Indian and non-Indian, have not been able to finish reading it. With the most recently published novels, however, it is possible to detect the beginning of a new trend; *Winter in the Blood, Indians' Summer*, and *Ceremony* all appear to be aimed at a reading audience that assumes a higher proportion of Native American readers.

Almost without exception the Native American novelist has been a kind of cultural hybrid, or cultural half-caste, somewhat dislocated from his traditional heritage. The fact that these writers as a whole have been so highly educated in the white man's sense separates them from their people, as we have seen illustrated in a number of their fictional characters. Momaday has a Ph.D. in English literature; Mathews, Oskison, Chief Eagle, Bedford, Pierre, Silko, and Welch all went on for postgraduate work, the last in creative writing. Several (Momaday, Bedford, Silko) are or have been academics, yet even the earliest (Pokagon and Mourning Dove) were highly educated by the standards of their day. Exposure to non-Indian education is clearly, then, the most distinguishing mark of their non-representativeness, and one might suspect that the theme of Western education is implicit in all of their works—not just in those novels in which the protagonists spend time attending the white man's schools.

Closely related to the problem of education and its marked influence upon these novelists is the curious fact that, with one or two exceptions, these writers have published only one novel each. John M. Oskison is an exception—and his work is the most tenuously related to the Indian heritage of all the novels discussed here. As I complete this study, a new novel by D'Arcy McNickle has been announced for publication, forty years after the appearance of *The Surrounded*.[1] One suspects that there is no simple explanation for this tendency toward singular publication, but that, rather, the creativity of many of these writers has been smothered by a number of pressures: the difficulty of finding publishers receptive to their work, the general lack of interest in Indian culture among American readers (until the most recent years), the disappointment at having to direct their writings toward non-Indian readers, even the problems of writing in what may be a second and less rewarding language. Furthermore, there is the larger emotional problem of distance, of never quite being able to get far enough away from the real-life situation that consumes all of one's psychic powers—a problem these writers share with a number of black American writers whose literary productivity has also remained minuscule.

I would speculate, too, that some of these novelists have written themselves into a quasi no-man's-land from which there is no escape. This appears to be true of N. Scott Momaday, whose publications since *House Made of Dawn* have been marred by a kind of repetitive preciousness and pretentiousness, indicating that Momaday has become trapped in a literary holding pattern (or a kind of circle, to use an image from his novel) from which it is impossible to move forward or backward. With a vision as bleak as his, one wonders whether Momaday can write another novel about the Native American without making a complete reversal and thereby undermining the validity of his earlier work.

The ethnic heritage, one might say, then, has placed many of these writers in a kind of double bind. If, on the one hand, Indianness has been the subject matter of their fiction, on the other it has been a tortuous experience to write about unless the writer has gained a certain distance from his past—at the expense of losing traditional ties and assimilating into the white world. Without their extensive educations, it is doubtful whether these writers would have come to write the novels that articulated their own distinct problems. The ethnic clash is often every bit as apparent in their writings as it has been in their lives; and the resultant novels, one assumes, were often written as a kind of ritual exorcism.

Yet these novels—especially the best of them, by Momaday, Storm, Welch, and Silko—are considerably more than literary purgations, since the writers, while grappling with the loyalties of their mixed ethos, have rarely fallen into the clichés invented by their non-Indian contemporaries. If, however, there are no Pocahontas figures in these novels—no Chingachgooks, no Indian Joes, no Chief Bromdens—neither are there any Bigger Thomases, Kunta Kintes, or Invisible Men. While Native American writers have avoided the pitfalls of literary stereotyping that have so often characterized the works of their white counterparts which include Indian characters, at the same time few characters in their works approach the stature of several of the more memorable protagonists in novels by black American writers (the other minority group it is possible to cite for comparison).

Not only did black American fiction emerge well before the first fiction by American Indians, but its intentions from the beginning were much more political. In the first novel by an Afro-American writer, William Wells Brown's *Clotel* (published in 1853), the author's abolitionist position is always predominant. Brown wrote his novel to expose the atrocities of slavery, and his novel, read today, is still an unsettling experience. By contrast, the protest dimension of Pokagon's *Queen of the Woods* is much more subdued, since it is directed at only one aspect of the white man's world: liquor. Without much of a strain on the imagination, it is possible to substitute any other racial group for Pokagon's Indian characters, and the story (with its didacticism) would remain much the same. A similar substitution with *Clotel* is impossible, because of the novel's racial and political overtones.

By the time Oskison, Mourning Dove, and Mathews were publishing their novels in the 1920s and 1930s, black American artists were in the midst of a cultural explosion known as the Harlem Renaissance, largely made possible because earlier figures (such as William Wells Brown, Frederick Douglass, W. E. B. DuBois, and James Weldon Johnson) had already expressed their rage, had articulated the collective anger of their people. The vindictive intent one finds in the works of any number of black American novelists (Brown, Frank Webb, Richard Wright, William Attaway, James Baldwin) never surfaces so bluntly in the works of their Native American contemporaries, though N. Scott Momaday's come the closest.

This is not to suggest that the emergence of Native American fiction has been less dynamic or interesting than fiction by black American writers. Rather, its course has been more steadfast, largely because the political dimension has not dominated it. In the early assimilationist novels by Native authors, one finds none of the overt protest that dominates the fiction of their Afro-American counterparts. While William Wells Brown, Frank Webb, and their contemporaries often developed their narratives by cataloging a steady barrage of atrocities inflicted by whites upon black people, little of such horror surfaces in the works by Pokagon, Mourning Dove, Oskison, or Mathews. To be sure, assimilation for them meant passive acquiescence, suffering, and confusion; the more vocal criticism against white America in the works of the post-Momaday writers is simply absent from the earlier novels.

Nor is the reaction against the white world in the later novels ever as hostile as it is often depicted in Afro-American fiction. Confrontation between the races is generally one-sided—whites against Indians, rather than the other way

around. It could be no other way because of the superior
military advantage always held by whites. Storm describes this
"warfare" as so many shots in the back; the Indian could do
little to defend himself. Momaday and Silko present us with
the contemporary embodiment of victimization, urban and
reservation derelicts, who usually lack both the ability and the
means to fight back. Protagonists in Native American fiction
(Mathews's Chal Windzer, McNickle's Archilde, Momaday's
Abel, many of Storm's Plains Indians) appear almost to a man
to be incapable of acting decisively, of fighting back against
the world that surrounds and encapsulates them. Instead,
they wait and endure, many of them capitulating in the process.

Even in the most recent novels, except for Bedford's *Tsali*,
there are only minor changes in this defeatist pattern. Rather,
the theme of race appears to be disappearing from American
Indian fiction, as the writers begin to turn back to the smaller
cultural unit—the family, and its extension, the tribal group.
The problems of Welch's unnamed protagonist are not the result of his Indianness vis-à-vis the white establishment. In *Autumn's Bounty*, *Ceremony*, and *Indians' Summer* (the last in
spite of its symbolic confrontation with the United States government) one can identify a kind of isolationist attitude concerning tribal life today—especially on the reservation—
emphasizing Indian life as a separate reality, apart from the
white man's surrounding domain. Thus, the cycle of Indian
fiction has moved from assimilation, through rejection, to,
most recently, qualified separatism.

In all of these novels Indian consciousness is something
that extends beyond race, toward some much more ethereal
or spiritual construct, far removed from the mundane realities
of the Indian/white confrontation. At base, that consciousness
is expressed in the writers' shared attitudes toward the land
and the rituals that give life its inner meaning, lifting it
beyond the temporal toward some higher, more transcendent
significance.

A timely urgency runs through all of these works, pleading
for the retention of the ancestral lands before they are broken
up, destroyed, further allotted or terminated—before they disappear forever. In the earliest works, the power of the land

emerges through the frequently romanticized attitudes toward the Earth Mother. Pokagon (the character) is immediately struck by the force of the wilds when he returns home from his studies; Oskison's characters are successful only when they respect the land, taking their rightful share without exploiting it; Chal Windzer's journey into the white man's world slowly cuts him off from the earth's magnetic pull. The sacredness of the tribal lands is a major theme of *Winter Count*, *Seven Arrows*, and *Tsali*, each story concentrating on the removal of Native peoples from their traditional locale. In the novels by Momaday, Welch, and Nasnaga, the land again asserts its force—in contrast to the urban ghettos where Indians have been relocated at the price of their contact with the earth. In *Ceremony*, land and ritual merge together in one great chain of being: the cattle, the uranium shaft, the pollen, the Laguna faces duplicated in the Japanese ones. Everything is connected; as in *Seven Arrows*, destruction of a part is felt by the whole. The earth weeps if a single individual ceases to care.

The rituals that permit one to retain an inner harmony with the environment are arduous and complex, particularly in the face of the unending advance of white civilization. The sun dance, the sweat lodge, the ritual hunt, the night chant, the sacred pollen and ash, the tobacco pouch and the pipe, the recitation of exemplary tales and songs (the power manifested in the word)—all of these ceremonies combine to give life its richer meaning, its spiritual and circular wholeness. If there are few dynamic protagonists in these novels, we can always identify those characters who have kept in touch with the earth and the circle of past traditions: Lonidaw, in *Queen of the Woods*; Archilde's mother in *The Surrounded*; Hawk, Night Bear, the Peace Chief, Thunder Bow, Hide on the Wind, and Green Fire Mouse, in *Seven Arrows*; Tsali; Yellow Calf in *Winter in the Blood*; Josiah, in *Ceremony*; even Stemteema in *Cogewea* and Jeff's various shamans in *The Wokosani Road*.

Ultimately, Indian consciousness in these works extends far beyond the arena of Native peoples themselves. The redeeming nature of the Indian world view—its ability to reconcile or absorb opposites and evolve through radical change into a new syncretic vision—potentially embraces the very people long considered its oppressors. Like the persona of Walt

Whitman's *Leaves of Grass*, the narrator of *Seven Arrows* announces at the beginning of his story a similar egalitarianism:

> Come sit with me, and let us smoke the Pipe of Peace in Understanding. Let us Touch. Let us, each to the other, be a Gift as is the Buffalo. Let us be Meat to Nourish each other, that we all may Grow. Sit here with me, each of you as you are in your own Perceiving of yourself, as Mouse, Wolf, Coyote, Weasel, Fox, or Prairie Bird. Let me See through your Eyes. Let us Teach each other here in this Great Lodge of the People, this Sun Dance, of each of the Ways on this Great Medicine Wheel, our Earth. (p. 1)

The end of Storm's novel fulfills this fusion of the red and the white man's visions, represented in such disparate opposites as "the songs, the bibles, the cities, and the dreams" (p. 371). A similar reciprocity or cultural mingling is manifested at the end of Silko's *Ceremony* in Tayo's vision of the universe: a world with no boundaries, where all living things, including the earth itself and all of its different peoples, are connected and made whole by the enrichment of one another's ways. This syncretic world view is also implied in *Winter in the Blood* through Welch's depiction of his narrator as just another American boy who grew up on the land. In Nasnaga's *Indians' Summer*, in spite of its suggestions of separation, the author implies that those whites unhappy with their own way of life will be accepted into the Indian nation. In *The Wokosani Road*, Mockingbird similarly pictures the Kanawan as capable of absorbing white members.

What emerges at this stage in the unfolding of Native American fiction is a vigorous, young literature, in many ways still undergoing the pains of parturition, yet in its wisdom and sense of tradition, years ahead of the culture that has often tried to subdue it. As the works discussed here are only the beginning, a small portion of those that will follow, so this account of the emergence of Native American fiction is only the first of what will soon be other interpretations, both from inside and outside of the circle. The Indian is no longer an opaque shadow, hidden away in the great forest, but a figure now looming on its outer perimeters, singing proudly in his own distinct voice.

APPENDIX 1

Cogewea: The Half-Blood

As in the works of Chief Simon Pokagon, John Oskison, and John Mathews, the theme of assimilation is central to Hum-Ishu-Ma's (Mourning Dove's) Co-Ge-We-A: The Half-Blood (1927), the account of a mixed-blood girl's infatuation with a white man. Outwardly, the story is a romance in the manner of Oskison's Wild Harvest, published two years earlier, yet the triangular love theme also bears a strong resemblance to the black writer Charles W. Chesnutt's The House Behind the Cedars (1900), a novel of "passing." In that work the young heroine, Rena Walden, belatedly discovers that the white man she intends to marry is not worthy of her love, and that she should have married Frank Fowler, the faithful childhood friend of her own race. In Cogewea, the young protagonist not only discovers that Alfred Densmore is out for her money, but also that James LaGrinder, her old mixed-blood friend, is a much more worthy candidate for her hand. Thus the theme of racial identity (and desired assimilation) is central to another work by an early Native American novelist.

From the very beginning, the reader knows that Cogewea should marry faithful Jim (James LaGrinder) and not fall into the trap set by Alfred Densmore. The novelist's concern, as in Wild Harvest, is to construct obstacles which prevent Cogewea from discovering that Jim is her ideal mate. For much of the novel, he is riding the range or involved in cattle roundups (the subtitle of the novel is "A Depiction of the Great Montana Cattle Range"). Cogewea's attraction to Densmore develops when he breaks his arm falling from a bronco—the result of a trick played on him by other cowboys after his arrival at Horseshoe Bend Ranch. Cogewea (whose name means "chipmunk") nurses him back to good health, and Densmore slowly convinces her to marry him.

The racial theme is ubiquitous in Mourning Dove's novel. The first paragraph identifies Cogewea as a mixed blood: "a 'breed'!—the socially ostracized of two races."[1] Shortly thereafter we learn that her mother was a full-blooded Indian; her father, who deserted them, a white man. When her mother died, Cogewea and her two sisters were brought up by their grandmother. As the girl says to one of the ranchhands,

> "We are between two fires, the Red and the White. Our Caucasian brothers criticize us as a shiftless class, while the Indians disown us as abandoning our own race. We are maligned and traduced as no one but we of the despised 'breeds' can know." (p. 41)

Nowhere is this "breed" theme (that is, rejection by both races) more obvious than in a scene that takes place during the Fourth of July celebrations. Dressed in Euro-American clothing, Cogewea enters the "ladies' " horse race. Although she wins the race, the white judge denies her the prize money, calling her a "squaw." When she enters the contest for Indian girls, she is in turn rejected by them. One of them says to her, " 'You have no right to be here! You are half-white! This race is for Indians and not for *breeds!* ' " (p. 66). As she explains later to Densmore,

> "The Indian is a peculiarly mysterious race; differing from all others. . . . We breeds are half and half— American and Caucasion [*sic*]—and in a separate corral. We are despised by both of our relatives. The white people call us 'Injuns' and a 'good-for-nothing' outfit; a 'shiftless', vile class of commonalty. Our Red brothers say that we are 'stuck-up'; that we have deserted our own kind and are imitating the ways of the despoilers of our nationality. . . ." (p. 95)

Cogewea's dilemma is much like Chal Windzer's in *Sundown*; she cannot decide whether she should live as an Indian or as a white. Early in the narrative, she states, " 'If permitted, I would prefer living the white man's way to that of the reservation Indian, but he hampers me' " (p. 41). She prefers the Euro-American lifestyle, but she understands that most whites will reject her. Her entire infatuation with Densmore results from her desire to be white. Jim proposes to her well before Densmore does, but she rejects him because to accept would mean living as an Indian. (By contrast, Jim has no doubts about his identity. As he tells Cogewea's grandmother, " 'I am not proud of my white blood' " [pp. 226–27].)

Much of the story is sentimental and stylized; Alfred Densmore is in every way a stock villain straight out of nineteenth-century melodramas. Ironically, it is Cogewea who hires him to work at her brother-in-law's ranch; and it is this initial error (Densmore knows nothing about cowpunching) that leads to the string of events which nearly result in her death. Almost from the beginning, the narrator supplies the reader with side comments about Densmore's genuine feelings for Cogewea. He is wont to talk aloud to himself, as if he were a character in a drama instead of in a novel: " 'What a fool! I am not really falling in love with that squaw! Ridiculous! What of my club associates? My sisters would never tolerate it, and it would break my mother's heart' " (p. 81). And somewhat later, " 'I like the girl only as any pleasing chattel. As a game, she affords amusement, but hardly a dividend. The wild Brownie will be forgotten when I return to civilization' " (p. 90). Densmore's racial slurs against Cogewea are matched by Mourning Dove's characterizing tags about him: "the crafty Easterner" (p. 133), "the plotter" (p. 161), "the wily schemer" (p. 234), "the arch conspirator" (p. 252).

Though Densmore does not tie Cogewea to the railroad tracks, his final designs are essentially the same: " 'A light marriage ceremony—acquirement of property title—accidental drowning while pleasure boating—fatal shooting accident while hunting—sudden heart failure—or safer still—the divorce court' " (p. 254). Because of a misunderstanding, Densmore has been misled by the other ranchhands into believing that Cogewea is wealthy, the owner of vast amounts of land and cattle. The denouement begins with the crafty villain's attempts to elope with her and steal her money, but all too quickly—even before they are married—he discovers that she is not an heiress. Outraged, he steals the $1,000.00 Cogewea withdrew from her bank account and ties her to a tree, where she is shortly discovered by Jim LaGrinder.

Mourning Dove cannot resist making one final stab at

Densmore and providing a happy ending for her story. In the final chapter of the novel, which takes place two years later, Jim again proposes to Cogewea and is accepted; on the same day, she receives a letter informing her that her father has died in Alaska, leaving an estate worth several million dollars. True to his whiteness, however, the old man had remarried and had " 'made a will bequeathing his three daughters twenty dollars each, and the remainder of his fortune to his widow, a young white woman from New York!' " (p. 282). However, " 'It transpired that owing to a technical flaw in daddy's will, we girls come in for a share in some of his fortune, amounting to a quarter million dollars each' " (p. 284). The novel concludes,

> In a cheap boarding house in an eastern city a few weeks later, a young man with a selfish mouth, suddenly turned pale as he read in a western paper an account of the settling of the great McDonnald mining estate in Alaska, and the marriage of his half-blood daughters. One of them a graduate of Carlisle [Cogewea], to the "Best Rider of the Flathead" [Jim LaGrinder], also a half-blood. The younger daughter known as the "Shy girl", had departed with her husband, Eugene LaFleur, a polished and wealthy Parisian scholar, on a honeymoon tour of Europe. (pp. 284–85)

A number of interesting ironies in this concluding paragraph suggest that the narrative voice within the novel has been split in two. Just as Cogewea cannot decide whether she wants to be Indian or white, so Mourning Dove obfuscates the ending by also trying to have it both ways, preaching one thing while having her characters do another. Cogewea learns her lesson about white men when Alfred slaps her on the face and ties her to a tree, supposedly to die. White people cannot be trusted, Mourning Dove tells us, yet there is apparently nothing wrong with Cogewea and her sisters inheriting their father's tainted money or with one more intermarriage (between Mary, "known as the 'Shy girl' " and Eugene LaFleur). (Mourning Dove may have considered him safe since he was French and not American.)

Further obfuscation within the narrative voice is suggested

by the author's strange blend of the comic and the serious. A number of the comic chapters in the book, describing the high jinks on the range, are oddly juxtaposed with the more serious "protest" sections that classify *Cogewea*, like Pokagon's *Queen of the Woods*, as a kind of "protest romance," though Mourning Dove's novel is the bleaker of the two. The criticisms of the white man's world, so inconsistent with the novel's romantic theme, suggest that the text of the novel may have been altered by an editor. Besides the rather manic-depressive plot, the author's use of language is often artificial; there is a superabundance of clichés, as well as stilted dialogues that are foreign to the characters involved. (Cogewea says to Jim, " 'I was contemplating the possibilities of becoming an authoress, of writing a book' " [p. 33]. Later she tells Densmore about Indian pipes, explaining, " 'Perhaps these were closely contemporaneous with the non-angular variety, showing the funnel-like orifice for both the stem and tobacco' " [p. 120].)

Additional tampering with the text is suggested by Mourning Dove's didacticism, which often includes ethnographic comments about her people. At the end of a fairly lengthy tirade against alcoholic consumption, for example, she concludes,

> This is the heritage of the white man's civilization, forced—like the opium traffic of China—upon a weaker people by the bayonets of commercial conquest. It overshadows all of the good resultant from the "higher" life. (p. 40)

Even when these asides are briefer ("The music, discordant and monotonous to the whites, is all rhythm to the Indian ear" [p. 73]), the result is often a temporary interruption in the narrative flow.

Many of the antiwhite sentiments in the novel are expressed by Stemteema, Cogewea's hundred-year-old grandmother. She represents the voice of reason (the past), and almost all of her stories (interpolated in the text) are woeful tales of Indian exploitation at the hands of white men—usually involving Indian women and white men. In her earliest warning about Densmore, she states,

"My grandchild! you talk too much to that pale face. He does not mean right by you! he is having sport with you. He wants to make a fool of you, that all the young people may laugh. You think he has love because he follows you. Not so! He is blinding you with false words. He is here to cheat you; all that any white man wants of the Indian girl. It is only to put her to shame, then cast her aside for his own kind—the pale faced squaw. Do not be foolish! my Cogewea. Do not bring grief to my old age; do not wound my heart. . . ." (p. 103)

Stemteema tells Cogewea the tragic story of the arrival of the first white men among her people; somewhat later, as a warning against intermarriage, she gives an account of her own sister's marriage to a white man who left her to return pregnant to her people. When Stemteema asks Jim to construct a sweathouse for her ("where she communes with the Great Spirit" [p. 238]), the reader understands that this is her final attempt to prevent Cogewea from running off with Densmore and abandoning her own people.

To be sure, Cogewea is also quite aware of the cruelty inflicted upon her people though the years by the white man:

Cogewea reflected bitterly how her race had had the worst of every deal since the landing of the lordly European on their shores; how they had suffered as much from the pen as from the bayonet of conquest; wherein the annals had always been chronicled by their most deadly foes and partisan writers. (pp. 91–92)

Talking to Densmore about Christianity, Cogewea states, " 'The white man's God has not saved my people from the extermination which came hand in hand with this "spiritual light bursting on a darkened New World" ' " (p. 134). Later, about the government's treatment of Indians, the narrator states,

The Indian Bureau was a blighting curse; its officials, with an army of employees, when not down right thieves conniving with favor-currying politicians and grafters, were, in the main, blundering incompetents, who could not for one day make good in any well regulated and honest business. . . . (p. 140)

There is, thus, a confusing voice apparent throughout much of the novel—in almost all of the passages quoted above—suggesting that *Cogewea* was not only "Given through Sho-Pow-Tan," as the title page indicates, but also edited by Lucullus Virgil McWhorter, whose name also appears there. I can think of no other explanation for the novel's many inconsistencies, its two opposing voices. What else can we make of a passage such as the following?

> The Indian is a strange race. Most of the old people do not make use of English, although the majority of them understand many words and can speak them but will not do so unless absolutely necessary. If alone with the whites, they will talk if occasion demands; but if in the presence of the younger Indians, they can hardly be induced to do so. (p. 118)

I am disturbed by that first sentence: "The Indian is a strange race." Would Mourning Dove decribe her people in that way? How are we to interpret the following passage, which appears near the end of the novel?

> This was not that she was ashamed of the Red race, but since civilization was the only hope for the Indian, it would, she reasoned be better to draw from the more favored and stronger, rather than to fall back to the unfortunate class so dependent on their conquerors for their very existence. (p. 274)

To whom may we attribute the statement "civilization was the only hope for the Indian"? To Julia (Cogewea's sister, who is referred to in the sentence)? To Cogewea? To Mourning Dove? Or to someone else? It is impossible to tell.

Mourning Dove (an Okanogan Indian) had sufficient education to write *Cogewea*. The introduction to the book, by Lucullus V. McWhorter, explains that, unlike her heroine, who was half white, Mourning Dove had only a "tinge of Caucasian blood . . ." (p. 12). She was born near Bonner's Ferry, in Idaho, about 1888 and attended Sacred Heart Convent for a year when she was seven and then for another year when she was twelve. From her seventeenth to her twenty-first years, she attended government schools and, somewhat later, during "the winter of 1912–13 . . . enrolled in a Calgary, British Columbia, business college" (p. 12). Earlier, in 1908, "she witnessed the last grand roundup of buffaloes on the Flathead Indian Reservation, Montana" (p. 11), which later became the setting for her novel.

Cogewea is the only early novel written by an American Indian who was a female, a work of fiction that is as much a hybrid as its main character. It is regrettable for the student of Indian fiction that Mourning Dove relied on others for help in writing the book, since it is impossible to determine the extent of the editor's coloring of her story with his own interpretations and judgments.[2] Although the novel might have been less polished if she had written it herself, the author's stance toward her Indian subject (and toward white culture) might not have been so ambivalent.

APPENDIX 2

The Wokosani Road

The Pan-Indian theme is of central importance to Jon Mockingbird's *The Wokosani Road* (1962), though the issue is often submerged in the author's wild and fantastic narrative. The story records a middle-aged Indian's attempt to make contact with and gain membership in " 'one of the most secret outfits in the world' "[1]—the Kanawan, an ancient brotherhood of Native peoples composed of men from differing tribal groups. In the course of establishing contact with and becoming accepted for initiation into the Kanawan, Jeff Hanson (a half-blood Apache) undergoes a series of difficult tests that symbolically prepare his body and mind for the higher life represented by the cult. Always there is a sense of the past, of age-old traditions of tribal life that continue in the present, sustaining it, giving it a sense of fulfillment and balance.

The novel begins during World War II when Jeff Hanson, a communications expert in the Navy on the S.S. *Cape Fear*, is temporarily stationed on an island called Tarawa, one of the Gilbert Islands in the South Pacific. After a day of heavy fighting, Jeff meets Cahuro Joligo (alias Joe Brown), an Indian from another ship. Cahuro has been severely wounded but refuses medical attention. The two them spend the afternoon drinking Four Roses, during which time Cahuro, who appears to have a sense of his imminent death, tells Jeff about the Kanawan:

"Up till about four hundred years ago we were a people made up of many tribes. We lived in and controlled most of the country from the Mississippi to the Rio Grande. From these people the Kanawan got its members, and that is mostly true today. We have many meeting places, but the main one is in the south, at the great medicine spring itself, where every member of the clan must go at least once in his lifetime." (p. 26).

181

Cahuro makes Jeff a Dog Soldier in the society and then leaves the ship to return to the battlefront. The next day Jeff learns that Cahuro has died in the fighting.

From his singular encounter with Cahuro Joligo, Jeff Hanson vows to become a fully recognized member of the Kanawan. He has, in fact, been "hooked" on the organization, as Mockingbird has obviously hoped his reader will be on his story. Although there are nearly a hundred additional pages discussing Jeff's subsequent activities in World War II, a sense of suspense has already been established by the secrecy and intrigue surrounding the brotherhood itself, hints of a vast hidden fortune owned by the cult, the existence of a fountain of youth (Cahuro looks about thirty years old but tells Jeff that " 'Twice that would be a lot nearer' " [p. 25]).

All of the opening section of the novel is set in the South Pacific during Jeff's war days. In contrast to the other works treated in this study, *The Wokosani Road* begins on foreign territory. A thin connection exists with Momaday's *House Made of Dawn*, though there is a more obvious link between Mockingbird's novel and Leslie Silko's *Ceremony*, in which the World War II arena is also the Pacific. Episodes from the war influence Jeff's subsequent activities and thinking. A Japanese prisoner named Tomo, for example, foreshadows Jeff's later suicide when he explains the Oriental concept of honorable death:

> "Japanese fight to death for many reasons. One is that they really believe, as Americans don't really, that there is a Heaven waiting where brave and faithful will be honored and made happy. To go Heaven now is certain for them. If they surrender, they can never be received as worthy of anything but to be cast out. In life, cast out; in death, cast out. Is it not better to die than to surrender, if you believe like that?" (p. 98)

Only much later is Jeff able to draw a connection between the two concepts: "These men of the Kanawan believed in that strange way that the Japs believed—those Japs that Jeff had seen help their enemies to kill them rather than do anything that would compromise them in the eyes of their gods . . ." (p. 328).

After the war, Jeff retires from his years in the Navy, returns to the United States, and marries a white woman named Doris. In 1951, they settle in Oklahoma, near the Red River Valley, and Jeff begins his search for the sacred Medicine Spring Cahuro Joligo had described ("He reasoned that once he had found the Medicine Spring, getting in touch with the Kanawan people would be simple" [p. 117]). In time, he locates what he believes is the spring, buys land adjacent to it, and begins farming. Shortly thereafter, he notices mysterious figures coming to the spring, especially during the night and the early morning. One of these persons turns out to be Joligo's son, who looks exactly like his father. In spite of his advanced age, Jeff is accepted by the order as a novitiate.

Much of the remainder of the novel is an account of the elaborate rites and rituals that Jeff Hanson must undergo before he is accepted into the Kanawan. He is sworn to secrecy about the organization itself (" 'No one should ever mention anything about our church or tribal affairs to anyone who is not known to be a fellow member' " [p. 332]); he learns the function of the "double salute"; the eschatology of their beliefs (" 'Tirawa is the Supreme Creator of Laws by which the whole of everything operates, exists, or ever shall exist' " [p. 340]); and in time comes to regard the Kanawan as a form of freemasonry, permitting adherence to other doctrines and faiths.

Jeff's most difficult ordeal is not with his mind but with his body: stomach ulcers, high blood pressure, a cancerous prostate gland, clogged sinuses, a fungus infection on his hand. He is a storehouse of diseases, which the Kanawan medicine men must cure before he will be permitted to undertake the physical test (swimming the Great Buffalo Water during the spring floodtime) that culminates one's initiation into the brotherhood. The cure for many of these ailments is undertaken by Yellowwolf, a Kanawan shaman, with the aid of a drink known as wokosani (composed partly of water from the Medicine Spring). Jeff never learns exactly what the secret ingredient in wokosani is because he does not complete his initiation, but he does know that the drink has significant medicinal powers and that it " 'is a tranquilizer to a considerable extent' " (p. 207). During a conversation about wokosani, Redwolf tells him it is "Tirawa's Gift":

"Without it you wouldn't have much. With it you have
one of the nicer things that Tirawa has given His children. After you emerge on the other shore, knowledge
like what this liquid is, where it comes from, and its uses
will be some of the secrets you will keep and guard for all
time. As a medicine man grows he receives more and
more of such secrets. Finally, like a seer of the Rosicru-
cians, he receives the Great Knowledge itself, and is or-
dained a shaman." (p. 206)

Elaborate discussions about medicine in *The Wokosani Road*
suggest that the author of the book may be a doctor, a layman
interested in medicine, or perhaps even an Indian medicine
man himself. Mockingbird makes it apparent that Jeff Hanson
is cured of his various ills not by the white man's scientific
knowledge but by Indian medicine. (By contrast, Jeff's white
doctor dies of cancer of the throat, while Jeff's own cancer of
the prostate gland is cured by Yellowwolf.) Lengthy conversations highlight the curative powers of traditional Indian folk
medicine, its ability to counteract curses and witchcraft. All of
the Indians of the Kanawan look about half their actual
ages—the result, we are told, of drinking wokosani and water
from the Medicine Spring.

Jeff's plans for completing his initiation as well as his desires
to become a medicine man are thwarted by one of his
neighbors, Arvil Pisstubby, identified as "a rather large, flabby
half-breed of Choctaw lineage" (p. 126) and "an unredeemable
moonshiner" (p. 126). Pissto (as he is called) has for many
years tried unsuccessfully to become a member of the Kanawan and has been tolerated by the brotherhood since they
have considered him harmless. However, Pissto becomes jealous of Jeff, poisons his cattle and other farm animals, and
generally makes the latter's life miserable. When his activities
become increasingly violent, the brotherhood decides to dispose of him ritualistically, but the plan backfires. Pissto is shot
by one of the brotherhood, and his body is discovered by his
family before it can be disposed of. Jeff is brought to trial for
murdering the man and found guilty by the jury.

The events concerning Arvil Pisstubby's murder are important because they generate Jeff's final moral dilemma. The
problem, as Jeff's legal counsel and fellow brother informs

him, is that " 'it would be awfully hard to defend a case like this without much about the Kanawan becoming public knowledge or conjecture' " (p. 311). Thereafter, the novel rapidly disintegrates into a number of clichés ("One played one's cards as Tirawa dealt them . . ." [p. 311]), designed to support Jeff's final action. After he loses his trial, Jeff chooses to commit suicide rather than go through a retrial, which, he is certain, would expose the Kanawan to the public.

The suicide and the subsequent events bring about a number of startling surprises, even though they are faithful to Mockingbird's Indian theme. Jeff tells Redwolf that he would " 'prefer to go the the HHG [Happy Hunting Ground] a little early, rather than go to prison' " (p. 339). When he asks Redwolf if suicide will eliminate his chances for entering the HHG, his friend replies, " 'That would be entirely up to you. . . . If you think it the correct thing to do, then it would not grate on your conscience, so it wouldn't mar your heaven in any way' " (p. 339). Tirawa permits the individual to do whatever he wants. (As the younger Cahuro later tells him, " 'If one Truly Believes and has the right mental attitude, just about anything is possible' " [p. 369].)

In a ludicrous scene, Jeff shoots his horse, dog, and cat; then he calls the mortuary and the sheriff. After the latter arrives, Jeff lies down on the stretcher and shoots himself. Yet there is more to the end of the novel than this. Although it is related in the third person, the entire story has been told through Jeff's consciousness and continues now to describe a number of incidents (witnessed by Jeff) *after* his death. Kutnahin (Tirawa's messenger) guides him to the HHG, where he rejoins his domestic animals. Jeff watches Doris return to the courthouse and throw the jar containing his ashes at the corrupt judge who presided over his trial. Later, a very old medicine man

> reported that he had seen Kutnahin in full regalia emerge from the dome of the courthouse, a most unusual place, and carry into the West the form of a white squaw [that is, Doris]. . . . He remembered very well because this was the first time he had ever seen Kutnahin conduct anyone other than an Indian who Truly Believed. (pp. 377–78)

In this brief epilogue, the judge gets his comeuppance and reluctantly begins treating minority people more fairly.

This description of *The Wokosani Road* excludes a number of the novel's most engaging attributes. For example, the author has made extensive use of visions and hallucinations within the context of the narrative, anticipating the subsequent works by Carlos Castaneda. In the first of these, while Jeff is still in the South Pacific, he has a vision of his father's death—an Indian riding a horse and a voice which seems to say to him, " 'The Indian of Death [is] taking your daddy in to the West' " (p. 74). At the funeral of another Indian GI, Jeff has his first vision of Kutnahin taking an Indian to the HHG: " 'Kutnahin takes to the Happy Hunting Ground all Indian dead who Truly Believe' " (p. 87).

Two hallucinatory sequences are important evidence of Jeff's own spiritual maturity. The first of these takes place during a religious service he attends with his Kanawan brothers:

> a man's head began to rise up out of the fire. It was the head of that other Cahuro Joligo, dressed in a war bonnet of eagle feathers. It rose slowly until there, standing above the fire, was the figure of the man of Tarawa.[2] Now Jeff could see quite plainly the arrow protruding from the right shoulder, and he knew that it was Kutnahin himself who was standing there. Kutnahin stepped from the smoke above the Fireplace and stood before the Moon. He looked around and smiled as naturally as a newly arrived friend might have smiled. (p. 238)

The vision of the HHG continues as Jeff sees a number of "animal friends of the long-ago" (p. 240) as well as his deceased father. A further hallucinatory episode of the HHG occurs shortly before Jeff takes his own life; this time he feels as if he is moving through time and space at a fantastic speed, returning to a scene from his youth.

What is particularly interesting about these vision sequences as well as the other passages that concern Native religion is the syncretic world depicted therein, such as we have already seen in Storm's *Seven Arrows* or can be found in the religious activities of the Native American Church.[3] Members of the Kanawan are expected to be members of other organized religions: Methodists, Presbyterians, and so on. During the religious ceremony when Jeff has his first lengthy vision, he is aware of the mixing of Indian and Western (especially Christian) customs: traditional Indian dancing and music, for example, blended with Handel's *Messiah*, "The Twelfth Street Rag," and "By the Waters of Minnetonka"; short prayers, talks by various people, and periods of dancing (p. 230), plus the consumption of wokosani.

Equally important is the author's attitude toward his white characters, since it suggests a further blending of cultural beliefs and practices. Jeff is more than surprised when he sees the Indian of Death guiding his father to the HHG. He is further pleased that Doris, his Caucasian wife, is accepted by members of the cult. The final scene, where Kutnahin unites Doris with her husband, implies a kind of salvation or spiritual redemption for whites within the framework of traditional Indian beliefs. Since Jeff has already noted a strong affinity between Oriental religions and his own, there is the added suggestion of an international brotherhood, embracing the enlightened peoples of disparate races and creeds.[4] In this sense, *The Wokosani Road* is one of the most optimistic novels about the relations between Indians and whites considered in this study—an attitude it shares with other, more recent works by American Indians, where protest is not usually the author's first concern.

A similar syncretic belief is implied in the Kanawan cult itself. Jeff worries about how he will communicate with Indians of other tribes once he arrives at the HHG:

> "What about language up there in the HHG? Will we be able to talk to such people as Cochise or Pontiac if we ever got to visit them? Reckon they'll speak some common language, or will we have to talk through an interpreter, or what?"
>
> "Whatever you think will be, will be," said Cahuro a little oracularly.
>
> "That would make it more of a dream world than a real one, wouldn't it?"
>
> "There's nothing on this earth or in the universe except Tirawa's thoughts. Things are what they appear to you only because you join in Tirawa's thoughts and think them real." (pp. 353–54)

This Pan-Indian theme of cultural unity has been expressed in a number of earlier passages in the novel, including a reference to the origins of the Kanawan society several hundred years ago: "The Kanawan had members in every tribe, and in some tribes just about every man was a Soldier" (p. 339). The Kanwan is, if fact, a brotherhood founded upon the highest moral principles, uniting the most enlightened Native peoples of the land.

Whatever possessed Jon Mockingbird (whoever he is) to write such a curious novel? Only a few clues in the book help answer this question. In the prologue, the author identifies himself as half Apache (his father was white, his mother an Indian). Talking about himself in the third person, Mockingbird says that as a child he liked to read and tell stories, especially Indian legends, and since his father's death, "Jon has 'gone white' and has woven into novels and allegories as much of the legends, the traditions, the religion of the Indians of the Lower Mississippi and of the Southwest as he can remember and adapt" (p. 13). The biographical account of the author on the jacket of the book states that Mockingbird "bases this book largely on his own experiences . . . it is 'forty per cent autobiography, forty per cent Indian legends and twenty per cent romance.' He did himself stand trial for a murder on a trumped-up charge, but unlike Jeff Hanson, he was acquitted." The jacket copy concludes, quoting the author, " '. . . having an Indian in my immediate background, I went out and put in some ten years studying legends and digging for information which I finally got "corralled" into this book.' "

That last statement is the most revealing, suggesting that Mockingbird does not think of himself as an Indian. I have been unable either to substantiate or to disprove the existence of anyone by the name of Jon Mockingbird.[5] For reasons best known to himself, the author apparently chose a pseudonym. Probably he is part Indian—enough to be interested in researching his past and writing about it. The reasons for publishing his novel with a vanity press are also difficult to assess. *The Wokosani Road* is a considerably better novel than most books published at the author's own expense. The style is impressive; the story is well plotted and, if not always credible, at least entertaining. The major weaknesses are the author's frequent gosh-oh-golly tone and the rather heavy-handed treatment of some of his own biases. There are too many passages such as the following one:

> "We make slaves all right, but those slaves are our own people. . . . It is called tax slavery. Our own country makes us American slaves work one day out of each three to pay our taxes. We can have what we make the other two days. Nice, no? The country then often uses the money we make on that one day, to go around the world making other people free and happy. Many peoples to whom we give money pay less taxes than do our own people. It is great good luck, Tomo, to lose a war to us." (p. 101)

Despite the novel's flaws, the author's enthusiasm for his subject matter is difficult to criticize. There is enough material for ten novels here, yet much of the fascination with Mockingbird's novel lies in the author's naïveté about fictional matters. Simply put, the novel is refreshing because the author never tries to put anyone on, never tries to impress anyone. Rather, *The Wokosani Road* appears to have been written spontaneously, without awareness of or interest in the several-hundred-year tradition of Western fiction.

Notes

Chapter 1   The Emergence of American Indian Fiction

1. Charles R. Larson, "*Seven Arrows*: Saga of the American Indian," *Books Abroad* 47 (1973): 88–92.

2. Letter from D'Arcy McNickle, October 6, 1975.

3. John M. Oskison, *Brothers Three* (New York: Macmillan Co., 1935). (From the book jacket.)

4. Though Dunbar (1872–1906) published four novels between 1898 and 1901, only one has identifiable black characters. Chesnutt (1858–1932) published three novels between 1900 and 1905—the first, *The House Behind the Cedars* (1900) a novel of "passing." At the beginning of their writing careers, both authors tried to conceal their racial origins.

5. Hum-Ishu-Ma, Co-Ge-We-A, *The Half-Blood* (Boston: Four Seas Co., 1927).

6. Harvey Chalmers, *West to the Setting Sun* (Toronto: Macmillan Co., 1943), p. vi.

7. Ted C. Williams, *The Reservation* (Syracuse, N.Y.: Syracuse University Press, 1976), p. vii.

8. Chief Simon Pokagon, *Queen of the Woods* (Hartford, Mich.: C. H. Engle, 1899), p. 35.

9. Harold E Diver, *Indians of North America* (Chicago: University of Chicago Press, 1969), p. 528.

10. Shirley Hill Witt, "Nationalistic Trends Among American Indians," in Stuart Levine and Nancy O. Lurie, eds., *The American Indian Today* (Baltimore: Penguin Books, 1968), p. 122.

11. Richard Wright, "How 'Bigger' Was Born," in *Richard Wright's Native Son: A Critical Handbook*, ed. Richard Abcarian (Belmont, Calif.: Wadsworth Publishing Co., 1970), p. 30.

12. Ibid.

13. Pokagon, *Queen of the Woods*, unnumbered page.

14. Ibid., p. 1.

15. Letter from John J. Mathews, June 22, 1976.

16. Denton R. Bedford, *Tsali* (San Francisco: Indian Historian Press, 1972), p. viii.

17. Hyemeyohsts Storm, *Seven Arrows* (New York: Harper & Row, 1972), p. 10.

18. "Northern Cheyenne Discuss 'Seven Arrows' Book; Criticism Is Expressed," *Wassaja* 2 (April/May 1974): 12.

19. *The Novel in the Third World* (Washington, D.C.: Inscape Corp., 1976), pp. 67–87.

20. Marshall Sprague, Review of *House Made of Dawn*, *New York Times Book Review*, June 9, 1968, p. 5.

191

Chapter 2   The Children of Pocahontas

1. "Introduction," in *The Capture and Release of Captain John Smith* (Ann Arbor, Mich.: Clements Library Association, 1960), p. 7.

2. Philip Young, "The Mother of Us All: Pocahontas Revisited," *The Kenyon Review* 14 (1962): 412.

3. Ingri d'Aulaire and Edgar Parin D'Aulaire, *Pocahontas* (New York: Doubleday & Co., 1946), p. 11.

4. Ibid.

5. Ibid., p. 45.

6. Marie Lawson, *Pocahontas and Captain John Smith: The Story of the Virginia Colony* (New York: Random House, 1950), p. 145.

7. Leslie A. Fiedler, *The Return of the Vanishing American* (New York: Stein and Day, 1968), p. 70.

8. Authorities differ on Pocahontas's age when she rescued Smith, usually agreeing, however, that she was between ten and fourteen. Since puberty was at approximately thirteen, my own guess is that she was no older than twelve, and possibly as young as ten. Had she been past puberty, her attire would have been different from what was described by witnesses who saw her.

9. This fact is first mentioned by William Strachey in *The Historie of Travel into Virginia Britania* (1612) and ignored by many of Pocahontas's acolytes. (Not, however, by her most serious biographers such as Philip Barbour or Frances Mossiker.)

10. Young, "The Mother of Us All." p. 413.

11. *The Capture and Release of Captain John Smith*, p. 18.

12. This question has been asked by innumerable critics. See, for example, Bradford Smith, *Captain John Smith: His Life and Legend* (Philadelphia: J. B. Lippincott Co., 1953), p. 106.

13. Frances Mossiker, *Pocahontas: The Life and the Legend* (New York: Alfred A. Knopf, 1976), p. 274.

14. Philip L. Barbour, *Pocahontas and Her World* (Boston: Houghton Mifflin Co., 1970), p. 127. See also Bradford Smith, Frances Mossiker, and John Gould Fletcher.

15. Grace Steele Woodward, *Pocahontas* (Norman: University of Oklahoma Press, 1969), p. 169.

16. Barbour, *Pocahontas and Her World*, p. 32.

17. David Garnett, *Pocahontas or the Nonparell of Virginia* (1933; New York: Doubleday & Co., Anchor Books, 1958), p. 203.

18. Ibid., p. 224.

19. Ibid., p. 226.

20. Mossiker, *Pocahontas*, p. 244.

21. Ibid., p. 275.

22. Noel B. Gerson, *First Lady of America* (Richmond, Va.: Westover Publishing Co., 1973).

23. Noel B. Gerson, *Daughter of Eve* (New York: Doubleday & Co., 1958).

24. Barbour, *Pocahontas and Her World*, p. 1.

25. John E. Cooke, *My Lady Pocahontas, A True Relation of Virginia* (Boston: Houghton Mifflin Co., 1879), p. 54.

26. Mossiker, *Pocahontas*, p. 226.

27. Garnett, *Pocahontas*.

28. Cooke, *My Lady Pocahontas*, p. 131.

29. Young, "The Mother of Us All."

30. Mossiker, *Pocahontas*, p. 321.

31. William Strachey, Ralph Hamor, Ben Johnson, Samuel Purchas, Robert Chamberlain, Robert Beverley.

32. At the height of her popularity, Pocahontas became a kind of cult figure, responsible for a rash of "Indian" dramas. According to Frances Mossiker, "at least forty plays [were] written (if not all produced) between the years 1830–1850—a last-minute rush to glorify the Noble Savage on the stage ere he was exterminated on the Plains" (*Pocahontas*, p. 325).

33. See especially John Barth, *The Sot-Weed Factor* (New York: Doubleday & Co., 1960).

34. Garnett, *Pocahontas*, p. 248.

35. A similar attitude toward the Indian has existed down through the years, especially during the period when government policy favored allotment. If Indians could be made into landowners (farmers), there would be no Indian problem.

36. Albert Keiser, *The Indian in American Literature* (1933; rpt. New York: Farrar, Straus and Giroux, 1975), p. 10.

37. I am referring here to the cannibalism which was recorded at the Jamestown settlement two years later, during the Starving Time (the winter of 1609–10).

38. Mossiker, *Pocahontas*, p. 264.

39. Woodward, *Pocahontas*, p. 55.

40. Bradford Smith, *Captain John Smith*, p. 116.

41. Ibid., p. 117; John Gould Fletcher, *John Smith—Also Pocahontas* (New York: Brentano's, 1928), p. 114; and elsewhere.

42. Fletcher, *John Smith*, p. 262.

43. Ibid., p. 263.

44. Young, "The Mother of Us All," p. 394.

45. Woodward, *Pocahontas*, p. 8.

46. Ibid., p. 191.

47. Mossiker, *Pocahontas*, p. 316.

48. Barbour, *Pocahontas and Her World*, p. 214.

49. Ibid.

50. Mossiker, *Pocahontas*, p. 177.

51. Roy Harvey Pearce, *Savagism and Civilization* (Baltimore: Johns Hopkins University Press, 1965), p. 49.

52. Keiser, *The Indian in American Literature*, p. 299.

Chapter 3   Assimilation: Estrangement from the Land

1. Chief Simon Pokagon, *Queen of the Woods* (Hartford, Mich.: C. H. Engle, 1899), p. 7. Subsequent page references will appear in the text.

2. See Cecila B. Buechner, *The Pokagons*, Indiana Historical Society Publications, vol. 10, no. 5 (Indianapolis, 1933), pp. 316–28.

3. Talented Tenth: "A term coined by W. E. B. DuBois . . . and used synonymously with 'Negro middle class.' " (Robert A. Bone, *The Negro Novel in America* [New Haven: Yale University Press, 1965], p. 13.)

4. John M. Oskison, *Wild Harvest* (New York: D. Appleton and Co., 1925), p. 16. Subsequent page references will appear in the text.

5. Allotment (the parceling out of land for each Indian) was designed to hasten the Indian's assimilation into the white man's world. If he could be made to work the land (that is, to farm a specific plot of land) his nomadic days would come to an end, and he would become self-supporting. The major problem with allotment was that,

traditionally, Native Americans regarded the land communally—not individually. As Oliver La Farge wrote in *As Long as the Grass Shall Grow* (1940):

If ownership in common were broken up . . . if each Indian owned a plot of his own, and freedom for wandering, visiting, hunting, were ended, the backbone of their resistance would be broken. The pride and responsibility of individual property would soon make them competitive, thrifty, individualistic. . . .

So, with no opposition at all from those who wished to get as much as possible of the remaining reservations for their own use, the famous Allotment Act [Dawes Act] was passed in 1887. . . .

Each member of the tribe then received an allotment of land, the sizes varying. . . . Since all history had shown that the Indians were bound to become extinct, and they were in fact dying off fairly rapidly, there was no need to make any allowance for a larger population in the future. Therefore, when the allotment [of a reservation] was finished, all remaining land was declared "surplus," bought cheap, and thrown open to white settlement. (p. 26)

6. John M. Oskison, *Black Jack Davy* (New York: D. Appleton and Co., 1926), p. 259. Subsequent page references will appear in the text.

7. John M. Oskison, *Brothers Three* (New York: Macmillan Co., 1935), p. 71. Subsequent page references will appear in the text.

8. John J. Mathews, *Wah'Kon-Tah* (Norman: University of Oklahoma Press, 1932), p. 332.

9. John J. Mathews, *Sundown* (New York: Longmans, Green and Co., 1934), p. 22. Subsequent page references will appear in the text.

10. In Mathews's historical account of his people, *The Osages* (Norman: University of Oklahoma Press, 1961), he notes that as early as the turn of the century, the Osages were referred to as "the wealthiest people per capita on earth" (p. 731). Oil royalties to the tribe reached a peak of $13,000 per capita in 1925, but had fallen to $712 in 1933" (p. 775).

11. Joseph Epes Brown, *The Spiritual Legacy of the American Indian* (Wallingford, Penn.: Pendle Hill Publications, 1964), p. 22.

12. Buechner, *The Pokagons*, p. 328.

13. Ibid.

14. See "When the Grass Grew Long," *The Century Magazine* 62 (1901):247–50. Another story is described in Oskison's *New York Times* obituary (Feb. 27, 1947, p. 21) as follows: " 'The Greater Appeal' told of a man who could not resist the 'call of the wild' and returned from civilization to an aboriginal existence." I have been unable to locate a copy of this story.

15. Margaret Szasz, *Education and the American Indian* (Albuquerque: University of New Mexico Press, 1974), p. 10.

16. Ibid., p. 8.

Chapter 4   Rejection: The Reluctant Return

1. D'Arcy McNickle, *The Surrounded* (1936; Albuquerque: University of New Mexico Press, 1978), p. 1. Subsequent page references will appear in the text.

2. N. Scott Momaday, *House Made of Dawn* (1968; New York: New American Library, Signet Books, 1969), p. 13. Subsequent page references will appear in the text.

3. This theme of outside meddling or intervention is not entirely new here. In James Fenimore Cooper's *The Prairie* (1827), Ishmael Bush, an embittered

backwoodsman, similarly regards himself as exempt from society's regulations. (Bush, however, does not simply ignore the game laws; he has no reverence for man or nature and his crimes are ultimately the pillage of both.)

Note also the similarity between Archilde's comments on Indian hunting rights in this scene and more recent arguments by Northwest Indian tribes to try to alter court decisions that have restricted their fishing rights. In the mid 1960s, hundreds of Indians participated in fish-ins to try to change these restrictions. The arguments were essentially the same as Archilde's: the white man's laws have altered the Indian's sacred relationship with his environment. (See Stan Steiner, *The New Indians* [New York: Harper & Row, 1968].)

4. The careers of McNickle and La Farge overlapped considerably. Both were trained anthropologists, pursuing the American Indian in their field work and "fictionalizing" their findings in their creative writings. La Farge reviewed *The Surrounded* for *The Saturday Review*, praising the novel and stressing the need for indigenous writing:

> . . . a number of white men have seen that the American Indian was a natural for them, [writing novels] mainly concentrating their interest on the most picturesque, least complex situations of the "blanket Indians" in the Southwest, or turning their faces toward the past. The real job must be done, one has felt, by men of Indian blood who partook of the life they described as most good sectional writers do.

It was clearly out of respect for him that McNickle wrote a biography of La Farge: *Indian Man: A Life of Oliver La Farge* (Bloomington: Indiana University Press, 1971).

5. McNickle published one other fictional work, *Runner in the Sun* (1954), a novel for adolescents included in the Holt, Rinehart and Winston "Land of the Free" series. The story focuses on a sixteen-year-old boy named Salt, who helps restore stability within his village when the Spider Clan tries to control the six other clans. A subplot involves Salt's journey to the South (to the Aztec civilization in Mexico) in search of a new variety of corn that will grow better in the lands of his people. Much of the story is spent creating a sense of intrigue and making certain that the forces of good win over evil. The most interesting aspect of the novel is that it takes place before the arrival of the white man, thus making it the only work of fiction by a Native American not concerned with some aspect of the white man–Indian conflict.

6. Momaday is obviously using the term in an ironic sense, since the word is usually applied to Indians who have had little or no exposure to the white man's world. In their book, *The Navaho* (rev. ed.; New York: Doubleday & Co., Anchor Books, 1962), Clyde Kluckhohn and Dorothea Leighton cite the term in an overheard conversation:

> They overhear remarks by those same groups of whites who had goaded them to give up "those ignorant Indian ways": "You can never trust these school boys." "Give me a 'long hair' every time. They may be dumb but they are honest and they work hard." "Educated Indians are neither fish nor fowl. They give me the creeps." (p. 170)

Abel is educated about the white man's world, but he still acts like a longhair.

7. Carole Oleson, "The Remembered Earth: Momaday's *House Made of Dawn*," *South Dakota Review* 11 (1973):72–73.

8. In addition to these family names (Tosamah and his grandmother, Aho), Momaday has based a number of the other characters and events upon the people he knew or incidents he witnessed as a child. Thus, Francisco Tosa, a shepherd at Jemez Pueblo, is the source for Abel's grandfather; the chicken pull and the Pecos bull run, described in more detail in *The Names*, are rituals Momaday observed as a youth.

9. In his provocative article, "Incarnate Grace and the Paths of Salvation in *House Made of Dawn*" (*South Dakota Review* 12 [1974-75]:115-25) Harold S. McAllister makes an interesting case for Angela as "a model of salvation," noting a number of relationships between her and the Virgin Mary. McAllister suggests that Momaday's novel "may be a Christian morality play; its subject is spiritual redemption in a squalid, hellish temporal world."

10. For additional commentary on the significance of the chicken pull, see *The Names* (New York: Harper & Row, 1976), pp. 144-45.

11. Jeanette Henry, "Momaday's Novel Wins Pulitzer Award," *The Indian Historian* 2(1969):38.

12. Lawrence J. Evers, in his article "Words and Place: A Reading of *House Made of Dawn*," *Western American Literature* 11 (1977):297-320, posits an equally fascinating interpretation: "The White Man Abel kills is, in fact, a white Indian, an albino. He is the White Man in the Indian; perhaps even the White Man in Abel himself" (p. 309).

From Harold S. McAllister I have further learned that there is considerable resentment against Momaday for basing his albino upon an actual Jemez Indian.

13. Martha Scott Trimble, *N. Scott Momaday* (Boise, Idaho: Boise State College Western Writers Series, 1973), p. 23.

14. Marian Willard Hylton, "On a Trail of Pollen: Momaday's *House Made of Dawn*," *Critique* 14 (1972): 68.

15. Ibid., p. 69.

16. Trimble, *Momaday*, p. 20.

17. Oleson, The Remembered Earth," pp. 77-78.

18. McAllister, "Incarnate Grace," p. 117.

19. Ibid., p. 125.

20. There is a possibility that Momaday intends us to interpret Abel's running at the story's end as a kid of parody of the rites of passage, an ironic initiation into death instead of adulthood. This is hinted at by the ashes rubbed on his arms and chest, and also by the placement of Francisco's death immediately before Abel's. (Francisco comes of age by killing a bear—an event that makes him a man. Abel takes part in no such experience.)

21. N. Scott Momaday, Note to "Three Sketches from *House Made of Dawn*," *Southern Review* 2 (1966):933.

22. Trimble, *Momday*, p. 5.

23. *The Names* (New York: Harper & Row, 1976), p. 167.

24. Alberto Moravia, *Which Tribe Do You Belong To?* (New York: Farrar, Straus and Giroux, 1974), p. 64.

Chapter 5   History of the People

1. Hyemeyohsts Storm, *Seven Arrows* (New York: Harper & Row, 1972), p. 243 (I). Conversations that are conducted in sign language are indicated by italics. Rather than place them in italics here, they are indicated by an "I" after the page number. Subsequent page references will appear in the text.

2. Denton R. Bedford, *Tsali* (San Francisco: Indian Historian Press, 1972), p. 253. Subsequent page references will appear in the text.

3. Dallas Chief Eagle, *Winter Count* (Colorado Springs: Denton-Berkeland Printing Co., 1967), p. 1. Subsequent page references will appear in the text.

4. As noted in the introduction, Chief Eagle's book was accepted by a New York

publisher on the provision that the scene involving Custer's suicide be changed to the usual (white) interpretation.

Chief Eagle is not the only writer to suggest that Custer's death was a suicide. A similar thesis was formulated by Thomas B. Marquis (1869–1935), in the 1930s. Marquis's conclusion—that many of Custer's men panicked and committed suicide—was so unpopular that he was unable to find a publisher for his book during his lifetime, despite the fact that he had written widely on American Indians. The manuscript remained unpublished until 1976 (*Keep the Last Bullet for Yourself: The True Story of Custer's Last Stand* [New York: Two Continents Publishing Group]).

5. Dee Brown, *Bury My Heart at Wounded Knee* (New York: Holt, Rinehart and Winston, 1970), p. 296.

6. See, for example, Douglas C. Jones's *The Court-Martial of George Armstrong Custer* (1976) which, for reasons best left to the author's own fancy, brings Custer back alive from the massacre and places him on trial for his crimes.

7. Charles Eastman, in *The Soul of an Indian* (1911; Rapid City, S.D.: Fenwyn Press Books, 1970), describes this evolution of the Sun Dance as the result of exposure to the white man: "It is noteworthy that the first effect of the contact with the whites was an increase of cruelty and barbarity, an intensifying of the dark shadows in the picture! In this manner the 'Sun Dance' of the Plains Indians, the most important of their public ceremonials, was abused and perverted until it became a horrible exhibition of barbarism, and was eventually prohibited by the Government" (pp. 55–56).

8. Brad Steiger, *Medicine Talk* (New York: Doubleday & Co., 1975), p. 114.

9. Ibid., p. 111.

10. Ibid.

11. Ibid., p. 116.

12. Ibid., p. 119.

13. Ibid., p. 110.

14. Ibid.

15. Arlene B. Hirschfelder, *American Indian and Eskimo Authors* (New York: Association on American Indian Affairs, 1973), p. 18.

16. Steiger, *Medicine Talk*, p. 117.

17. Chief Standing Bear, *Land of the Spotted Eagle* (Boston: Houghton Mifflin Co., 1933), pp. 165–66.

18. Steiger, *Medicine Talk*, p. 133.

19. Chief Standing Bear, *Land of the Spotted Eagle*, p. xix.

20. Ibid., p. 27.

21. John G. Neihardt, *Black Elk Speaks* (1932; New York: Pocket Books, 1972), pp. 164–65.

22. Eastman, *Soul of an Indian*, p. 9.

23. Chief Standing Bear, *Land of the Spotted Eagle*, p. 168.

24. In *Medicine Talk*, Dallas Chief Eagle notes of traditional life: "We are only passing through life on our way to the Spirit World of our ancestors" (p. 113).

25. Eastman, *Soul of an Indian*, p. 22.

26. In an attempt to duplicate the symbolic nature of Storm's novel, I have from time to time capitalized significant words from the narrative. As Storm states in "The Circle,"

> Within *Seven Arrows*, and particularly within the old Stories, the words to which the Teller would have given inflections are capitalized. *These words are symbolic Teachers, and it is very important that you approach them symbolically rather than literally.* (p. 11; italics in original.)

27. Eastman, *Soul of an Indian*, p. 39.

Chapter 6   Survivors of the Relocation

1. Nasnaga, *Indians' Summer* (New York: Harper & Row, 1975), p. 137. Subsequent page references will appear in the text.

2. See *The Return of the Vanishing American* (New York: Stein and Day, 1968).

3. There appears to be some discrepancy concerning Chief Pierre's chieftaincy. The dust jacket and the title page of the novel identify the author as "Chief George Pierre, Colville Confederated Tribes of Washington." In a letter to me, Pierre describes himself as a hereditary chief, for life, an office he inherited in 1963, after the death of his father (who had been chief for fifty years). Information supplied by the Bureau of Indian Affairs states that Pierre was appointed chief by the governor of the state, but that he no longer holds this office.

4. Chief George Pierre, *Autumn's Bounty* (San Antonio, Texas: Naylor Co., 1972), p. 5. Subsequent page references will appear in the text.

5. One can discover innumerable parallels with Hemingway's novel: as was true of Santiago, the Cuban fisherman, Alphonse's wife died long ago; both are old men who have been ostracized by their people; Alphonse's defeat of the mountain lion is a parable of the indomitable spirit of man, a spiritual victory in the face of seemingly insurmountable odds (the packs of rabid coyotes, the loss of the knife and the gun, the first snowstorm of the autumn), a test of survival (Santiago's marlin is devoured by sharks; Alphonse's mountain lion by coyotes); both are sustained by their memories of past victories.

6. James Welch, *Winter in the Blood* (1974; New York: Bantam Books, 1975), p. 3. Subsequent page references will appear in the text.

7. James Welch, "The Only Good Indian, Section I of a Novel in Progress," *South Dakota Review* 9 (1971):54.

8. In a letter answering my query about the meaning of "borrow pit," Welch said it was "the ditch on either side of a road which the road builders gouge out to use the dirt to build the road bed . . . the builders borrow the dirt on either side of the road, then push it up to create a raised bed, on which they lay asphalt or cement or whatever."

9. Leslie Marmon Silko, *Ceremony* (New York: Viking Press, 1977), p. 195. Subsequent page references will appear in the text. (As this book went to press, a paperback edition of *Ceremony* was published—too late to cite quotations in it [New York: New American Library, Signet Books, 1978].)

10. Silko is also a published poet.

11. There is an interesting parallel here with the attitude a number of African intellectuals—the proponents of *négritude*—shared about World War II. The Western world, they felt, had become sterile by overmechanization; the war was seen as the logical culmination of the white man's inability to control his destiny since his ties with nature had been completely severed.

Chapter 7 The Figure in the Dark Forest

1. *Wind from an Enemy Sky* (New York: Harper & Row). Scheduled for publication in 1978.

Appendix 1: *Cogewea: The Half-Blood*

1. Hum-Ishu-Ma (Mourning Dove), *Co-Ge-We-A (The Half-Blood)* (Boston: Four Seas Co., 1927), p. 15. Subsequent page references will appear in the text.

2. The Library of Congress cross-indexes *Cogewea* under Lucullus McWhorter, whose most famous book, *Yellow Wolf: His Own Story* (1940), was published by The Caxton Printers, in Caldwell, Idaho. Seven years earlier, The Caxton Printers published Mourning Dove's second book, *Coyote Stories*. A note on the title page of that volume reads as follows: "Edited and illustrated by Hester Dean Guie, with notes by L. V. McWhorter. . . ."

Appendix 2: *The Wokosani Road*

1. Jon Mockingbird, *The Wokosani Road* (New York: Exposition Press, 1963), p. 27. Subsequent page references will appear in the text.

2. Note the similarity between "Tarawa" (the island in the South Pacific where Jeff first met the elder Cahuro Joligo) and "Tirawa." It is difficult to determine whether this similarity is intentional. For further reference to "Tirawa," the Pawnee word for God, see Alice C. Fletcher, *The Hako: A Pawnee Ceremony*, Twenty-second Annual Report of the Bureau of American Ethnology, part 2 (Washington, D.C., 1904).

3. For a discussion of the amalgamation of Christian ideas and beliefs by the Native American Church, see Earl Shorris, *The Death of the Great Spirit* (1971; New York: New American Library, Mentor Books, 1972), especially pp. 20–32.

4. The author also suggests a connection between the Kanawan and a religious cult composed of Tibetan monks in the Himalayas (see pages 114–15).

5. See chapter 1 for discussion of establishing ethnic authenticity.

Coincidentally, there are a number of parallels between the fictional Jeff Hanson and George Pierre, the author of *Autumn's Bounty*. In a descriptive handout currently given to customers at "Chief George Pierre's Trading Post" in Torrance, California, the author describes his military experience as follows: "At age 16, July 15, 1942, enlisted in the Marine Corps and served in the South Pacific. Wounded at Tarawa November 20, 1943. . . ."

Bibliography

Primary Sources

Bedford, Denton R. (Minsee.) *Tsali*. San Francisco: Indian Historian Press, 1972.

Chief Eagle, Dallas. (Sioux, b. 1925.) *Winter Count*. Colorado Springs, Colo.: Denton-Berkeland Printing Co., 1967. Reprint Denver: Golden Bell Press, 1968. Second Reprint Boulder, Colo.: Johnson Publishing Co., 1968.

Mathews, John Joseph. (Osage, b. 1895.) *The Osages*. Norman: University of Oklahoma Press, 1961.

———. *Sundown*. New York: Longmans, Green and Co., 1934.

———. *Wah'Kon-Tah: The Osage and the White Man's Road*. Norman: University of Oklahoma Press, 1932.

McNickle, D'Arcy. (Flathead, 1904–77.) *Indian Man: A Life of Oliver La Farge*. Bloomington: Indiana University Press, 1971.

———. *Runner in the Sun: A Story of Indian Maize*. New York: Holt, Rinehart and Winston, 1954.

———. *The Surrounded*. New York: Dodd, Mead, and Co., 1936. Paperback reprint Albuquerque: University of New Mexico Press, 1978.

———. *Wind from an Enemy Sky*. New York: Harper & Row, scheduled for publication in 1978.

Momaday, N. Scott. (Kiowa, b. 1934.) *House Made of Dawn*. New York: Harper & Row, 1968. Paperback ed. New York: New American Library, Signet Books, 1969.

———. *The Names*. New York: Harper & Row, 1976.

———. "Note to Three Sketches from *House Made of Dawn*." *Southern Review* 2 (1966):933.

———. *The Way to Rainy Mountain*. Albuquerque: University of New Mexico Press, 1969. Paperback reprint 1976.

Nasnaga [Roger Russell]. (Shawnee, b. 1941.) *Indians' Summer*. New York: Harper & Row, 1975.

Oskison, John M. (Cherokee, 1874–1947.) *A Texas Titan: The Story of Sam Houston*. New York: Doubleday, Doran and Co., 1929.

———. *Black Jack Davy*. New York: D. Appleton & Co., 1926.

———. *Brothers Three*. New York: Macmillan Co., 1935.

———. *Tecumseh and His Times: The Story of a Great Indian*. New York: G. P. Putnam's Sons, 1938.

———. *Wild Harvest*. New York: D. Appleton & Co., 1925. Reprint Chicago: White House Book Club, 1925.

Pierre, Chief George. (Colville Confederated Tribes, b. 1926.) *Autumn's Bounty*. San Antonio: Naylor Co., 1972.

Pokagon, Chief Simon. (Potawatomi, 1830?–99.) *The Red Man's Rebuke*. Hartford, Mich.: C. H. Engle, 1893.

———. *Queen of the Woods*. Hartford, Mich.: C. H. Engle, 1899. Reprint Berrien Springs, Mich.: Hardscrabble Books, 1972.

Silko, Leslie Marmon. (Laguna, b. 1948.) *Ceremony*. New York: Viking Press, 1977. Paperback ed. New York: New American Library, Signet Books, 1978.

Storm, Hyemeyohsts. (Northern Cheyenne, b. 1933.) *Seven Arrows*. New York: Harper & Row, 1972. Paperback ed. New York: Ballantine Books, 1974.

Welch, James. (Blackfoot, b. 1940.) "The Only Good Indian: Section I of a Novel in Progress." *South Dakota Review* 9 (1971):55–74.

———. *Winter in the Blood*. New York: Harper & Row, 1974. Paperback ed. New York: Bantam Books, 1975.

Hum-Ishu-Ma (Mourning Dove). (Okanogan, 1888?–?.) *Co-Ge-We-A, The Half-Blood: A Depiction of the Great Montana Cattle Range*. Boston: Four Seas Co., 1927.

———. *Coyote Stories*. Caldwell, Idaho: The Caxton Printers, 1933.

Mockingbird, Jon. (Apache?, 1903?–?). *The Wokosani Road*. New York: Exposition Press, 1963.

Additional Works Cited:

d'Aulaire, Ingri, and d'Aulaire, Edgar Parin. *Pocahontas*. New York: Doubleday & Co., 1946.

Barbour, Philip L. *Pocahontas and Her World*. Boston: Houghton Mifflin Co., 1970.

———. *The Three Worlds of Captain John Smith*. Boston: Houghton Mifflin Co., 1964.

Barth, John. *The Sot-Weed Factor*. New York: Doubleday & Co., 1960.

Berger, Thomas. *Little Big Man*. New York: Dial Press, 1964.

Bird, Robert Montgomery. *Nick of the Woods* (1837). Reissue New Haven, Conn.: College and University Press, 1967.

Bone, Robert A. *The Negro Novel in America*. New Haven, Conn.: Yale University Press, 1965.

Brown, Dee. *Bury My Heart at Wounded Knee*. New York: Holt, Rinehart and Winston, 1970.

Brown, Joseph Epes. *The Spiritual Legacy of the American Indian*. Wallingford, Penn.: Pendel Hill Publications, 1964.

Brown, William Wells. *Clotel* (1853). Paperback ed. New York: Macmillan Co., Collier Books, 1970.

Buechner, Cecila B. *The P9kagons*. Indiana Historical Society Publications, no. 10 (Indianapolis, 1933), pp. 316–28.

Chalmers, Harvey. *West to the Setting Sun* (1943). Reprint Toronto: Macmillan Co., 1943.

Cooke, John E. *My Lady Pocahontas: A True Relation of Virginia* (1879). Reprint Ridgewood, N.J.: Gregg Press, 1968.

Driver, Harold. *Indians of North America*. 2d. ed., rev. Chicago: University of Chicago Press, 1969.

Eastman, Charles. *The Soul of an Indian* (1911). Reprint Rapid City, S.D.: Fenwyn Press Books, 1970.

Ellison, Ralph. *Invisible Man*. New York: Random House, 1952.

Evers, Lawrence J. "Words and Place: A Reading of *House Made of Dawn*." *Western American Literature* 11 (1977): 297–320.

Fiedler, Leslie A. *The Return of the Vanishing American*. New York: Stein and Day, 1968.

Fletcher, Alice C. *The Hako: A Pawnee Ceremony*. Twenty-second Annual Report of the Bureau of American Ethnology, Part 2 (Washington, D.C.: Smithsonian Institution, 1904).

Fletcher, John Gould. *John Smith—Also Pocahontas*. New York: Brentano's, 1928.

Garnett, David. *Pocahontas or the Nonparell of Virginia* (1933). Paperback ed. New York: Doubleday & Co., Anchor Books, 1958.

Gerson, Noel B. *Daughter of Eve.* New York: Doubleday and Co., 1958.

——. *First Lady of America.* Richmond, Va.: Westover Publishing Co., 1973.

Henry, Jeanette. "Momaday's Novel Wins Pultizer Award." *The Indian Historian* 2(1969):38.

Hirschfelder, Arlene B. *American Indian and Eskimo Authors: A Comprehensive Bibliography.* New York: Association on American Indian Affairs, 1973.

Hylton, Marian Willard. "On a Trail of Pollen: Momaday's *House Made of Dawn.*" *Critique* 14(1972):60–69.

Jones, Douglas C. *The Court-Martial of George Armstrong Custer.* New York: Charles Scribner's Sons, 1976.

Keiser, Albert. *The Indian in American Literature* (1933). Reprint New York: Farrar, Straus and Giroux, 1975.

Kahn, E. J. "A Reporter at Large: 1970 Census—II." *The New Yorker,* October 22, 1973, pp. 105–32.

Kluckhohn, Clyde, and Leighton, Dorothea. *The Navaho* (1946). Rev. ed., paperback, New York: Doubleday & Co., Anchor Books, 1962.

La Farge, Oliver. *As Long as the Grass Shall Grow.* New York: Alliance Book Corp., 1940.

——. "Half-Breed Hero" (review of *The Surrounded*). *Saturday Review,* March 14, 1936, p. 10.

——. *Laughing Boy.* Boston: Houghton Mifflin Co., 1929.

Larson, Charles R. *The Novel in the Third World.* Washington: Inscape Corp., 1976.

Lawson, Marie. *Pocahontas and Captain John Smith: The Story of the Virginia Colony.* New York: Random House, 1950.

Loving, Boyce. *The Origin of Necking, a Travesty on the Pocahontas–John Smith Episode.* Richmond, Va.: Whittet and Shepperson, 1932.

Marquis, Thomas B. *Keep the Last Bullet for Yourself: The True Story of Custer's Last Stand.* New York: Two Continents Publishing Group, 1976.

McAllister, Harold S. "Incarnate Grace and the Paths of Salvation in *House Made of Dawn.*" *South Dakota Review* 12 (1974–75):115–25.

McLuhan, T. C. *Touch the Earth.* New York: Simon and Schuster, 1971.

McWhorter, Lucullus. *Yellow Wolf: His Own Story.* Caldwell, Idaho: The Caxton Printers, 1940.

Moravia, Alberto. *Which Tribe Do You Belong To?* New York: Farrar, Straus and Giroux, 1974.

Mossiker, Frances. *Pocahontas: The Life and the Legend.* New York: Alfred A. Knopf, 1976.

Neihardt, John G. *Black Elk Speaks* (1932). Paperback ed. New York: Pocket Books, 1972.

"Northern Cheyenne Discuss 'Seven Arrows' Book; Criticism Is Expressed." *Wassaja* 2 (April/May 1974):12.

Oleson, Carole. "The Remembered Earth: Momaday's *House Made of Dawn.*" *South Dakota Review* 11 (1973):59–78.

Pearce, Roy Harvey. *Savagism and Civilization.* Baltimore: Johns Hopkins University Press, 1965.

Shorris, Earl. *The Death of the Great Spirit* (1971). Paperback ed. New York: New American Library, Mentor Books, 1972.

Smith, Bradford. *Captain John Smith: His Life and Legend.* Philadelphia: J. B. Lippincott Co., 1953.

Smith, John. *The Capture and Release of Captain John Smith*. Ann Arbor, Mich.: Clements Library Assoc., 1960.

Sprague, Marshall. Review of *House Made of Dawn*. *New York Times Book Review*, June 9, 1968, p. 5.

Standing Bear, Luther. *Land of the Spotted Eagle*. Boston: Houghton Mifflin Co., 1933.

Steiger, Brad. *Medicine Talk*. New York: Doubleday & Co., 1975.

Steiner, Stan. *The New Indians*. 1968. Paperback reprint New York: Harper & Row, 1975.

Szasz, Margaret. *Education and the American Indian: The Road to Self-Determination, 1928–1973*. Albuquerque: University of New Mexico Press, 1974.

Trimble, Martha Scott. *N. Scott Momaday*. Boise, Idaho: Boise State College Western Writers Series, 1973.

Whitman, Walt. *Franklin Evans, or the Inebriate* (1842). Reprint New York: Random House, 1929.

Williams, Ted C. *The Reservation*. Syracuse, N.Y.: Syracuse University Press, 1976.

Witt, Shirley Hill. "Nationalistic Trends Among American Indians." In *The American Indian Today*, edited by Stuart Levine and Nancy O. Lurie. Baltimore: Penguin Books, 1963.

Woodward, Grace Steele. *Pocahontas*. Norman: University of Oklahoma Press, 1969.

Wright, Richard. "How 'Bigger' Was Born." In *Richard Wright's Native Son: A Critical Handbook*, edited by Richard Abcarian. Belmont, Calif.: Wadsworth Publishing Co., 1970.

Young, Philip. "The Mother of Us All: Pocahontas Reconsidered." *Kenyon Review* 24 (1962):391–415.

Index